PRAISE FOR *THE NEW LANGUAGE OF BUSINESS*

"This book clearly shows how today's industry pressures and business challenges mandate renewal of the contract between organizations and their IT assets and people—and it illustrates how a service-oriented approach to IT can help organizations go through the necessary transformation. The role of governance in bringing IT and business closer together is particularly well explained, and the book is worth reading for that alone."

—Neil Ward-Dutton, Research Director, Macehiter Ward-Dutton

"It's easy to pay lip service to the concept of business/IT alignment, but in The New Language of Business, Sandy Carter walks the walk. Few treatments of SOA ground this admittedly difficult topic in the world of business as thoroughly as Sandy has here. I'd recommend this book to any business reader who wants to leverage IT to make their business more agile and innovative, and to any technical reader who wishes to understand how to place SOA in the business context where it belongs."

—Jason Bloomberg, Senior Analyst and Principal, ZapThink LLC

"A very valuable read. In today's globally connected marketplace profitable growth requires business flexibility and continuous innovation, both of which are increasingly proving to be impossible without business modularity and the new table-stakes technology SOA."

—Ron Williams, Professor, Kenan-Flagler Business School,
University of North Carolina at Chapel Hill

"Sandy has provided a pragmatic and holistic perspective on Service Oriented Architectures. She adds credibility by sharing IBM's in-depth customer research as well as case studies to support the findings. The book is a strong source book for those wanting to get started with SOA."

—Judith Hurwitz, President & CEO, Hurwitz & Associates, coauthor,
Service Oriented Architectures for Dummies

"Few people have thought as long or as hard about SOA as Sandy Carter. This book embodies her invaluable work and the work of many at IBM to research, define, deploy and make SOA happen. Useful not just from a SOA perspective, but also as a concise articulation of the contemporary concepts fundamental to understanding where business and IT are heading."

—Carol Baroudi, coauthor *Service Oriented Architecture
For Dummies*, Senior Analyst, Aberdeen Group

The New Language of Business

of Business

SOA & Web 2.0

The New Language
of Business

SOA & Web 2.0

Sandy Carter

IBM Press
Pearson plc

Upper Saddle River, NJ • Boston • Indianapolis • San Francisco
New York • Toronto • Montreal • London • Munich • Paris • Madrid
Cape Town • Sydney • Tokyo • Singapore • Mexico City

ibmpressbooks.com

IBM Press Program Managers: Tara Woodman, Ellice Uffer
Cover design: IBM Corporation

Associate Publisher: Greg Wiegand
Marketing Manager: Kourtnaye Sturgeon
Publicist: Heather Fox
Development Editors: Sheri Cain and Laura Norman
Managing Editor: Gina Kanouse
Designer: Alan Clements
Senior Project Editor: Kristy Hart
Copy Editor: Krista Hansing Editorial Services, Inc.
Indexer: Lisa Stumpf
Compositor: Jake McFarland
Proofreader: Water Crest Publishing
Manufacturing Buyer: Dan Uhrig

Published by Pearson plc
Publishing as IBM Press

IBM Press offers excellent discounts on this book when ordered in quantity for bulk purchases or special sales, which may include electronic versions and/or custom covers and content particular to your business, training goals,marketing focus, and branding interests. For more information, please contact:

U. S. Corporate and Government Sales
1-800-382-3419
corpsales@pearsontechgroup.com.

For sales outside the U. S., please contact:

International Sales
international@pearsoned.com.

 **This Book Is Safari Enabled**

The Safari® Enabled icon on the cover of your favorite technology book means the book is available through Safari Bookshelf. When you buy this book, you get free access to the online edition for 45 days. Safari Bookshelf is an electronic reference library that lets you easily search thousands of technical books, find code samples, download chapters, and access technical information whenever and wherever you need it.

To gain 45-day Safari Enabled access to this book:

- Go to http://www.awprofessional.com/safarienabled.

- Complete the brief registration form.

- Enter the coupon code I1JK-KKDK-JNWJ-8MKH-DDH8.

If you have difficulty registering on Safari Bookshelf or accessing the online edition, please e-mail customer-service@safaribooksonline.com.

Library of Congress Cataloging-in-Publication Data

Carter, Sandy, 1963-

The new language of business : SOA & Web 2.0 / Sandy Carter.

p. cm.

ISBN 0-13-195654-X (hardback : alk. paper) 1. Business—Data processing. 2. Business enterprises—Computer networks—Management. 3. IBM software. 4. Information technology—Management. 5. Management information systems. I. Title.

HD30.2.C3747 2007

658'.05—dc22

2006038699

ISBN-10: 0-13-195654-X
ISBN-13: 978-0-13-195654-4

Text printed in the United States on recycled paper at R.R. Donnelley in Crawfordsville, Indiana.

First printing, February 2007

10 09 08 07   7 6 5 4

Dedication

To my parents, for their encouragement of risk taking; my angel daughters, Maria and Cassie, from Russia with love; and my wonderful husband, Todd—the love of my life!

Contents

PART II   A Flexible Business Requires Flexible IT

Foreword

If you're reading this book, you've likely heard about the business benefits of a service oriented architecture (SOA), or, at a minimum, you're aware of the term *SOA* and are seeking more information on what it is, what it isn't, and what exactly it's going to do for your company. And, let's face it, you want to know what SOA is going to do for—or to—your career.

Before you skip ahead to the chapters on SOA governance, Web 2.0, and, my favorite, top ten don'ts, it's important to first understand what SOA is—and what it isn't.

First, SOA is not a product. An SOA is not something that you can order off the shelf or online that can be shipped overnight. SOA is a journey. Second, SOA is not new; the use of technology to drive business goes back to the days of the abacus. Third, SOA is not a fad that will be usurped by the "next big thing."

So what exactly is SOA? Although several definitions have surfaced, the one that most accurately describes

it is this: *An SOA is an evolutionary approach to building information technology (IT) systems that is focused on solving business problems.*

More specifically, it's important to understand what SOA is in the context of the organization. SOA is not a product; the key word is *architecture.* Creating an SOA is a lot like building a house. You design your blueprints, set your foundation, and build from the inside out—making sure that, all the while, you can freely move from one room to another without being hindered by walls or doors. We call those walls and doors proprietary applications.

Second, if SOA isn't new, why are we talking about it? Well, the reality is that since the time of the Tower of Babel, people have always been trying to communicate using a common language. The challenge could be as simple as an American trying to understand the nuances of the Queen's English or as complex as a CFO trying to reconcile monthly financial reports from offices around the world. Only now has technology evolved in such a manner— enter SOA—that will help break down those barriers among teams, departments, and divisions, to ensure consistency in reporting across the organization.

And although the term *SOA* is relatively new, the actual functions that it facilitates are not. The sheer fact that SOA has been evolving for years rules out the notion of a passing trend. However, what is new is that, as an industry, we've come to realize that the need to easily connect different parts of the organization is best served through an SOA. Until the need to increase revenue, expand market presence, and streamline business processes disappears, SOA will continue to be the driving force behind successful organizations. Of course, the *SOA* moniker may shift over time. However, the ability to address core business needs and help organizations realize true business value won't disappear.

With more SOA books on the market, why this one? Why now? I could tell you that this book is in response to the growing demand among our customers and business partners, who realize that an SOA is the most effective and efficient way to maximize the value of their existing IT investments.

Another answer is that many industry and IT leaders today are hearing about the business value of SOA and want a more specific roadmap on how, where, when, and why to jump on this moving train.

A little less bashful response is that only IBM has the most comprehensive portfolio designed to enable customer success through SOA, and we want to share this inner circle knowledge.

And still another reply is that this is the only book of its kind that is based on thousands of interviews with customers, prospects, and industry analysts.

The truth can be found in all of these answers. *The New Language of Business: SOA & Web 2.0* is based on the collective feedback from industry leaders at organizations of all sizes, in more than 50 countries, who shared their views, experiences, and challenges of aligning technology with business goals. Regardless of their current business issues or anticipated future challenges, it was clear to these organizations that SOA was unanimously the best way to address those challenges. This book is their story. It provides that much-needed roadmap and features proven best practices learned in the field by the IBM SOA community. That community includes software and services experts, customers, partners, analysts, and now you. Welcome to the SOA journey!

Steve Mills
Senior Vice President and Group Executive
IBM Software Group

Acknowledgments

This book represents a dream that I have had for a number of years, starting when I first heard Lou Holtz speak about having a list of your top 100 things that you want to do with your life. But I would not even have started writing this book as one of my top items, had I not met and chatted with Don Tapscott at a recent CIO conference. He encouraged me to write from the heart and to give it a go after he had listened to me present at that CIO conference. "Tell your story," he said, with much the same passion as Lou.

I love telling stories—in fact, my favorite quote is from an old Indian proverb: "Tell me the facts, and I'll learn. Tell me the truth, and I'll believe. But tell me a story, and it will live in my heart forever." Stories are the heartbeat of life. This is our SOA story, one that I believe in firmly. I was inspired by this story because it adds value to so many of my customers and partners, and will change the IT industry forever.

It would not have been possible without the help of many people, including Lou and Don.

First, thanks to God, who blessed me with determination and talent so that I was able to persevere and write this book and learn from so many phenomenal people.

Second, thanks to my family—Todd, Cassie, and Maria, who supported my weekends writing, and my parents, who always told me I could do anything. Thanks also to my in-laws, who cheered me on!

Third, thanks to the IBM SOA Specialty partners for their encouragement and tales of customer value. Acutuate, Adminserver, Alcatel Shanghai Network Support, Aldata, Alphinat, Amazon, Amberpoint, Ametras, Argo Data Resource, Bison Group, Business Objects, Celequest, China Systems, Chordiant, Clear Technology, Clear2Pay, Cognizant, Cognos, Convansys, CSC–Hogan, Crea-Union, Curam, Cylande, Dassault–Enovia, Dassault–MatrixOne, Dassault–Smarteam, Dexterra, Eastcom, eMeter, Eniac, Gillardon, I2, IBS, IEnterprises, Infor–SSA, Initiatiate, Itemfield, J&J Dreger, JWare, Lawson, Logo Business Solutions, Mincom, Miracle Software, MRO, Napersoft, NetManage, Neusoft, Nimaya, Parametric, Technology Corporation, Procilon, Prostep, RIM, SAS, Sateri, SEEC, Sterling Commerce–Yantra, Summa Technologies Inc., Syncron, Sysdat GmbH, Systar, Transworks, TrueDemand, Twinsoft, Ultramatics, Unisys, Webify, Weblayers, Wizart, Wondertek, and xAware.

Fourth, thanks to my customers for their great sharing of their learnings, especially Abbott, ACI Global, Audi AG, Banca Intesa, Bendigo Bank, Bombardier, Broward County School Board, businessMart AG, Caixa Economica Federal, Cargill, Cathay Life Insurance Co. Ltd., CashCall Inc., Coldwater Creek Inc., COSCO Group, Delaware Electric Cooperative, Finnish Defence Forces, H. Gautzsch Großhandel GmbH & Co. KG, Harley-Davidson Inc., ING Group, Mitsui-Soko Co. Ltd., Pacorini S.p.A., Pep Boys, Porto Media, PostFinance (a division of Swiss Post), Prudential Financial, Region Västra Götaland (VGR), Renault, Royal Bank of Canada, Sony Ericsson, Sprint Nextel, Standard Life group of companies, Storebrand Group, St. George Bank Limited, s.Oliver Bernd Freier GmbH & Co., Telefonica Chile, The People's Bank of China, Toyota, United States Tennis Association, University of Pittsburgh Medical Center, Wachovia Corporation, Xerox Corporation, and Yanmar Information System Service CO. LTD.

Fifth, thanks to the IBM visionaries on SOA whom I truly admire: Steve Mills, Robert LeBlanc, and Ginni Rometty.

Sixth, thanks to my SOA team—what a team! They are the most talented and passionate team I've ever worked with! The entire team inspired me, but, in particular, I would like to call out those who helped me in the book: Paul Brunet, Kareem Yusuf, Jason Weisser, Becky Michel, Janell Straach, Barbara Formichelli, Michael Holmes, Dave Wilson, Michael Liebow, Peggy Vaughan, Rob High, Howie Miller, Eric Baxley, Leif Davison, John Choi, Michael Curry, Kramer Reeves, Deb Cascino, Anthony Karimi, Scott Neuman, Kathy Keating, Georgina Castanon, Lidia Gasparotto, Katie Kean, Tom Rosamilia, Anthony Karimi, Caroline Poser, Sara Peck, Glenn Hintze, and Max Anderson.

Seventh, I would like to thank Aberdeen Group, Forrester Research, Gartner, and International Data Corporation (IDC) for the use of their materials in this book. I would also like to thank the IT analysts for their insight—in particular, Aberdeen Group, AMR Research, Forrester Research, Gartner, Hurwitz & Associates, IDC, RedMonk, Wohl Associates, and ZapThink.

And finally, thanks to my new friends at Pearson Education, Greg Wiegand and Laura Norman!

About the Author

Sandy Carter is Vice President, SOA and WebSphere Strategy, Channels and Marketing, where she is responsible for IBM's cross-company, worldwide SOA initiatives. In this role, Sandy helps oversee the company's SOA strategy across software, services, and hardware, and sets the company's SOA direction. Sandy has played a critical role in helping to identify SOA acquisition targets and ensure the successful integration of these organizations into the IBM SOA portfolio. Additionally, she directs messaging, content, and presentations, and leads a global team responsible for driving marketing campaigns that maximize customers' and IBM's business partners' success through SOA.

Sandra's track record speaks for itself. Under her SOA leadership, she has grown the WebSphere business, led the brand to win seven industry awards, and helped IBM's SOA initiatives consistently earn third-party validation and top leadership rankings by analysts and pundits alike; at the time of this writing, WebSphere

has realized 32 consecutive quarters of growth. Sandra is a frequent speaker at industry events sponsored by *Infoworld* magazine, Gartner Group, IDC, and Women in Technology (WITI). Sandra holds a Bachelor of Science degree in math and computer science from Duke University and an MBA from Harvard; she is fluent in eight programming languages. For more information, visit Sandy's blog at www-03.ibm.com/developerworks/blogs/page/SOA_ Off_the_Record or BooksBySandy.com.

I

Start at the Beginning—
The Business

1

The Innovation Imperative

Managers have seen dramatic changes in the last ten years on what they focus on in building their businesses. Spurred on by extraordinary advances in technology, we can expect the next ten years to be just as interesting. After the dot-com boom, which in 1999 accounted for nearly 80% of the $5.2 trillion increase in the total value of U.S. corporate equities, CEOs refocused on cutting costs to stay competitive. Investors demanded leanness after what was seen as a period of excess during the tech boom. More than 340,000 payroll jobs were lost in the San Francisco Bay Area from 2000 to 2004.

You could characterize the view of technology over the last ten years and its role in the businesses bottom line as the swinging of a pendulum. During the late 1990s, traditional companies became caught up in the dot-com boom and were wildly throwing money at IT (the technology vendors didn't help the situation), with the belief that return on investment (ROI) was guaranteed and that the first business in would gain the competitive advantage. When the ROI didn't materialize, the

pendulum swung to the other extreme, with the belief that IT had been commoditized and should be managed like any other utility—managing costs down and not expecting business advantage because everyone is equal.

Today the pendulum has settled in the middle, where the connection between business and IT will deliver the promised business value. A new language has emerged as the common point between business and IT, with flexibility as the driver and service oriented architecture (SOA) as the enabler. For the next few years, this new language will drive a new agenda that is very simple: Innovate and grow your business. Because of amazing technology such as video face recognition, radio frequency identification (RFID), SOA, and other emerging technologies that companies now possess, CEOs are looking to harness IT and process advances to exponentially grow their businesses. Innovation need not be technological. Ron Williams, a professor at UNC Kenan-Flagler Business School, points to a great example: When McDonald's applied the production-line process to producing restaurant food, it could use low-skilled workers to quickly produce large amounts of food of a standard quality, thus inventing the fast food industry.

This new focus on not just new products, but new business models, is part of the changing world, where sustaining growth is the key. It has always been very difficult to build profitable growth and far more difficult to sustain it. But in today's environment, this is required. Innovatively gaining business flexibility to grow your business is the focus of this book. Becoming flex-pon-sive* will become a key success factor. Flex-pon-sive* is the description of a company that responds with lightning speed and agility to rapidly changing business needs, leveraging the new language of business.

FOCUS ON GROWTH

To better understand the focus of the new world, IBM conducted a survey of 456 CEOs from around the world in conjunction with *The Economist* magazine and Nikkei Research to find out what topics will drive the business agenda for the immediate future. These CEOs represent every major industry sector and represent

assets in the trillions of dollars globally. It was the largest survey ever undertaken based on in-person CEO interviews and provides a comprehensive view of the business agenda for the next two to three years.

This survey of CEOs yielded several important findings (listed here according to importance):

- Growth—top-line revenue
- Flexibility—a core competence
- Skills

THE GROWTH AGENDA

Growth is back on the CEO agenda. But achieving growth is not easy. Historical evidence shows that only a tiny fraction of firms have ever succeeded in doing so over time. Of the original Forbes 100 announced in 1917, GE is the only one of the remaining 68 that has surpassed the return on the S&P over the 70-year time period ending in 1987. Most firms' long-term business growth at best keeps up with the growth in the economy, and their revenue increases hover around the national inflation rate.

So the hardest challenge—growing the top line—is at the top of the list, outpacing cutting costs. As one CEO said, "Now it is about growing the top line while keeping the bottom line in check." How do CEOs believe the growth will come? More than 64% of CEOs believe that they'll grow by introducing new products into the market and differentiating their products through their service over the next five years. As one CEO commented, "In order to grow and differentiate the business, the only way is for us to develop new products and services and in spaces we have never dealt in before." More than half look to new markets to drive revenue growth, and, with no surprise, China is clearly identified as the most important. Experts predict that the country's combined imports in the next five years will reach US$150 billion to US$200 billion. In fact, members of the Association of Southeast Asian Nations (ASEAN) saw a 27% increase in exports to China in the first ten months of this year.

In addition to new products and markets, CEOs believe that by leveraging customer information to make more loyal customers, they can grow. More than 60% feel they need to do a better job capturing and understanding customer information rapidly to make swift business decisions. Growth is shown to come from businesses mining their current customer base more efficiently and effectively. One bank focused on growth by differentiating a service based on customer loyalty factors and saw a 15% growth in its top line.

FLEXIBILITY: A CORE COMPETENCE

Another major change in priorities is that CEOs are no longer simply looking for efficient organizations, but are building organizations that are flexible—organizations that not only respond to market changes, but that can even cause those changes to happen. CEOs want responsiveness to be a competitive advantage instead of a defense mechanism. Most CEOs believe their companies are not agile enough to identify and chase new market opportunities. Eighty percent cited the ability to respond rapidly to changing market forces as high priority, but only 13% of CEOs rated their organizations as "very responsive" to changing business conditions. The majority of CEOs see their IT groups as inhibitors of flexibility and not a mechanism to gain a competitive advantage.

Interestingly, it is this core competency that CEOs believe will drive their ability to grow and innovate. Why? Because growth requires innovation, and innovation requires change. Without flexibility, change does not come at the speed and cost required in the marketplace. Thus, this whole concept of flex-pon-sive* becomes central to our discussion.

SKILLS: ORGANIZATIONAL CHALLENGES WITHIN A COMPANY'S FOUR WALLS

A skills revitalization is crucial to making growth a reality in the corporate world today. CEOs are looking at how to make their people more effective—to enable people with tools, information, and

skills to work across the organization. Why? Sixty percent of CEOs felt that the leadership, skills, and capabilities of their employees are a major barrier to making the necessary changes to grow a business. Less than 10% of respondents rate their company's record of change management as having been very successful. More than half of those surveyed believe that they do not have the requisite skills to move into new markets and capture emerging growth opportunities, yet they feel that it is critical to future success.

THE INNOVATION IMPERATIVE

Addressing these three challenges is what becoming an on demand business is all about. In 2002, Sam Palmisano, IBM's chief executive officer, defined *on demand*:

> An on demand business is an enterprise whose business processes—integrated end to end across the company and with key partners, suppliers, and customers—can respond with flexibility and speed to customer demand, market opportunity, or external threat.

Innovative businesses think about business processes end to end. They look at their business processes for best practices, overlaps, and inefficiencies by continuously improving business processes, and they use that to grow and to become more flexible. Companies such as Harley Davidson, VW, and Nestlé are never satisfied or finished with their current business processes and models. And in today's competitive environment, no one runs without it. When a company improves a process, someone has to change the associated business systems and, therefore, IT. This integration of process, people, and information is a competitive advantage for business results. It is the new language of business and IT, the focus on process flexibility enabled by IT. These companies need to become flex-pon-sive*!

In a recent follow-up study to our Global CEO Study 2006, 765 CEOs in every major industry told us that the pressures to achieve profitable growth had introduced a new mandate—the need to innovate:

- Two-thirds of the CEOs we spoke to believe their organizations will need to introduce fundamental, radical changes in the next two years to respond to competitive pressures and external forces.
- CEOs need to innovate to reach their growth and flexibility through their process focus.

CEOs need to innovate to reach their growth and flexibility through their process focus.

FOCUS ON PROCESS AND INFORMATION IS KEY

Most IT organizations have technology that runs faster than their focus on business process. But the successful companies are those in which business and IT are aligned in their focus. To achieve proper business/IT alignment, it takes more than just integrating IT into your business processes. Flexible businesses require flexible IT.

In today's environment, processes are constantly changing. In the past, processes changed about once a year. Now processes change every month and, in some cases, every week. See the "Business Process Importance" case study for an example.

And on and on these changes to process may go. But being able to drive these changes in process to grow and being flexible affects your bottom line. Thinking about business processes end to end and beyond the four walls of a company is taking leaders beyond just incremental gains and is breaking new ground. A separate study by IBM shows that, when compared to others in their industry sectors, companies that have gone the furthest in developing their flexibility capabilities have, on average, experienced superior three-year growth in key areas of business performance.

The study sampled major companies across the Americas, Europe, and Asia Pacific (AP). Using the results of a quarterly survey, the study identified companies that had advanced the furthest in building their on demand capabilities and compared their business performance with that of their industry peers in general.

CASE STUDY
BUSINESS PROCESS IMPORTANCE

Retail Payments is a business process area within banking but also has natural interfaces to other industry applications, such as retail distribution. The payments business service area is characterized by the need for both internal and external connectivity and work-flow among multiple organizational entities. The end-to-end supply chain is varied and dynamic. Requirements for adherence to standard interfaces and regulatory requirements are high. This is a business process service in which IT flexibility, availability, scalability, and proactive manageability are key. As banks adapt to business requirements to grow revenue and reduce costs in the area of electronic payments, the need for IT flexibility is heightened.

In this area of payments processing, changes in the market have required that competitive companies allow for direct client access. A common process change could simply allow through a browser an approval application. Now, this process change may seem simple, but think of the human and IT changes that must occur to make this happen. But it doesn't stop here. Processing specific types of payments can be offloaded to partner banks. These suppliers can be swapped in or out, depending on costs and quality of services provided. The related IT services supporting these business services need to allow for these requirements. Another business process change may be driven by the need to lower costs. In countries where checks are used, check processing is an area where economies of scale make a difference. This business service may be outsourced in order to achieve lower costs.

The most advanced companies were those that had made the most progress in integrating business processes and infrastructure, both internally and with their suppliers, customers, and other external partners. Not only had they achieved high levels of integration and automation of key processes, but they were able to manage

those processes in a dynamic, flexible, and highly responsive manner, building capabilities that are critical to supporting on demand initiatives.

The results were impressive. Companies that have displayed the attributes of flexibility and this link between IT and business have shown clear gains in business results when compared to their peers.

We found that, on average, these companies grew earnings 17 points faster than their peers and experienced 1.3 points of improved net profit margin, 1.3 points better difference in ROI, and .7 points better difference in return on assets (ROA).

In the battle for growth, each point can make a difference in market leadership. For example, for a company with $5 billion in revenues, a single-point gain in gross profit margin (GPM) yields $50 million. A 2-point gain in GPM for a company with $40 billion in revenues yields $800 million.

So as you can see, most CEOs are looking beyond product or service innovation, and more are looking to business process model innovation as a key differentiator. As one CEO put it, "Products and services can be copied. The business model is the differentiator." But I believe this focus on business model innovation is also connected to this newfound realization of the power of flexibility. To innovate, the aperture is opened further and we see the market shift from a mindset of "invented here" to "innovation everywhere." It's a natural next step to envision business processes that formalize that innovation through collaboration. The key is to begin to focus on what differentiates you the most and have partners to help do the rest. The new business process becomes more open, and firms begin to partner more extensively. The world becomes flat. So what technology most expedites flexibility, collaboration, and innovation?

In this book, we discuss how the new technologies of SOA and Web 2.0 allow this new competitive world to exist. They are the new language of business because they enable a focus on processes through business services. This new language assists companies in becoming flex-pon-sive*.

SUMMARY

A flex-pon-sive* business is about business effectiveness enabled by thoughtful, well-designed investments in IT focused on business models and processes. Companies that go down that path show, on average, significantly better business results than their peers. Business flexibility, through approaches like SOA and Web 2.0, enables leaders to take informed, decisive action to achieve the agility they need for market success.

So the imperative of becoming an innovative business is one that leads to growth and flexibility required to compete in today's world but also, more important, in tomorrow's more competitive world.

2

What Is Flex-pon-sive*?

More than 75% of CEOs place a high priority on the ability to respond rapidly, yet only one in ten CEOs believes that his or her organization has the capability to be very responsive to react to changing market conditions. Companies need to establish effective, real-time response capabilities by establishing business flexibility in their business processes. Competitive advantage comes from aligning these processes with IT infrastructure. Business Process Management transforms a company by integrating and automating key business processes and IT processes across the enterprise for increased business flexibility. Flex-pon-sive* becomes table stakes in today's environment.

WHAT DOES FLEX-PON-SIVE* MEAN?

Business flexibility is a key element in a company's growth strategy. The terrain for today's businesses is fraught with competitors, complexity, regulations, consolidation, demanding customers, and business models that must change quickly and precisely. To navigate

successfully, these organizations must be flexible, from both a business and an IT perspective. That's the core of flex-pon-sive*.

> What is flex-pon-sive*? It is the description of a company that responds with lightning speed and agility to rapidly changing business needs. This company must have a focus on processes that are enabled for change through IT.

It is not just looking at the business side or the IT side, but knowing that the power comes from linking the two. It is the ability to become more responsive to changing market conditions, including opportunities, customers, and competitive actions.

Companies need to be flexible enough to identify new opportunities and respond to them rapidly and economically, and to react to any customer or partner demand as well as to external threats. They need to accurately plan and manage demand, shorten the product-development lifecycle, and consolidate systems and information from constant merger and acquisitions activity. Some examples of business flexibility challenges include the ability to establish a single view of customers as a means to drive sales, connect supply chains to better respond to customer demand changes (such as out-of-stock products or the need for new products), or provide consistent multichannel access for customers to increase customer loyalty.

So we are not just talking about any flexibility, but the flexibility that matters to a company's bottom line. Flex-pon-sive* companies have the flexibility that drives them to not just respond to the environment, but drive the environment forward. They combine the power of IT and business to drive the market to new places. Flex-pon-sive* companies enable flexibility and quick reaction time, which are very important qualities in uncertain situations. Remember from Chapter 1, "The Innovation Imperative," the key statistics from the CEO survey: Two-thirds of CEOs believe they'll need to respond to change in the next two years. Flexibility is required.

WHAT DRIVES FLEXIBILITY TODAY?

As you are reading this, you are probably thinking, "Business flexibility is not a recent requirement." Businesses have always wanted to do more and do it quickly, but in today's environment, changes have made this more than just a desire—it's now a need. In the past, the IT infrastructure was inflexible. As a result, more IT efforts focused on what was possible from an IT perspective instead of what was required and needed from a business perspective. Because there were no real threats in the marketplace, companies began to accept inflexibility because there was no incentive to radically change.

Today we see that business flexibility is required. A flex-pon-sive* company is one that will succeed because of the change required. Combine globalization and regulatory requirements—both business drivers that dictate that your company must become flexible if it is to succeed—with the recent technology advancements of SOA, Web 2.0, and open standards that make IT flexibility possible, and the market is ready to not only change, but also demand flexibility.

The following list describes the two major drivers of the increasing need for flexibility today that make it more of an imperative than it was yesterday.

- **Economics**—As the marketplace globalizes, new markets, new workforces, and new competitors are making companies look for ways to adapt more quickly. Companies that can't differentiate themselves are being forced to compete with what *BusinessWeek* calls "The China Price," defined as 30% to 50% less than what something can possibly be made for in the U.S. The struggle against commoditization is happening across all industries and countries. Differentiation is driven by innovation, continuously creating innovative products and services and, in most cases, leveraging standard components, transforming and improving business processes again and again. Think like today's leading companies that are never content

with the status quo. Every time they change a process to stay ahead of their competitors, the associated business systems need to change to support the revised business process. It's never-ending.

- **Speed of market**—The cycle time is shrinking between changes in business processes. Whereas we might have seen companies make significant changes to processes yearly in the past, you'll see the same level of change on a monthly or even weekly basis. The challenge in today's world? With ever-increasing pressure on time and cost, how does a business coordinate all of its activities: selling around the globe, sourcing products and labor internationally, and designing and building the latest products that customers want from components that are rapidly changing? Motorola delivered 60 new cell phones in 2004, all made from standard components. To avoid commodity hell, companies must create a very different set of innovative business capabilities on a responsive basis—faster and faster. It is like *Alice in Wonderland*, with Alice having to run as fast as she can just to stay in the same place.

Companies must reduce their cycle times and their time to design, develop, and deliver products to market. But it doesn't stop there; they must reduce the time to transform processes, the time to respond to customer problems, and the time to build relationships with customers and partners. They must coordinate inside and outside of the enterprise and build responsive supply chains with very little inventory by effectively planning and sharing information.

Flexibility seems like a natural goal. What's the inhibitor?

CASE STUDY
BOMBARDIER AEROSPACE: BUSINESS FLEXIBILITY STRATEGY TAKES FLIGHT

By way of history, Bombardier Aerospace has a legacy of innovation that consolidates more than 250 years of aviation history. The company produced 14 new aircraft programs in the past 14 years. Based in Montreal, Quebec, Canada, the company has more than 28,000 employees worldwide and in locations that include Toronto, Canada, as well as Wichita, Kansas, United States, and Belfast, Northern Ireland.

Since competition in the international aerospace industry is intense, many aerospace companies are trying to gain an advantage by making their internal processes more efficient and more flexible. Bombardier is no exception.

The company was faced with significant business challenges around flexibility and cost containment. First, they needed to gain a more visible view into their supply chain; second was the need to extend critical information to customers and partners; and third was Bombardier's need to integrate the people and processes that resulted from significant shifts in the business. All of these challenges would allow them to have more business flexibility.

More specifically, Bombardier needed to be able to track products, fulfill customers' orders faster, and maintain better control over the products in its warehouses. Additionally, the company was faced with a lack of visibility in identifying spare parts information across multiple manufacturing lines, which often resulted in duplicate orders and shipment delays. Adding to the complexity was the fact that Bombardier had recently undergone several significant mergers and acquisitions, which resulted in various silos of information throughout the company.

Bombardier leveraged on demand business techniques to ensure their flexibility by doing the following:

continues

- Integrating disparate sources of information throughout the company.

- Streamlining business processes and accelerating the supply chain.

For example, Bombardier can now place orders through its ERP system and have instant access to what has been ordered and what parts are required to fill the order. As a result, the solution has significantly reduced the time required to fulfill customers' orders and provided Bombardier with the ability to have increased competitiveness through business flexibility.

In addition, this added business flexibility allows Bombardier to take advantage of dramatically reduced cycle times, which results in cost savings, efficient handling of spare parts, and a consolidated view of the purchasing process and supply chain. The company has been able to decrease that 40-day complex interface building process down to 10 days and, more important, has realized a cost savings of between 50% and 60% in what was previously allocated to development, support, and maintenance.

As the Bombardier case study shows, solving immediate business problems while simultaneously laying the groundwork for flexible IT that is capable of adapting to quickly changing business conditions is key. Although these solutions were implemented by Bombardier to address specific business needs, the basic concepts are universal. Concepts such as reuse of existing business functions, improvement of business processes, easier application connectivity using open standards, and separation of back- and front-end systems are relevant to virtually every enterprise that uses IT.

The future success of IT will be based on how easily services can be pieced together to quickly create new business solutions. SOA, backed by robust standards, technologies, and best practices, will enable this success.

BUSINESS RESPONSE: WHAT DOES IT TAKE TO BE A WINNER?

As we have seen, a focus on business process and business models is a key to business flexibility. Beyond product or service innovation, most companies are looking to business model innovation as a key differentiator. A company needs to directly address its flexibility strategy by emphasizing monitoring and management of both business and IT processes and models. By managing both business and IT processes within an integrated framework, enterprises are better able to align IT resources to meet business priorities. While enterprise business executives examine the results of core business process execution, they obtain business views of the IT infrastructure to recommend IT specific actions that will generate the greatest benefit to the business.

To start to achieve competitiveness in flexibility, unprecedented levels of integration are required to realize these improvements to the business environment. Integrations starts with the ability to model and simulate a business process, and optimize that process through simulation proactively before expending resources to put it into production. Then businesses need to integrate people, processes, and information throughout the enterprise and to connect with customers and partners for efficient business-to-business operations. Finally, companies should be able to monitor, analyze, and manage business processes from start to finish.

For example, business managers should be able to monitor the supply chain minute by minute, be alerted of abnormalities, and adjust manufacturing activities to meet overall business goals. Many companies have started to integrate their business processes and manage their overall IT infrastructure to gain efficiencies; they need to adapt these resources more effectively for greater time and cost savings. Today managers are able to analyze historical data and static reports from their operations to identify trends and communicate business results. Now they want access to real-time information, on demand, to make effective decisions faster. Ultimately, they want a solution that supplies timely information, proactively makes recommendations, and provides a dynamic mechanism for the underlying systems to respond.

Enterprises can improve business performance by evolving from an environment of manual or isolated business functions with limited feedback to one that provides automated, connected, and integrated processes with highly visible metrics. For example, they can provide higher levels of service to customers when Internet operations are linked with back-office systems or when e-commerce systems are synchronized with retail business operations and other customer channels. And the business can be more effective when intraenterprise business systems such as customer relationship management (CRM), enterprise resource planning (ERP), and supply chain management (SCM) are connected. Many companies use balanced scorecards that assess performance based on financial metrics. Although these are certainly useful, they provide a significantly delayed tool for managing performance and helping to ensure success. Business Process Management puts key performance indicators, in addition to financial results, in front of business executives to give them greater insight into their operations in real time.

A focus on process and business models provides the benefit of anticipating and responding to client needs, competitive threats, regulations, and the ability to see business information and understand and adapt business processes and IT infrastructure accordingly. It consists of a set of capabilities to analyze and model processes, monitor business performance in real time, track current performance against goals and historical trends, and align IT management with business priorities.

We take a deeper look at processes, how to determine which ones are of value for your company to focus on, and how to leverage that focus to align business and IT. With a set of tools that will help you apply a flex-pon-sive* view to your processes, we look at this as a journey through a set of projects. But as the new business model and focus on processes becomes more open and distinct, and as firms begin to partner more extensively globally, they will require a technology that expedites this focus. That technology focus will be service oriented architecture (SOA).

SOA is a business-driven IT architectural approach that supports integrating your business as linked, repeatable business tasks or

services. It helps today's businesses innovate by ensuring that IT systems can adapt quickly, easily, and economically to support rapidly changing business needs. SOA helps customers increase the flexibility of their business processes, strengthen their underlying IT infrastructure, and reuse their existing IT investments by creating connections among disparate applications and information sources.

SUMMARY

Business flexibility is a mandate in today's economic and fast-moving market.

Businesses are under pressure to expand aggressively and reduce costs while doing so. Balancing these demands requires ability to act upon business decisions quickly, economically, and with minimal disruption to the business. In this environment, the agility to recognize and react to rapidly changing opportunities ahead of competitors has never been more important. All to often, business processes that are shackled to rigid, complex, silo'ed IT systems reduce companies' agility and, therefore, competitiveness. This inflexibility and rigidity can keep leaders from taking bold action to reach their objectives. As business processes grow more and more dependent on the IT systems that support them, line-of-business executives are working more closely with CIOs and demanding more from them. CIOs need to find ways to use IT systems to enhance agility rather than constrain it.

Flex-pon-sive* companies know that flexibility is not an option, but a mandate. With the recent technology advancements and the move toward standards, companies today can actually become flex-pon-sive* quickly. Technology no longer will stand in the way of innovation. The market has the technical means, the technical foundation, to innovate. It is an era of massive reinvention, innovation, and expansion.

This is not to say that technology is an end in itself. It's a means to something else. Though in its infancy now, SOA promises to democratize information and unleash capability much as the

Internet—which, I believe, was the last technology revolution of comparable magnitude—has.

How can you prevent it from turning into anarchy, chaos? How do you manage and govern it all? These are pressing questions because, as experience has continually reminded us, the only way to capture the benefits of freedom is to corral and direct it, not to suppress it. These aren't technical challenges. These are process challenges and cultural issues. They speak to the very character and nature of your firm.

To address flexibility requires first a focus on the alignment of business processes and models with your company's objectives. This Business Process Management view is the starting point for ensuring your company's competitiveness. Now the environment is ripe for change. The next step is to determine which of your business models and processes will play the most significant role in your transformation. In the rest of this book, I will help you take stock of where you are today; identify your goals and priorities for making your business more flex-pon-sive* and agile; chart a course to get from where you are to where you want to be; start your journey with focused, well-defined entry point projects and build on them as your maturity and sophistication grow.

3

Deconstructing Your Business: Component Business Model

To gain business and IT alignment, you must focus on the right business processes. Your company must view your business processes as a set of linked components that address the strategic, technical, operational, organizational, and financial issues that businesses deal with today. Because industries and enterprises are disaggregating themselves and spreading the implementation of individual business tasks to the parties that can best deliver these specialized services (for example, in electronics, financial services, and automotive), they need tools and insight that help them determine their competitive advantage and how to drive growth based on their unique value proposition to customers. Having a view of the processes, both those that you have built over the past years and the new ones that you need to grow, enables your company to spot areas where you need to improve and differentiate. This enables you to focus on the right set of processes and the outcomes that you need to achieve to drive the business. This is another step in becoming a flex-pon-sive* company.

To assist your company in this step, you need to do the following:

- Deconstruct your business by breaking it up into logical components

- Decide what's differentiating and what is commodity overhead

- Decide how to invest:

    1. Analyze costs to figure out what each activity costs you.

    2. Combine duplicate activities.

    3. Outsource expensive commodity activities.

    4. Invest greater resources in differentiating and cost-competitive activities.

COMPETING IN AN ERA OF SPECIALIZATION

In the new economy, CEOs must respond to unstoppable forces and demanding stakeholders. Fortunately, firms can leverage new technologies to rethink their organizational models and industry positions. Virtually every industry has been moving down the path of external specialization. Firms must decide where to play so they can maximize their growth and optimization while satisfying three demanding stakeholders groups: customers, employees, and shareholders. A recent IBM paper hypothesized that, by 2010, the world's most successful firms will be "specialized enterprises" focusing on critical components or building blocks. The new ideal model structures the enterprise as a network of modular business building blocks. To begin to develop modular business building blocks, start by deconstructing your business into logical component processes, determine your differentiation, and analyze the benefits that you can measure.

STEP 1: DECONSTRUCTING YOUR BUSINESS

To focus on the right areas, a business first needs to deconstruct its business model—break it into discrete business components (see Figure 3.1).

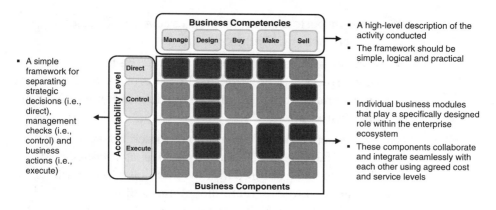

Source: IBM Business Consulting Services

Figure 3.1 Business component model

First, let's look at the terminology we use.

- **Business component**—A business component's *purpose* is the logical reason for its existence within the organization, as defined by the value it provides to other components. Examples of a business component are those that obtain customer insight or deliver products. Components require *resources*—the people, knowledge, and tangible assets that support their activities. Each component conducts a mutually exclusive set of *activities* to achieve its business purpose, and serves a unique purpose and collaborates with other components within the business model by using agreed cost and service levels. Similar to a stand-alone business, each business component provides and receives *business services*.

- **Accountability levels**—These refer to a simple framework for separating strategic decisions (direct), management checks (control), and business actions (execute). The three accountability levels imply different priorities.

  - **Direct**—Components at this level provide strategic direction and corporate policy for other components. They also facilitate collaboration with other components.

  - **Control**—These midtier components serve as checks and balances between the "direct" and "execute" levels. They

monitor performance, manage exceptions, and act as gate-keepers of assets and information.

- **Execute**—These components provide the business actions that drive value creation in the enterprise. They process assets and information for use by other components or the end customer.

At the "execute" level, for example, the emphasis is on keeping people fully occupied and productive. Components at this level tend to be structured in ways that make information easily available. From a technology standpoint, speed of data entry and real-time availability are key. When customers go to an ATM, for instance, they want a simple interface that provides accurate information in a straightforward format: How much money is in my account?

Contrast this with activities related to the "direct" tier, where such high-level activities as launching new products are handled. This level houses a small number of people who have a very large impact on shareholder value, so the design imperatives are nearly the opposite of those at the "execute" tier. Launching a new product requires collaboration among several elements, including marketing, risk, finance, regulatory, and credit. Input from all of these stakeholders is needed to make the launch a success, so workflow is a key requirement. From a technology standpoint, activities typically require people to discern patterns and trends from rich, multidimensional data, usually stored in a data warehouse. So systems at the direct level are not designed for speed of data entry, but rather for ease, breadth, and depth of analysis. Real-time interfaces are not needed because data is often months old and is processed in batches.

- **Business competencies**—A business competency is a high-level description of the type of business value provided to the enterprise. The description should be a simple, logical, and practical set of activities that make up the description, and those activities should be mutually exclusive and collectively exhaustive. A generic description across all types of businesses could be "Manage, Design, Buy, Make, Sell," but other frameworks can be used for specific firms and industries.

Manage is about directive and support activities that are strategic or administrative in nature. *Design* is a set of product- and service-creation activities that ensure future business growth. *Buy* is procurement and aggregation activities that serve as inputs to the make function. *Make* is manufacturing and other value-added activities that create the end product or service. *Sell* is sales, marketing, delivery, and service activities that connect with customers. Business competencies should be industry specific and should provide a simple framework for organizing components (see Figure 3.2).

Industry Examples of Business Competencies

Key	
Sales	Business competency
▪Billing	Sample components

Consumer Products Firm

Business Administration	Manufacturing	Supply Chain and Distribution	Customer Relationship	Consumer Relationship
▪ Corporate strategy ▪ Regulatory compliance ▪ HR administration	▪ Production planning ▪ Procurement ▪ Assembly	▪ Supply chain strategy ▪ Logistics ▪ En route inventory	▪ Relationship strategy ▪ Account management ▪ Account servicing	▪ Brand strategy ▪ Product management ▪ Consumer service

Financial Services Firm

Business Admin.	Financial Mgmt.	Product Mgmt.	Product Operations	Customer Portfolio	Customer Accounting	Customer Service
▪ Planning ▪ Facilities ▪ Acquisitions	▪ Risk ▪ Securitization ▪ Treasury	▪ Marketing ▪ Development ▪ Directory	▪ Authorizations ▪ Processing ▪ Inventory	▪ Analysis ▪ Profiling ▪ Correspondence	▪ Policies ▪ Reconciliations ▪ Billing	▪ Planning ▪ Case handling ▪ Sales

Pharmaceuticals Firm

Business Admin.	Business Development	Research & Development	Manufacturing	Distribution	Channel Management	Patient Relationship
▪ HR planning ▪ Quality oversight ▪ Accounting	▪ Strategy ▪ Performance ▪ Licensing	▪ Portfolio mgmt. ▪ Monitoring ▪ Discovery	▪ Planning ▪ Oversight ▪ Packaging	▪ Wholesaling ▪ Logistics ▪ Tracking	▪ Pricing strategy ▪ Brand mgmt. ▪ Customer service	▪ Strategy ▪ Research ▪ Advertising

Source: IBM Business Consulting Services

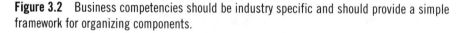

Figure 3.2   Business competencies should be industry specific and should provide a simple framework for organizing components.

No doubt, you have an organizational chart describing your sales organization. But do you have a chart like Figure 3.3 that tells you what it does? Everything it does? Do you know which things it does that other parts of the organization also do? Are other groups throughout the enterprise in need of something similar? Do you know what each process costs you?

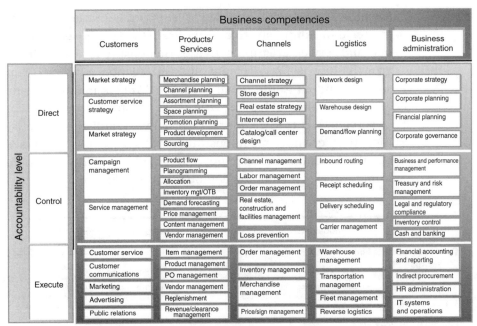

Business competencies				
Customers	Products/ Services	Channels	Logistics	Business administration

Accountability level

Direct
Market strategy	Merchandise planning	Channel strategy	Network design	Corporate strategy
	Channel planning	Store design		Corporate planning
Customer service strategy	Assortment planning	Real estate strategy	Warehouse design	
	Space planning	Internet design		Financial planning
	Promotion planning			
Market strategy	Product development	Catalog/call center design	Demand/flow planning	Corporate governance
	Sourcing			

Control
Campaign management	Product flow	Channel management	Inbound routing	Business and performance management
	Planogramming	Labor management		
	Allocation	Order management	Receipt scheduling	Treasury and risk management
	Inventory mgt/OTB			
Service management	Demand forecasting	Real estate, construction and facilities management	Delivery scheduling	Legal and regulatory compliance
	Price management			
	Content management		Carrier management	Inventory control
	Vendor management	Loss prevention		Cash and banking

Execute
Customer service	Item management	Order management	Warehouse management	Financial accounting and reporting
Customer communications	Product management	Inventory management		
	PO management		Transportation management	Indirect procurement
Marketing	Vendor management	Merchandise management		HR administration
Advertising	Replenishment		Fleet management	IT systems and operations
Public relations	Revenue/clearance management	Price/sign management	Reverse logistics	

Source: IBM Business Consulting Services.

Figure 3.3 Example component business model

Figure 3.4 shows an example of the Component Business Model (CBM). This example shows a company in the consumer packaged goods industry, but this approach can be applied to organizations in any industry. It reveals where you can consolidate, reorganize, and outsource—what it takes to make your business flexible in the face of uncertainty. The bottom line: You must break it down before you can build it up. The issues and opportunities might differ by industry, but this methodology for analyzing potential new business designs doesn't. The methodology combines in-depth industry expertise with sound methodology.

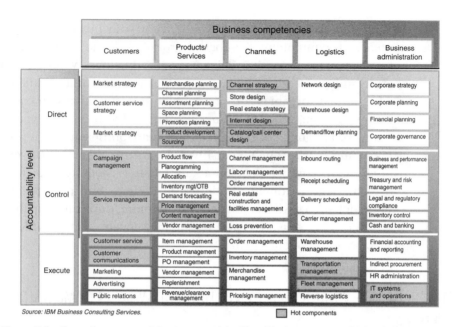

Business competencies				
Customers	Products/ Services	Channels	Logistics	Business administration

<table>
<tr><td rowspan="3">Accountability level</td><td rowspan="4">Direct</td><td>Market strategy</td><td>Merchandise planning</td><td>Channel strategy</td><td>Network design</td><td>Corporate strategy</td></tr>
</table>

Direct

	Customers	Products/Services	Channels	Logistics	Business administration
	Market strategy	Merchandise planning	Channel strategy	Network design	Corporate strategy
		Channel planning	Store design		Corporate planning
	Customer service strategy	Assortment planning	Real estate strategy	Warehouse design	
		Space planning			Financial planning
		Promotion planning	Internet design		
	Market strategy	Product development	Catalog/call center design	Demand/flow planning	Corporate governance
		Sourcing			

Control

	Customers	Products/Services	Channels	Logistics	Business administration
	Campaign management	Product flow	Channel management	Inbound routing	Business and performance management
		Planogramming	Labor management		
		Allocation	Order management	Receipt scheduling	Treasury and risk management
		Inventory mgt/OTB			
	Service management	Demand forecasting	Real estate construction and facilities management	Delivery scheduling	Legal and regulatory compliance
		Price management			
		Content management		Carrier management	Inventory control
		Vendor management	Loss prevention		Cash and banking

Execute

	Customers	Products/Services	Channels	Logistics	Business administration
	Customer service	Item management	Order management	Warehouse management	Financial accounting and reporting
	Customer communications	Product management	Inventory management		
		PO management		Transportation management	Indirect procurement
	Marketing	Vendor management	Merchandise management		HR administration
	Advertising	Replenishment		Fleet management	
	Public relations	Revenue/clearance management	Price/sign management	Reverse logistics	IT systems and operations

Source: IBM Business Consulting Services.    Hot components

Figure 3.4 Example component business model with critical components highlighted

NOTE

Over the past two years, the IBM Business Consulting Services and IBM Research and Development teams have come together to do a lot of work with CBMs. Although the concept has been around for a long time, they have focused on taking the component notion from generic to industry specific and from conceptual to highly practical and operational. This includes creating a methodology around linking a business component (and all of its parts—people, strategy, operations, and so on) through to the technology (applications and infrastructure) that will enable it. The teams have created CBMs for 69 industries. These models are designed to simplify the way a business looks at itself by identifying the unique set of business building blocks (components) it's made up of, allowing a more effective coupling between changes in business operations and the underlying technology infrastructure. This strengthens your ability to connect change and investments with the business outcomes and returns that you anticipate.

To start deconstructing your business, view your business components. Each component is a logical grouping of the people, technology, and resources that deliver specific business value or can operate independently. Create a map of the essential "building blocks" of your organization in a tabular structure that can easily fit on a single page. The value of this map is that it enables you to see how well aligned your organizational capabilities are with your strategy and how strongly your investments are aligned with your strategy; then you can develop a step-by-step integrated business and technology roadmap to address key issues and pain points. This model shows where you have overlapping/duplicate capabilities on both the business and technology levels, and provides a clear path to reconcile them.

STEP 2: DECIDE WHAT'S DIFFERENTIATING AND WHAT IS COMMODITY OVERHEAD

Step 2 is all about differentiation. After you break down the business into its components, you can look at which of these processes can really help you differentiate your business from the competition and which are simply the things you have to do to maintain your business. In our example, in Figure 3.4, we have highlighted this example company's differentiation. The component map provides a basis for developing strategic and operating insights for the business. By gauging the relative urgency of different areas of the map, executives can determine which components demand immediate attention. Given the company's strategy, which components are the most important? Which have the potential to create absolute advantage? What proportion of the value the firm creates can be attributed to each component?

Another consideration is sequence. After the initial areas are componentized, what logic will the course of improvement initiatives follow? This type of analysis yields a "heat map" that highlights areas where focus of additional resources promises the greatest return on investment in the shortest time frame. For example, near-term changes that enhance the firm's strategic differentiators are likely to be designated as "hot" areas. Low-hanging fruit could be areas where your company is already leveraging the concept of

a shared service. Pursuing such "quick wins" makes sense because efficiencies gained in the first round of componentization can be used to support subsequent rounds.

STEP 3: DECIDING HOW YOU INVEST

Step 3 involves deciding how you invest in certain business components and how they tie into the business outcomes. In particular, here is where your company would review a typical business case approach:

- Analyze costs to figure out what each activity costs
- Decide where you are combining duplicate activities
- Determine whether you outsource expensive commodity activities
- Place greater resources in differentiating and cost-competitive activities

Analyzing costs enables you to determine and size your next steps. For instance, you might want to combine duplicate activities to save costs and to make your business more effective. This might not be a differentiated task, but it might gain you some short-term benefits. A lot of companies who have gone through a merger or acquisition focus on these duplicate activities first. In addition, in Step 2, you decided on your heat maps of your most differentiated components. You need to focus on your strategy of placing greater resources on areas that differentiate you and potentially outsource expensive commodity-type activities. These will also change over time. What is a differentiation today could end up being a commodity in the near future. The key is to focus on a set of business components that can drive your growth through differentiation.

Over time, the emphasis placed on any particular aspect will vary, depending on the firm, the industry, and the current level of specialization. Most firms find that they must iterate strategically, selecting priorities that position them for further progress. At every stage, the enterprise should align its strategy with opportunities that create the most value most quickly. An enterprise can evolve toward its component-based vision by developing a reinvention plan. In fact, many firms have already begun the journey.

CASE STUDY
POSTFINANCE

PostFinance is a major Swiss financial services company who has recently adopted a steady growth strategy to achieve its five-year business goals. The company's senior management knew such rapid growth would have an enormous impact on the bank's IT structure. The company needed a strategic Enterprise Architecture to understand the IT implications of the business changes, particularly to highlight where the existing IT environment would not be able to support the execution of the business strategy in medium and long terms. PostFinance needed to develop a structured approach to translating the new business strategy into itemized and measurable actions, in order to align the tactical business focus with the strategy.

They explored a possible Enterprise Architecture solution based on existing information and structures by using the Component Business Model (CBM) methodology. The study lists the benefits as well as the cost related to developing and maintaining an Enterprise Architecture, in particular with regard to a series of strategic aspects raised by the bank's executive management team.

The three-tier Enterprise Architecture proposed in the study encompasses PostFinance's business, application, and technical levels, linking each aspect with the help of financial management data structures.

- The Business Architecture is based on CBM heat map and describes the key business functions, the key activities, and the key resources within a business component. Furthermore, the Business Architecture includes the key performance indicators (KPI) for sizing the component, analyzing performance, and calculating costs.

- The Application Architecture describes the applications supporting the business components. For every application, a

detailed application pass provides information on linkage to business components, linkage to applications, functionality, service levels, security, and costs.

- The Technical Architecture provides information on systems and how they are linked to applications and other systems.

The outlined Enterprise Architecture solution highlights the IT implications of the PostFinance's business strategy and helps determine whether the current IT environment is capable of supporting the bank in achieving its goals.

PostFinance's benefits were both strategic and tactical. They gained additional business insight and a greater understanding of the relation among the underlying IT environment (applications and systems) and the alignment of business goals and IT objectives. Overall, this outlines short- and long-term cost/benefit ratio and positions PostFinance for growth and increased market share.

CASE STUDY
Porto Media

Porto Media, a new media service provider and development company in Ireland, shaved years off product launch times by developing a security standard for its product and develop and design the business and technical architecture to move it from startup to service provision in six months.

Porto Media had created proprietary technology for dual interface secure digital (SD) memory cards to enable very fast loading of digital content—2GB in 18 seconds. Porto Media envisioned a new digital content delivery service that would use kiosks set up in retail and other locations to allow customers to download music and movies onto high-speed SD card, and then play or watch that content on compatible devices such as hand-held players, compatible home media centers, or phones. The main barrier that Porto Media faced was a common one for companies seeking to

continues

establish such services—the need to be able to secure high-value content in order to drive user demand. Without a high level of content protection and strong usage constraints in place, it was doubtful that any provider of music videos or movies would allow its content to be included within the service.

Porto Media also needed to move quickly from a startup/development company to a viable service delivery company. To do this, it not only had to build a content delivery infrastructure from the ground up, but it also had to design the company's business processes and organizational structure to support the new business model.

First, Porto Media had to determine what an on demand media rental company would look like—what structures, processes, and organization would it need? They chose the Component Business Modeling methodology to map out the capabilities, organizational structure, and business processes, as well as a cost model. Porto Media sped its time-to-delivery of its first workable prototype and defined business model to six months—potential competitors have struggled for two to five years to produce a content-delivery model that content providers would embrace. The service oriented architecture (SOA) approach to the design of the delivery platform will cut development time for the platform in half, in comparison to competitors, and will enable Porto Media to operate as a truly on demand content business.

CASE STUDY
AN ELECTRONICS COMPANY

In the highly competitive consumer electronics industry, product profit margins continue to be compressed. Companies are looking to generate additional revenue and profit elsewhere in their business. An electronics company realized it had an opportunity

to transform its service and support operations from a primary warranty support operation to a services and solutions operation, generating additional revenues and margins. The company had two goals: Incremental services revenue growth two times current revenue and reducing "cost of quality" through transformation—significant double-digit recurring improvement to profitability.

They used the Component Business Model (CBM) methodology to develop a Growth and Transformation Roadmap that would help it meet its dual goals of positioning the services business to meet growth objectives, and improving the efficiency of and lowering costs for the services organization by optimizing business processes. The CBM methodology allowed them to map out the processes and performance of their Service After Sales Operations organization and benchmark it against key competitors.

The team identified several transformation initiatives for which it developed detailed business cases, operational models, and roadmaps. The work was a collaborative effort with the electronics company, who prioritize the initiatives and map out partnerships, vendor relationships, and launch plans for each. They identified 73 growth and 20 transformation opportunities based on market/savings potential and competitive trends.

By rapidly moving from concept to detailed executable plans across the transformation roadmap, the team was able to begin capturing significant benefits within the time frame of the initial engagement.

Working to define an aggressive yet manageable program, the joint team developed an initiative program, including quick-hits, which were self-funding—savings generated within the initial six-month period were used to fund subsequent execution initiatives in the growth and transformation areas.

PATTERNS OF SUCCESS

In examining companies that have begun this journey, we can identify three major patterns, check out their focus and flex-ponsive* nature.

First, firms that focus on bottom-line improvements by reducing costs and becoming more flexible succeed by creating efficiency and responsiveness. To overcome organizational inertia, they typically begin the journey with activities that already function as components. These "pre-existing" components—shared service centers are one example—provide a momentum-establishing foundation of quick wins (and a funding base for carrying the strategy through to subsequent stages). These companies focus on initiatives that are aligned with the component map, eliminating or adjusting initiatives that do not embrace the enterprise vision, especially those that add process complexity or incur excess costs. They prioritize the creation of components based on financial value, strategic value, and investment requirements.

The second pattern includes firms that have matched industry change through business model changes and transformed themselves. These companies are flexible and forward-thinking, maintaining market share and state-of-the-market performance throughout the transformation—a tall order indeed. They continuously monitor the market for value opportunities and risks, while constantly assessing their componentization plans based on the interplay between the enterprise (internal) and industry (external) views. This requires an ongoing measurement process that provides management with a feedback mechanism for reviewing the performance of components.

These company's adopters follow best practices, create component benchmarks to support excellence, and develop industry benchmarks within and across components. If internal components become best-in-class, they consider offering them externally to generate new revenues. If component performance lags, they leverage external partners.

The third pattern is found in firms that focus on top-line growth through the construction of networks and ecosystems. They try to

maintain market share and state-of-the-market performance by leveraging proven partners and offerings. In pursuing the network route, care must be taken to fight the right industry battles. Because absolute advantage is critical to success in a fully networked industry, it is vital for network players to carefully monitor competitors—both traditional rivals and new entrants—and to develop a thorough understanding of the trends that shape the industry network as it matures. Moving ahead of the market is a real risk, as is the chance that the industry will choose to rally around an open standard.

LEVERAGING CBM TO DELIVER VALUE

To compete in the emerging world of flexible, open-value networks, companies need to focus on the few activities in which they have a truly differentiating advantage in the value they provide or the cost at which they deliver compared to the competition. CBM points the way forward by giving executives leverage to drive flexibility, scalability, efficiency, and openness throughout the enterprise. On the external side, CBM enables firms to improve how they manage people, processes, and technology.

Aggregating people into cohesive groups allows them to focus clearly on what they know best, even as they learn to coordinate cross-organizational operations. Centralizing redundant processes into modules can drive scale gains and best practices across the organization. Finally, componentization reduces the number of technology gaps, overextensions, and duplications, allowing the firm to cut noncore investments and identify opportunities to develop new services based on excess capacity in existing technologies. In this new environment, proprietary industry value chains are an anachronism, and hardwired business structures are a liability. Today, if your business is struggling to align itself and decide on successful business priorities, a CBM might be the right starting point for you. It can assist you in addressing strategic issues aligning business capabilities to the overall strategy and identifying differentiating requirements. By ensuring that investments are aligned with the business strategy, you can ensure that all areas of the company are focused on the right priorities.

NOTE

In my world, I deal with a lot of customers who have gone through mergers and acquisitions. CBM enables a comprehensive, nonpolitical, and nonsiloed view of the organizational capabilities, and aids in creating a single roadmap for integration. In addition, a CBM can help prioritize your transformation initiatives by creating integrated business and technology transformation roadmaps that align with the overall strategy.

An example is a large CPG company, who recalls how they approached maximization of their recent merger. Initially, this client wanted to perform a finance benchmarking project. The results of this project highlighted the need to understand the overall key differentiators of the business, how the local business unit operating models needed to change to focus on these differentiators, and how they would connect the operating model vision to the technology strategy in the new merged company. Using the CBM approach helped this client answer these questions. The results of this analysis are operating model patterns for each business unit that directly link to the strategic positioning and technology strategies of the company maximizing their investments for the merger. These patterns also drive the development of an impact assessment, a transformation roadmap and the supporting business case. In the end, the company expects the benefits to focus on the elimination of duplicate business processes and organizational realignment, to reduce costs and increase focus on core business services.

SUMMARY

Breaking your business into a set of components involves a deep understanding of your business and the value the components bring to it. A key to success is deciding what's differentiating and what's simply operating from a process perspective. This differentiation is specific to your industry and, more particularly, to your business. Deciding which of the differentiating components to focus on involves deciding how your company approaches change: incrementally or as a market maker. Both have implications, and both have been used successfully. A component business model enables you to start linking the business and IT alignment for success. This discovery brings you closer to becoming a flex-pon-sive* company that can innovate for its competitive advantage. To innovate your business processes and business models, you need a technology that expedites and aligns business and IT. That technology focus is service oriented architecture (SOA).

II

A Flexible Business Requires Flexible IT

4

SOA as the DNA of a Flex-pon-sive* and Innovative Company

Service oriented architecture (SOA) is more than a buzzword; SOA is revolutionizing the way we think about IT and is a crucial element for all business leaders in becoming flex-pon-sive*. SOA is the IT enabler of flexibility, its core DNA. It is an evolutionary approach to building information technology (IT) systems that are focused on solving business problems. In my experience, it is the only way to support the business demands and innovation demands of the new flex-pon-sive* company. This innovation to IT structures is so revolutionizing that the proven successes of SOAs have enabled this segment to grow to a worldwide market opportunity of $60.3 billion in 2006. This is a 75% increase in growth compared to 2005, when the market was estimated at $34.6 billion. Moreover, the SOA market is expected to skyrocket, with an anticipated 54% compound annual growth through 2008, to reach $143 billion.

Why is that possible? Because SOA finally has the potential to make the concept of business flexibility real. Companies have been talking about flexibility for years

but have never been able to transform that talk into full-scale reality. Now, you might be asking, "How can SOA succeed where previous approaches have failed?" The standards, best practices, and governance models have finally matured to the point that business flexibility can actually work through reuse and modularity. SOA is the DNA for a company's business flexibility strategy.

In this chapter, the definition of SOA is discussed at a high level, and the SOA reference architecture is shown as a guiding roadmap for your company.

This chapter is just the start of this important concept. Chapter 5, "SOA Key Concepts," goes into a little more detail on the IT attributes that makes SOA the enabler for flexible IT. Chapter 6, "SOA Governance and Service Lifecycle," and Chapter 7, "Three Business-Centric SOA Entry Points," discusses why SOA is the key enabler for business flexibility. In addition, the rest of this book centers on this crucial innovation combined with Web 2.0 as the new language of business and IT.

WHAT IS SERVICE ORIENTED ARCHITECTURE?

What is SOA? Service oriented architecture (SOA) is a business-driven IT architectural approach that supports integrating your business as linked, repeatable business tasks or services. SOA helps today's businesses innovate by ensuring that IT systems can adapt quickly, easily, and economically to support rapidly changing business needs. It helps customers increase the flexibility of their business processes, strengthen their underlying IT infrastructure, and reuse their existing IT investments by creating connections among disparate applications and information sources.

Service oriented architecture begins with a service—a service being simply a business task, such as checking a potential customer's credit rating only opening a new account. It's important to stress that we're talking about a part of a business process here. Don't think about software or IT. Think about what your company does on a day-to-day basis, and break up those business processes into repeatable business tasks or components. (Think back to our

discussion of CBM, the act of breaking your business into these repeatable tasks!)

Service orientation is still focused on the business and is the way a company views the various functions that make up a company. Think about our discussion on deconstructing your business into a set of processes made up of components. These repeatable business tasks could be implemented by services. Services here are the building blocks of flexible IT systems that support your business processes. If your business views itself as a set of services connected to produce a particular outcome, then your business uses a service-oriented approach to bring high value goods and services to the market. This is becoming the pervasive way to view a business, and I believe it will soon become table stakes in the market.

SOA is an architectural approach that follows service-orientation principles to make software resources more flexibly available. SOA provides the technology underpinnings for working with services that are not just software or hardware, but rather business tasks. It is a pattern for developing a more flexible kind of software applications that can promote loose coupling among software components while reusing existing investments in technology in new, more valuable ways across the organization. SOA is based on standards that enable interoperability, business agility, and innovation to generate more business value for those who use these principles.

Most decisions that companies make to facilitate innovation and flexibility deem responding to a rapidly changing business force as a necessity. SOA makes change easier. Rigidly integrating IT systems together in short-sighted ways for today's immediate needs makes change difficult, time-consuming, and expensive. Instead, SOA breaks IT into building blocks that are easy to assemble and configure and reconfigure. These building blocks are called services. Because these services are built on open standards, they can be easily integrated with other IT systems without fear of vendor lock-in, and they inspire reuse. Because you can use what you already have in a service-enabled form (that is, you don't have to subject your company to the risk of modifying your current trusted applications and systems), and you can add new building blocks or services, or combine them with someone else's.

With this view of SOA, you can see how SOA helps companies become more agile by enabling the alignment of business needs and the IT capabilities that support these needs—the services that IT delivers support tasks that your business performs. Business drives requirements for IT; SOA enables the IT environment to effectively and efficiently respond to these requirements. SOA is about helping companies apply reusability and flexibility that can lower cost (of development, integration, maintenance), increase revenue, and obtain sustainable competitive advantage through technology.

It is very important to note that SOA is an evolution, not a revolution. Although its results are revolutionary, it builds on many technologies that we have been using in the marketplace, such as web services, transactional technologies, information-driven principles, loose coupling, components, object-oriented design/development, event-delivery models, EJB, and .NET. The beauty of SOA is that these technologies exist together in SOA through standards, well-defined interfaces, and organizational commitments to reuse key services instead of "reinventing the wheel." None of these technologies delivers SOA. SOA is not just about technology, but about how technology and business link themselves for a common goal of business flexibility.

Businesses have become increasingly complex over the past couple of decades. Factors such as mergers, regulations, global competition, outsourcing, and partnering have resulted in a massive increase in the number of applications any given company might use. Even if these applications were purchased or developed in the context of a logical master plan, the forces that influenced creation of that master plan will surely change. These applications were implemented with little knowledge of the other applications with which they would be required to share information in the future. As a result, many companies are trying to maintain IT systems that coexist but are not integrated.

When is a company ready for SOA? The answer is, anytime and every time. SOA is not a destination, but more of a mindset for running your company; different companies might find that different approaches and degrees of service orientation are right for them. Companies face a variety of business issues—Table 4.1 lists a subset of those.

Table 4.1   Business Issues and SOA Solutions

Business Issues	SOA Can Help...
■ Agents unable to see policy coverage information remotely ■ Calls/faxes used to get information from other divisions ■ Clinical patient information stored on paper in clinic ■ Complex access to supplier design drawings	Integrate *information* to make it more accessible to employees
■ High cost of handling customer calls ■ Reconciliation of off-invoice deductions and rebates ■ Hours on hold to determine patient insurance eligibility ■ High turnover leading to excessive hiring and training costs	Understand how *business processes* interact to better manage administrative costs
■ Decreasing customer loyalty due to incorrect invoices ■ Customers placed on hold to check order status ■ Inability to quickly update policy endorsements ■ Poor service levels	Improve customer retention and deliver new products and services through *reuse* of their current investments
■ Time wasted reconciling separate databases ■ Manual processes such as handling trade allocations ■ Inability to detect quality flaws early in cycle ■ High percentage of scrap and rework	Improve *people* productivity with better business integration and *connectivity*

SOME KEY DEFINITIONS

Business Process Management (BPM)—A discipline that combines software capabilities and business expertise through people, systems, and information to accelerate time between process improvements, facilitating business innovation.

components—A modular unit of functionality, accessed through one or more interfaces. A component might be composed of other components, but a component is not necessarily a service.

composite application—A set of related and integrated services that support a business process built on an SOA.

connectivity—One of the five SOA entry points. It enables your company to exchange information among all your assets within and outside of your business through a secure, reliable, and scalable

continues

messaging backbone for seamless communication among applications, people, and information sources.

Enterprise Service Bus (ESB)—A flexible connectivity infrastructure for integrating applications and services by performing the following actions between services and requestors: routing messages between services, converting transport protocols between requestor and service, transforming message formats between requestor and service, and handling business events from disparate sources.

information—One of the five SOA entry points. An information-centric approach to SOA yields context-rich information that can drive and enable new forms of innovation. Information as a service is an approach that unlocks information in all its forms from its repository, process, and application silos, providing it as a trusted service to the applications, processes, and decision makers who need it.

open standards—(Source: Wikipedia) Publicly available and implementable standards. By enabling anyone to obtain and implement the standard, open standards can increase compatibility between various hardware and software components because anyone with the necessary technical know-how and resources can build products that work together with those of the other vendors that base their designs on the standard. (However, patent holders may impose "reasonable and nondiscriminatory" royalty fees and other licensing terms on implementers of the standard.)

people—One of the five SOA entry points. A people-centric approach to SOA focuses on the front end of the user experience to help facilitate innovation and greater collaboration. People-centric collaboration is about enabling human and process interaction with consistent levels of service. Companies that focus on collaboration among people improve their productivity by giving their employees and trading partners the ability to create a personalized and consolidated way to interact with other people and information in the context of business processes. They need a role-based,

intuitive, and adaptive user experience. The people entry point interacts with SOA-based business services and composite applications through an enabling framework of tools and practices.

process—One of the five SOA entry points. A process has two meanings in SOA: 1) A process is a set of related business tasks spanning people, systems, and information to produce a specific service or product. 2) As an SOA entry point, the process entry point provides specific tools and services to help streamline and improve processes across the enterprise. The process entry point provides the foundation for IBM's business process management with SOA.

reuse—One of the five SOA entry points. It addresses methods of creating the services needed to execute business tasks by service-enabling existing IT assets, consuming reusable services from an external service provider, and creating net-new reusable services from scratch.

service—A repeatable business task supported by software deployed on network-accessible platforms provided by the service provider. Services are self-contained, reusable software that are independent of applications and the computing platforms on which they run. Services have well-defined interfaces and allow for a 1:1 mapping between business tasks and the exact IT components needed to execute the task.

Service Component Architecture (SCA)—A set of specifications that describe a model for building applications and systems using a service oriented architecture. SCA extends and complements prior approaches to implementing services, and SCA builds on open standards such as web services. It provides an open, technology-neutral model for implementing IT services that are defined in terms of a business function and makes middleware functions more accessible to the application developer. SCA also provides a model for the assembly of business solutions from collections of

continues

individual services, with control over aspects of the solution such as access methods and security. Vendors working to create SCA include BEA Systems, IBM, IONA, Oracle, SAP, Siebel, and Sybase.

Service Data Objects (SDO)—Complements SCA by providing a common way to access many different kinds of data. The specification reduces the skill levels and time required to access and manipulate business data. Today a multitude of APIs are used to manipulate data. These APIs tend to tightly couple the source and target of the data, making their use error prone and subject to breaking as business requirements evolve. SDO makes it easier to use and realize the value of these APIs without needing to code directly to them. Vendors working to create SDO include BEA Systems, IBM, Oracle, SAP, Siebel, Sybase, and Xcalia.

service orientation—An approach to integrate business tasks as loosely coupled, linked business services. We cover the concept of loosely coupled services in more depth in Chapter 6. Because SOA is the technology side, the matching concept on the business side is service orientation—looking at your business as a set of interconnected services.

service oriented architecture—A business-driven IT architectural approach that supports integrating your business as linked, repeatable business tasks or services. From a technology viewpoint, it is an architectural style structure of a software system in terms of its components and the services they provide, without regard for the underlying implementation of these components, services, and connections between components.

service registry and repository—A central reference point within a service oriented architecture that stores and manages services information (metadata). It stores information about what the services are, how they are used, and how they are interconnected with

other components. This information can be used to foster reuse of services' assets and to govern services throughout the life cycle. It finds services and obtains binding information (in the service descriptions) for services during development for static binding or during execution for dynamic binding. We cover the service registry and repository in more detail in Chapter 6.

SOA entry points—Five distinct but interrelated ways of undertaking SOA projects that encompass both a business and an IT component. These are people, process, information, connectivity, and reuse.

SOA Reference Architecture—A vendor-neutral pictorial representation that assists in visualizing and laying out projects from a service perspective and defines the comprehensive IT services that support your SOA at each stage in leveraging the SOA entry points.

COMPETING ON FLEXIBILITY

By definition, SOA is an architecture approach or style. At the same time, SOA is an approach to IT that can help solve immediate business challenges and begin paying for itself quickly. In fact, the number of opportunities for quick return on investment can be surprising. For example, many businesses are unaware of the number of duplicate processes that occur in separate departments and applications—and how much these duplicate processes are costing them. When you examine the costs and lost revenue attributable to redundant functions and duplicated efforts, you begin to see the value of centralized services compared to managing multiple competing and overlapping functions. Consolidating the number of moving parts in a business leads to simplification, lower costs, and greater flexibility.

SOA offers an approach that can be incrementally adopted as organizations start the necessary but sometimes daunting task of bringing order to what might have become chaos. The entry points into SOA outlined in the following sections have helped many

companies get started and move further along the SOA adoption path. But just as important, these entry points have produced clear and demonstrable business results. The SOA entry points have been developed by reviewing thousands of customer engagements on business flexibility leveraging SOA. The five SOA entry points are people, process, information, reuse, and connectivity (see Figure 4.1). In Figure 4.2, each of these are defined: two IT-centric entry points—reuse and connectivity—which provide the IT foundation; and three Business-centric entry points—people, process, and information. I'd like to focus on the two IT entry points: reuse and connectivity.

As companies use SOA to provide standardized services and business processes, the value of IT to overall business mission grows exponentially. When there is only one consolidated view of each customer, supplier, and business partner; only one shared, reusable service to support a repeatable task that is executed by many parts of the company; and only one business process for each specific business need, organizations can run more smoothly and put more of their energy into growing their businesses instead of taming their IT infrastructures. Just one example of an entry point's value is that of reuse. In the past, the prevailing belief was that the value of reuse was in eliminating duplicate development and maintenance. Now, however, it is widely accepted that the true value of reuse is in the standardization of business processes.

The following two projects help demonstrate how organizations have used SOA to their immediate advantage, while at the same time laying the groundwork for more flexible IT systems that can provide competitive advantage in the years ahead. This is why many in the industry conclude that, for businesses to be successful, SOA must be their glue for linking IT and business.

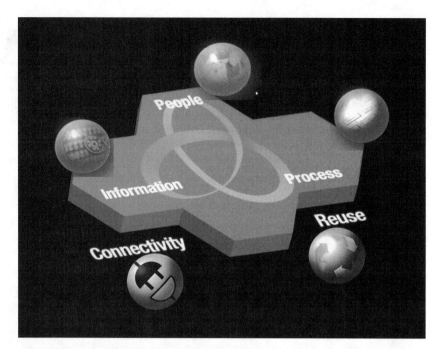

Figure 4.1   SOA entry points help companies get started.

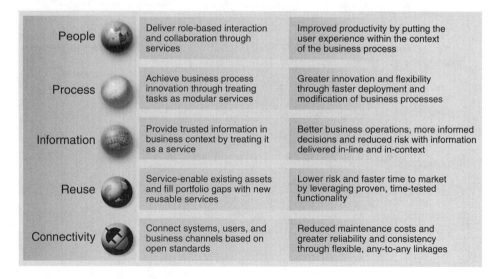

People		Deliver role-based interaction and collaboration through services	Improved productivity by putting the user experience within the context of the business process
Process		Achieve business process innovation through treating tasks as modular services	Greater innovation and flexibility through faster deployment and modification of business processes
Information		Provide trusted information in business context by treating it as a service	Better business operations, more informed decisions and reduced risk with information delivered in-line and in-context
Reuse		Service-enable existing assets and fill portfolio gaps with new reusable services	Lower risk and faster time to market by leveraging proven, time-tested functionality
Connectivity		Connect systems, users, and business channels based on open standards	Reduced maintenance costs and greater reliability and consistency through flexible, any-to-any linkages

Figure 4.2   SOA entry points and their value to companies

CASE STUDY
A RETAIL INDUSTRY COMPANY

This major retailer has estimated the revenue impact of its SOA project (as part of its broader business initiative) at $20 million. The project consisted of creating a centralized service used as a single source of information for delivery-date commitments. Many businesses can suffer in the marketplace because they do not provide the necessary means to effectively manage customer expectations. Consider what can happen when a service company makes an appointment to send a service representative to a customer's home to repair a problem.

When making the appointment, the company can commit only to having the representative arrive at any time during an eight-hour timeframe. Then, after the customer has waited at home for an entire day, the company calls to inform the customer that the service representative cannot make the appointment and needs to reschedule. This inability to manage customer expectations can result in alienating customers and even in losing some customers to competitors. This concern transcends industries and is important to any organization that depends on the quality of its customer service to maintain and grow its business.

In the retail industry, successful retailers are those who can manage, meet, and exceed customer expectations. Whether it is ensuring the quality of the merchandise, maintaining necessary inventory levels, or fulfilling orders expeditiously, companies must meet these high expectations by their customers. Delivery dates must be met, and if a date has changed, the customer must be informed, regardless of who is at fault. This issue prompted a retailer to undertake an SOA-based project.

The retailer's fulfillment chain comprised multiple systems, each of which could update the promised delivery date for an order. When someone changed a delivery date in one of the many fulfillment applications, the information wasn't consistently updated in the order-processing system. As a result, when a delivery date was adjusted, the customer was frequently not properly informed. Because these disparate systems didn't reliably communicate these updates to each other, customer representatives had to spend valuable time checking multiple order-management systems to try to answer customer queries or resolve a complaint when an order did not arrive on the expected day. The long wait for information and the inability to keep the customer informed of changes frustrated both customers and employees.

The solution—a centralized delivery-date service. Now, when a delivery date is changed, the fulfillment system sends a delivery-change notification to this event-driven service through the retailer's connectivity layer or Enterprise Service Bus (ESB). As a result, the order system database, and any other system that subscribes to this service, is immediately updated. This capability allows customer service representatives to respond to and address customer issues more quickly and accurately.

This is a simple SOA project. The total effort to create a centralized service and build a connectivity layer or ESB (the next chapter will go into detail on what an ESB is and its role in SOA) required four developers for four months. But the impact to the business is extensive. Customers are no longer disappointed with missed delivery dates and contradictory delivery information. The number of cancelled orders has declined, as have the number of delivery attempts that are unsuccessful due to scheduling confusion. Even more important, the retailer is profiting from the repeat business of customers who value the company's ability to meet its delivery commitments.

CASE STUDY
A FINANCIAL SERVICE COMPANY

Financial services organizations all over the world are struggling to reduce costs and increase customer satisfaction, while at the same time dealing with an increasingly complex array of security concerns. These competing challenges often result in situations where companies must choose to spend more or risk customer dissatisfaction. The financial services organization discussed in this scenario used SOA to help lower costs and improve customer satisfaction, all without compromising security.

A common thread among all industries is the movement to automate processes that are traditionally labor—and cost—intensive. Often the most expensive processes are those that are required to handle the exceptions in the everyday business. Whether it concerns reverse logistics within a supply chain or billing disputes for services rendered, handling such exceptions can be expensive because of the enormous amount of human intervention that is often required.

This project enabled a financial services organization to significantly decrease the labor-intensive processes and high costs associated with disputed transactions. Automating this process by creating a centralized service helped enable the organization to realize estimated cost savings of more than $200 million per year. It achieved these savings by replacing a manual and archaic set of processes with an automated service that was surprisingly simple to implement.

This financial services organization functions as a support network for many large retail establishments. The process this organization had in place to handle disputed charges is an example of an extremely expensive business exception. When a retail customer

disputed a transaction, the financial services organization would manually print all transactions and send them through ground mail to the customer to identify which transactions were being challenged. The customer would then have to sign these papers and send them back through ground mail to the financial services organization, which would then package them and send selected documents to the retail institution. After this paperwork was received, the retail institution would decide whether the charge should be removed. This process could take up to 20 days to complete and typically cost the organizations involved between $400 and $700 per transaction.

Because security was such an enormous concern, any new solution had to help ensure the integrity of the financial services organization's core transaction system. Protection of customer data was essential, so this financial services organization wanted to maintain only one access point to its transaction system. In the past, the organization had not been comfortable with integrating this system with its retail partners because it would have required a unique, point-to-point connection for each partner. Maintaining these point-to-point connections would have been cost prohibitive and would have most likely resulted in a higher-than-acceptable error rate. The financial services organization would allow partners to communicate with its transaction system only if it was possible for all of them to share the same connection—reducing the financial service's organizations security and maintenance responsibilities to a single connection. SOA turned this potential obstacle into an opportunity.

To create a solution, the financial services organization deployed a service in front of its core transaction system that allows retail partners to transmit dispute claims to the financial services organization on behalf of the partners' retail customers. To register a

continues

dispute, customers now simply log into the retail institution's website and view a list of transactions that have posted to their account. Customers can then select the transactions they wish to dispute. The website sends this request to the financial services organization's transaction-dispute service. The authentication that customers provide while logging on to the website enables the financial services organization to eliminate the need for paper documentation with a handwritten signature. Today the transaction-dispute process averages a total of three hours, reduced from 20 days, and costs only $40 to $70 per transaction, instead of the previous $400–$700 per transaction, representing a 90% reduction in costs.

CASE STUDY
COLDWATER CREEK

Having evolved from a home-based retailer of women's apparel into a 5,000-person enterprise doing business through stores, direct-mail catalogs, and a website, Coldwater Creek is focused on continuing its growth. However, by running each of its three sales channels on a unique system, the company was challenged to introduce new business initiatives quickly. For example, as it planned revenue-generating credit card and loyalty programs, it was faced with developing separate applications for each channel. Coldwater Creek needed to enhance its business while avoiding the delays and costs associated with lengthy development processes.

Coldwater Creek can now efficiently deliver improvements across the enterprise with a customized SOA design. The SOA allows the retailer to enhance all three of its sales channels at once with open standards–based web services. By creating two initial web services, Coldwater Creek quickly launched credit card and rewards programs for all channels that increase customer loyalty and drive

sales. By using open standards to integrate with different technologies, web services allow the retailer to maintain its separate systems but leverage a single set of business logic to enhance all of them at once. Once it established the SOA framework, the revenue-generating initiatives that Coldwater Creek had planned went live. They created a web service that facilitates a co-branded credit card program that customers can use with all of Coldwater Creek's sales channels, even at other businesses. A second web service facilitates a cardholder rewards program, through which Coldwater Creek can deliver targeted promotions that increase customer loyalty and encourage more sales.

Their SOA benefits to date include a monthly revenue increase with new credit card and loyalty programs, 100% ROI achieved in less than one day, and improved competitiveness with faster delivery of new business initiatives.

It is important to note that, in these case studies, we spend the time on the problem and then on the results that SOA brought to the table. We do this in extreme makeover style—that is, we show the problem and the value that SOA brought to the table, to illustrate the value the SOA has today for customers. The impact is actually larger than discussed. Because these companies have based their architecture on SOA, this approach will ensure future flexibility and reuse. As a result of their initial SOA project, they have set the SOA foundation in place for all future projects to leverage. So although you could accomplish some of the same goals listed earlier, you would not have been able to do them in the same timeframe with the same future benefits that will accrue for the project. A review of early case studies indicates that organizations that use an SOA can reduce integration project development and maintenance costs by 30% or more (see "Integration in a Service Oriented World," Forrester Research, Inc., July 2006 in Figure 4.3).

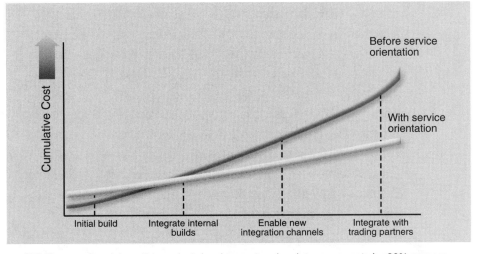

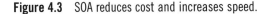

[SOA] can reduce integration project development and maintenance costs by 30% or more.

Source: Forrester Research, Inc.

Figure 4.3 SOA reduces cost and increases speed.

SOA CONNECTIVITY FOR FLEXIBILITY

The five SOA entry points (people, process, information, connectivity, and reuse) are the core to really understanding SOA. In the next two sections, we dive into the connectivity and reuse entry points. We tackle those two entry points first because they are considered to be prerequisites for really diving into people, process, and information. The ability to effectively connect your infrastructure enables you to pursue higher value SOA projects. To integrate the people, process, or information in your company, it is necessary to first provide the connectivity among the various services, applications, and data within your IT environment. Although connectivity has always been a requirement, SOA brings new levels of flexibility to these linkages. The days of brittle, hard-coded connections are over; SOA brings flexible connections between services and throughout your IT environment, typically through an Enterprise Service Bus (ESB). This kind of connectivity has distinct value on its own in addition to acting as a building block for more SOA initiatives.

SOA connectivity enables users to deliver an existing business process through a different business channel with minimal rework. For example, if you have a business process such as opening a new account that you deliver through a call center, you can deliver the same process through a website or a kiosk by leveraging this kind of connectivity. Doing so will ensure a secure, consistent user experience and save a great deal of cost. By the same token, SOA connectivity lets you reach out to your trading partners with secure, services-based connectivity beyond your firewall. McKinsey & Co. just came out with an article on "What's on CIO agendas in 2007." One of the two trends "of significant importance" in 2007, is a migration to service-oriented architectures. Forty-eight percent of all CIOs surveyed say they will implement SOA with a focus on external Partner Process integration in 2007. The full report is very powerful, and I encourage you to read it. The Enterprise Integration Challenge report from Software Strategies found that use of an ESB was two to four times less expensive than custom-built integration or FTP.

From a technical perspective, you can get the right level of connectivity for your business needs in multiple ways. You can deploy a messaging backbone based on web services and other messaging protocols as the foundation for SOA connectivity. Or, you can build on this backbone by implementing an ESB to add a mediation layer for connectivity among services, existing applications, and data. You can integrate using web services, JMS, or virtually any other endpoint for universal connectivity. Or, you can choose a hardware form factor and use SOA appliances to augment your connectivity and security.

REUSE THROUGH SOA FOR FLEXIBILITY

Reuse is the second SOA entry point for flexibility. Creating and reusing services lets you create flexible, service-based business applications. If you create a new department, open a new lab, or develop a new product, you probably wouldn't start completely from scratch. You'd tap into existing knowledge from your people, your proven best practices, and your information sources. The same is true with SOA.

To build an SOA, you look at what you already have (people, applications, business processes, and so on) and use existing resources to streamline business processes, cut development time, ensure consistency through the organization, and save money. Based on open standards, SOA enables a company to extend the value from its existing software by service-enabling it and then repeatedly reuse the business value that comes from that service.

One of the key value propositions of SOA is the value of reuse to save costs. By focusing on reuse, companies can:

- Enhance flexibility by reducing duplication of function and creating services to be shared across the enterprise
- Leverage proven core applications and functions through services enablement, wrapping, or other methods

In fact, a study by Software Productivity Research found that it is five times less expensive to reuse existing services and applications than to rewrite them.

OPEN STANDARDS

Because SOA is based on open standards, you can create solutions that are reusable. This means they are portable and/or interoperable. Open standards matter more today than ever before in the history of computing.

Because all companies live in a heterogeneous environment, they have made investments in a variety of systems. This concept previously bogged us down. Since SOA is based on open standards, the flexibility it provides enables companies to create solutions that are portable and/or interoperable.

Some of the key areas that you should review for SOA open standards are in web services standards. (We cover web services in detail in Chapter 6.) These standards provide the foundation upon which SOA was built. Standards organizations such as the W3C, OASIS, and the Web Services Interoperability Organization are developing the key standards for SOA. Some of the recently published or

ratified web services standards address the important areas of reliable messaging, security, transactions, and management. Within the management space, in particular, IBM, Microsoft, HP, and Intel recently published a management reconciliation roadmap to help pull together a fork in the standards road that was developing.

Going beyond the classic technology underpinnings for SOA, make sure your company is keeping an eye on the vertical industry standards, for example, in the areas of healthcare, life sciences, the automotive industry, and insurance. All these industries have something to gain from the new model of interoperation that SOA brings.

In the area of development tools and standards, a group of companies is providing Service Component Architecture (SCA), which provides for a simplified language independent component model, and Service Data Objects (SDO), which provides a high-level abstraction to help you get to data, no matter what form it is in (in a database, in an XML document, structured, unstructured, and so on).

In the area of Business Process Management, Object Management Group (OMG) is developing standards such as the Universal Modeling Language (UML) and the Business Process Modeling Notation. This essentially creates a standard way to depict business flows that can be shared with partners, thus fostering interoperation at even higher levels. At the high end of the so-called web services "stack" is the Business Process Execution Language (a.k.a. BPEL, pronounced "beeple"). BPEL provides a way to formally specify business processes and interaction protocols.

Last, but not least, is the area of management and governance. Critical to the success of the whole system is the ability to monitor and manage the piece parts. The Web Services Distributed Management standard (WSDM, pronounced "wisdom"), which was done in OASIS, helps you manage the new world of SOA services.

Make sure that as you explore SOA, you choose a vendor that supports these open standards, to increase interoperability among systems and prevent vendor lock-in.

You should take a step-by-step approach to creating and reusing services.

1. Use portfolio management to consider what kind of assets you need to support the business processes that make up your company. This step is one of the hardest because it involves leveraging the skills of people who understand both the business side of the process and the IT side, to look at the level of the process that your company might want to share. This step is about deciding what you want your business process to look like and then determining what kinds of services will be needed to support the tasks within that process, regardless of whether those services already exist.

2. Identify key high-value existing IT assets that make up parts of your business processes. These can come from functionality within your packaged or custom applications, your sources of information, or transactions in your core systems. This step is made much easier through the use of automated asset-analyzer tools that help search your environment to identify key software that can be reused as services. If you service-enable these key assets, you can more easily incorporate them in your broader IT environment. Previously, you might have needed very specialized skills to access and use some of these systems. By service-enabling them, you are expanding access to these systems to a much broader skill set and extracting greater value from these existing investments. You probably won't be able to satisfy 100% of your business needs through reuse, so it's usually necessary to fill in gaps by creating new services.

3. Explore a centralized way to access and control these reusable services. To do this step, your company will probably want to invest in a registry/repository to do things such as keep track of what services are available, record key information about these services, and enable interested parties to subscribe to notifications of updates and changes to services of interest to them.

THE SOA REFERENCE ARCHITECTURE

Earlier in the chapter, I referred to SOA as the DNA for on demand businesses because of the flexibility and innovativeness that an on demand business must have. In a human, DNA is genetic information that determines the structure, function, and behavior of the cell. To get to a competitive level of flexibility, the structure and behavior of a business must be intrinsically linked to SOA, and a roadmap of the requirements for this "DNA" must be plotted. The SOA Reference Architecture defines the comprehensive IT services required to support your company's SOA at each stage of your SOA entry point project. It is a vendor-neutral way of looking at and planning the set of services that go into building an SOA. As you can see from Figure 4.4, it is not a true architect's view of the architecture, but more a high-level view of the capabilities and services that your company should think through during deployment.

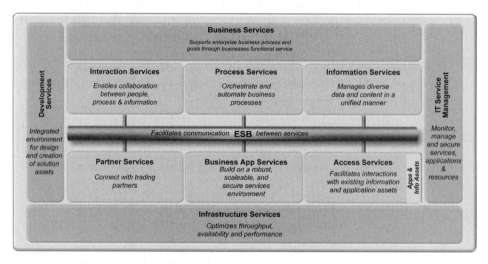

Figure 4.4   SOA Reference Architecture

SOA Reference Architecture includes capabilities that you need to consider when approaching SOA, regardless of what products and services are used. These capabilities can be implemented on a

build-as-you-go basis, allowing capabilities and project-level solutions to be easily added as new requirements are addressed over time. A key to any SOA entry point project is to start with a discrete project and then progress over time. Biting off more than you can chew will put success at risk.

For a business-savvy IT executive, it is important that you understand the elements of this reference architecture. The reference architecture is a great tool for laying out roadmaps for pursuing SOA. Regardless of what kind of project you're undertaking, it makes sense to lay it out on a reference architecture to see how the various services you're designing will interact with each other.

Let's start in the center of the figure, where the backbone of the reference architecture is the connectivity layer, or the Enterprise Service Bus (ESB), which facilitates communication between the services that we just discussed. The ESB delivers all the interconnectivity capabilities required to leverage the services implemented across the entire architecture. Transport services, event services, and mediation services are all provided through the ESB. We discuss the ESB and its value in more detail in Chapter 5.

Continuing through the SOA Reference Architecture, you see the set of services that are oriented toward the integration of people, processes, and information:

- **Interaction services** is the link to the people side of SOA. It provides the capabilities required to deliver IT functions and data to end users, meeting the end user's specific usage preferences.

- **Process services** provide the control services required to manage the flow and interactions of multiple services in ways that implement business processes.

- **Information services** provide the capabilities required to federate, replicate, and transform data sources that can be implemented in a variety of ways.

Although you do not directly see reuse on this architecture, the point is that all the services you see listed around the ESB or connectivity layer are built with reuse in mind. For example, in the

information services box in Figure 4.4, you could envision an account number for a customer to be represented as a reusable service. An application could leverage that shared information service to get consistent account information, to verify customer data, and to query customer records. Many of the services in an SOA are provided through existing applications; others are provided in newly implemented components, and others are provided through external connections to third-party systems.

Let's take a look again at Figure 4.4, to see the key areas for reuse:

- **Access services**—Existing enterprise applications and enterprise data are accessible from the ESB through a set of access services that provide the bridging capabilities among legacy applications, prepackaged applications, enterprise data stores, and the ESB.

- **Partner services**—These services provide the document, protocol, and partner-management capabilities required for business processes that involve interactions with outside partners and suppliers.

- **Business application services**—These services provide runtime services required for new application components to be included in the integrated system.

Moving out from the center boxes of Figure 4.4, you see the surrounding value areas. On the sides, you can see these service sets:

- **Development services**—Tools are an essential component of any comprehensive integration architecture. Development services are used to implement custom artifacts that leverage the infrastructure capabilities.

- **IT services management services**—These include capabilities that relate to scale and performance. For example, edge services, clustering services, and virtualization capabilities enable efficient use of computing resources based on load patterns.

Underlying all these capabilities of the SOA Reference Architecture is a set of infrastructure services, which are used to optimize throughput, availability, and performance.

The crowning glory of the SOA Reference Architecture is the link to the business side. That is the layer in the reference architecture of business services. Business services are used to monitor and manage the runtime implementations at both the IT and business process levels. They support the enterprise business process and goals through businesses functional service.

I have found this SOA reference architecture helpful in describing SOA to a variety of customers and in helping them plan their flexibility journey. However, one of the items that I always dive deep on is the interaction of the elements of the entry points and the reference architecture. In Figure 4.5, you can see where services originate and how they interact with each other to produce useful results for the flexible business.

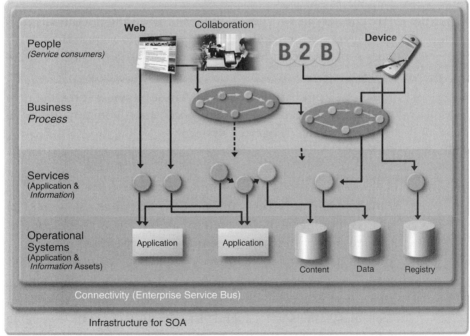

Source: SOA Community of Practice, SOA Solution Stack Project

Figure 4.5   How the entry points work together

At the bottom, you can see the operational systems; the applications, data, and content; the hardware; and even the registry. This is the "engine room," where the actual computing and information live. The next layer up is the services—some reused from existing applications, some information as a service, and other services newly built. These are the "contracts" that call and choreograph action down in the engine room. These services come together dynamically at runtime to support processes such as supply chain or a gift registry. At the top, you see the role that people play, now consuming the services and chains of linked services in a variety of ways. One of our discussion points in later chapters is the interaction among these five entry points to extract the most business value.

WHY SOA PROJECTS SUCCEED AND HOW TO LEVERAGE THEIR LESSONS

For every SOA success story, there lies an abandoned SOA project stuck in one of the various stages of deployment. Underscoring the successes and challenges of an SOA is the popularized theory that 50% of IT projects are deemed unsuccessful. This, of course, can make embarking on an SOA strategy rather intimidating.

Still, SOAs remain at the top of the executive and IT agenda based on their ability to more closely align technology with the needs of the business. Quickly dismantling the high statistics associated with IT project failures, SOAs have shown demonstrable return on investment.

When approached properly, SOA has proven itself as a way to increase flexibility, boost revenue, and drive down expenses. Still, some watchers out there are asking, "How can SOA succeed where previous approaches have failed?" and "How do I avoid becoming a statistic?"

These are powerful questions. Simply stated, a successful SOA strategy can be achieved because the standards, best practices, and governance models have finally matured to the point that reuse can actually work. After all, SOA is, by definition, an architecture as well as an approach to IT that can help solve immediate business challenges.

Although each company has different business needs and each industry faces its own set of challenges, common issues can lead to the failure of an SOA. In reviewing the engagements that I've seen, there are ten secrets for success:

1. **Get executive sponsorship**—Before presenting how you'll ensure your company's SOA success, be prepared to demonstrate successes and failures of other companies on their path to SOA, and articulate how you'll emulate proven practices and avoid pitfalls.

2. **Align the troops**—Converse to overcoming the obstacle of executive support for your SOA is the challenge of aligning your organization to work and think in new ways. To do this, identify and recruit critical champions for each part of the business who will support and even evangelize the SOA efforts.

3. **Consolidate views**—Eliminate the multiple views of information that are currently floating across your organization so that you are looking at only a singular, comprehensive, and consistent view of the business.

4. **Reuse**—Identify and maintain a repository of your current web services to avoid duplication of efforts. You might be surprised by how much work different pockets of your organization already have done.

5. **Integrate the silos**—In theory, many of today's IT organizations are seeking to integrate and avoid redundancies while maximizing their current IT investments, but the reality is that extraordinary efforts are being spent on still trying to maintain different IT systems that coexist but are not integrated. The penny-wise, pound-foolish approach to SOA simply does not work.

6. **See the forest through the trees**—Remember that an SOA is an architecture, not a combination of clumsily bundled point products that need to be force-fit. A true SOA is created with an open standards–based approach through four strategic stages: model, assemble, deploy, and manage.

7. **Hop on the Enterprise Service Bus**—An ESB provides the much-needed connectivity infrastructure that you can use to integrate services within an SOA. We do a deep dive on the ESB in Chapter 7 as well. Together, SOA and an ESB help reduce the number and complexity of interfaces, enabling you to focus on your core business issues instead of maintaining your IT infrastructure.

8. **Work step by step**—When the thought of rolling an enterprise-wide SOA becomes overwhelming, remember that the best approach is to continually test and modify while rolling it out first departmentally and then slowly throughout the organization, to identify issues while adding to your arsenal of best practices along the way.

9. **Avoid the *carpe diem* approach**—Remember that you're not building your SOA just for today or this year. This is an organization-wide approach to aligning IT with the needs of the business and must accommodate today's needs as well as those of the future. For example, be sure to include support for mobile and wireless devices, and ensure that you have enough flexibility to support future business processes.

10. **Prevent the accidental SOA**—Many organizations might discover that they have a healthy repository of web services that will comprise the majority of their SOA. Don't believe that the SOA starts and ends with a collection of web services. Remember that an SOA must go beyond web services to support all your business processes. It must also provide a flexible, extensible, and composable approach to reusing and extending existing applications and services, as well as constructing new ones.

CASE STUDY
WACHOVIA BANK AS AN EXAMPLE OF SERVICE ORIENTED ARCHITECTURE
VALUE IN ACTION

Wachovia Bank is one of the top six banks in the United States. One of the greatest business drivers is to be flexible for their customers. The goal is that the customers have a unified experience so whether they go to the Internet channel or an ATM, or call the call center, they get the same answer, the same process. In the past, each channel has been very silo driven and has written its own applications. We were doing point-to-point integration—and that's pretty much unmanageable, or very, very difficult to manage.

Now with service oriented architecture, Wachovia is able to turn these silos of applications into an integrated platform where all of the front end actually talks to a single back-end service. And that single service then can display the same information in different ways to the customers as they come to the bank through the different channels. Service oriented architecture allows Wachovia to, if you will, "skinny down" those channel delivery applications to make things simpler, skinnier, and more lightweight so that when they make a change, they can make it across all of the channel-delivery applications. If they have a new product that has to get to market or a new application to enable a new product, those things can happen much faster now since they have been using SOA.

As Ron Donson, IT Architect for Wachovia Bank said, "The biggest benefit is the reuse of functionality—so that Wachovia isn't building the same thing ten times. There is tremendous benefit there—great cost reduction. The customers are much more appreciative of the fact that they are receiving the same information no matter what channel they use to access the bank." Wachovia is very proud of the fact that they are rated as the bank with the highest customer satisfaction in the United States—and they can meet their customers' needs because their services are written and run on SOA.

SUMMARY

Service oriented architecture is the supporting IT infrastructure that enables companies to become more flexible through a focus on business processes. SOA starts with a business task, which has as its DNA the most flexible IT available. Although SOA is at the beginning of its maturity curve, many companies are already seeing the benefits of SOA. As Forrester says, "Now is the time to jump on SOA for business flexibility."

Make sure that before you begin your SOA project, you understand the concepts of reuse and connectivity as a foundational level and how SOA can help you with the flexibility to link people, process, and information. Together they all add up to a flex-pon-sive* company.

As you read through the next couple of chapters, you will see a complete picture of the five SOA entry points and how governance plays such a critical role in successful deployment. Over time, the focus on SOA will become table stakes for every company.

5

SOA Key Concepts

Old world meets new world. In Mark Colan's article on SOA (http://www-128.ibm.com/developerworks/web-services/library/ws-soaintro.html), he uses a great analogy to standards. In 221 B.C., Emperor Qin unified several formerly warring states into a new country, which we now call China. Perhaps one reason China has endured as a nation was Qin's introduction of standards, which consolidated cultures and facilitated trade. Some examples of the standards they used include a standard distance for wheels on carts that enabled them to travel efficiently on any road, and a common written language that everybody could use to exchange messages (even if they did not speak the same language). You could say that Qin developed the models for standards (such as web services) and a message transport and exchange (such as ESB) that provided China the flexibility to support its changing ways over time.

In much the same way, service oriented architecture is the key to a flexible IT infrastructure. Because both flexible business and flexible IT are required, it is

important for those companies striving to be flex-pon-sive* to make sure they understand both areas. In the last chapter, we discussed the importance of the IT thought process related to reuse, connectivity, security, and management, asserting that SOA is the DNA for a flex-pon-sive* company. Let's now dive deeper into some of the key concepts of that DNA for the IT professional in SOA. We will not go too deep; however, you need to understand some basics to be able to make intelligent decisions about your journey.

- Decide the interoperability standard you want for your organization (web services)
- Identify the service(s) you want and need (Business Services Registry and Repository)
- Connect the services Enterprise Service Business (ESB)

INTEROPERABILITY STANDARD: WEB SERVICES

Companies today have a variety of systems that have resulted in a heterogeneous environment. This heterogeneity used to bog us down with lack of interoperability. But because SOA is based on open standards, we're able to create solutions that draw upon functionality from these existing, previously isolated systems that are portable and/or interoperable, regardless of the environment in which they exist.

DEFINING WEB SERVICES

As you recall from our discussion earlier in the book, web services are an open standards way of supporting interoperability. According to Wikipedia, a web service is a software system designed to support interoperable machine-to-machine interaction over a network. Web services are frequently just application programming interfaces (API) that can be accessed over a network, such as the Internet, and executed on a remote system hosting the requested services. SOA is a style of architecture that enables the creation of applications that are built by combining

loosely coupled and interoperable services. These services inter-operate based on a formal definition (or contract, like WSDL) that is independent of the underlying platform and programming lan-guage. In SOA, since the basic unit of communication is a message rather than an operation, web services are usually loose coupled. Although you can do SOA without web services, the best-practice implementation of SOA for flexibility always involves web services because of their value proposition around interoperability for flexibility.

Technically, web services are based on Extensible Markup Language (XML). XML is a markup language for documents con-taining structured information. The technical specifics of XML's capabilities go beyond the scope of this book, but for our purposes, they support things such as e-commerce transactions, mathemat-ical equations, object metadata, server APIs, and a thousand other kinds of structured information. XML is a common data represen-tation that can be used as the medium of exchange between pro-grams that are written in different programming languages and execute different kinds of machine instructions. In simple terms, think about XML as the official translator for structured informa-tion. Structured information is both the content (word, picture, and so on) and the role it plays. For instance, even in this book, the content I use in a header or a footnote designates different meanings based on the context.

For me, the key here for us as business leaders is the unprece-dented vendor cooperation and buy-in. Unlike in the past, when each vendor went its own way, all the big guys (Microsoft, IBM, and others) have agreed on standards for web services. In addition, based on the standard bodies work, the web services standards build on each other, making each iteration one of value that builds on the last.

XML is the basis for all web services technologies and the key to interoperability; every web services specification is based on XML. (*Note:* In particular, SOAP formalizes the exchange of information written in XML, and WSDL describes the SOAP details in an XML vocabulary.)

Web services have these characteristics:

- Loose coupling
- Service granularity

LOOSE COUPLING

Part of the value of SOA is that it is built on the premise of loose coupling of services. Loose coupling is about the capability of services to be joined together on demand to create composite services, or disassembled just as easily into their functional components. Per Wikipedia, loose coupling describes an approach in which integration interfaces are developed with minimal assumptions between the sending and receiving parties, thus reducing the risk that a change in one application or module will force a change in another application/module.

Tight coupling refers to a semipermanent linkage between one chunk of code and another. This rigid and brittle connection was forged out of necessity because interfaces to and from these chunks of code were not well defined, and connections usually needed to be created via custom code. SOA services are linked dynamically and flexibly. Loose coupling is simply a way of ensuring that the technical details such as language, platform, and so on are decoupled from the service.

For example, look at currency conversion. Today all banks have multiple currency converters, all with different rate refreshes at different times. If you create a common service "conversion of currency" that is loosely coupled to all banking functions that require conversion, you are able to average the rates, times, and samplings to ensure that you are able to float treasury in the most effective manner possible. Another example is common customer identification. In most businesses, there is no common customer ID and, therefore, no way to determine who the customers are and what they buy for what reason, let alone being able to harvest any information about them. By creating a common customer ID that is independent of applications and databases, you are loosely coupling the service "customer ID" or "all customers virtual" to CRM, data, and applications without the application or database ever

knowing who it is or where it is. The service is simply called by way of a request message and the response, instead of through the use of APIs or file formats.

It could be any kind of process: something as mundane as a database call or something as critical as a financial transfer between two nations' central banks. The difference between traditional, tightly bound interactions and loosely coupled services is that, before the transaction takes place, the functional pieces (services) operating within the SOA are dormant and disconnected. When the business process initiates, these services momentarily interact with each other. They do so for just long enough to execute their piece of the overall process, and then they go back to their dormant state, with no long-standing connection to the other services with which they just interacted. The next time the same service is called, it could be as part of a different business process with different calling and destination services.

A great way to understand this is through the analogy of our telephone system. At the dawn of widespread phone usage, operators had to physically plug in a wire to create a long-standing, semi-permanent connection between two parties. Callers were "tightly bound" to each other. Today you pick up your cellphone and put it to your ear, and there's no dial tone—it's disconnected. You enter a number and push Talk, and only then does the process initiate, establishing a loosely coupled connection just long enough for your conversation. Then when the conversation is over, your cellphone goes back to "dormant" mode until a new connection is made with another party. As a result, supporting a million cellphone subscribers does not require that the cellphone service provider support a million live connections; it requires only supporting the number of simultaneous conversations at any given time. It allows for a much more flexible and dynamic exchange.

SERVICE GRANULARITY

I have worked with customers to deploy SOA, and I assert that the success depends on the design of the services and the service focus. A service is self-contained, reusable software that is inde-

pendent of applications and the computing platforms on which they run. Services have well-defined interfaces and enable a 1:1 mapping between business tasks and the exact IT components needed to execute the task. SOA services focus on business-level tasks, activities, and interactions. The relationship of a service to a process is critical. A business process is a set of related business tasks spanning people, systems, and information to produce a specific outcome or product. With SOA, a process is made up of a set of services.

Before SOA, the focus was on narrow, technical subtasks. You might have heard people call this a fine "level of granularity" or low "degree of abstraction." For simplicity's sake in SOA, we know there is more than just a simple one-to-one relationship between the steps in a process (such as checking a credit rating) and the services that are designed to support that flexible business process.

Every company has a different view of how granular it requires its service to be, based on its business design. Very simply, granularity is just the amount of function a service exposes. For example, a fine-grained service provides smaller units of a business process, and a coarse-grained service provides a larger business task that contains a higher number of substeps.

For me, this is like Goldilocks and the Holy Grail. Services cannot be too big or too small, but must be just right. Designing and deciding how granular your services should be is a success maker. If the service is too big, that yields less reuse. If the service is too small, you end up with performance hits and poor mapping between business tasks and the services that support them.

So granularity is sort of the Holy Grail; that is, determining how big or small to design a service is more a function of how atomic the composite function is. In loan origination, the granularity of the service might be quite coarse, as there are only so many different functions associated with loan origination. However, in manufacturing of pharmaceuticals, for example, the

trace development process of researching a drug has countless permutations of use versus nonuse; thus, the different "services" associated with managing the trace development process become quite atomic, which necessitates a good deal more granularity in the service design level. Remember, granularity is always a function of business process decomposition—the more detailed the business process, the more finely grained the services.

It is important to note that this concept of services is one of the keys to making SOA the language of business. Most business leaders could care less about SOA. Instead, they focus on the problem at hand—and rightly so. Because of these business services, this language and linkage of business services become a crucial piece of the solution to the problem on hand and the future strategic mission.

BUSINESS SERVICE REGISTRY AND REPOSITORY

One of the biggest questions that companies have to deal with is where to store and how to manage services, both the new ones created and the ones that are reused in the environment. Think about a library. A library is simply a place to store books—ones that have been reused repeatedly—and houses the system to find them, check them out, and update the books when new releases came. For services in your flexible IT environment, you need the same type of system that helps with visibility, reusability, adaptability, and manageability of services. The registry and repository is analogous to the card catalog within the library. It's not the shelves or the books themselves; it's the metadata about the books—where they're located, the author, the date of publication, and the cross-references.

This library again helps us with the business and IT linkage. It is a place where you can share best practices and knowledge about the business models and processes—albeit, in IT terms. This Business Service Registry and Repository (BSRR) is a key point of technology enablement for the flex-pon-sive* company.

WHAT IS A BUSINESS SERVICE REGISTRY AND REPOSITORY?

A Business Service Registry and Repository (BSRR) is a place where you store information about services in your systems (or in other organization's systems) that you already use, that you plan to use, or that you want to be aware of. It helps with service semantics and the business meaning that bridges the gap between the IT and the business world, and it provides a business-level view of the services. For example, an application can check the BSRR just before it invokes a service to locate the most appropriate service that satisfies its needs in terms of functionality and performance. Its primary role is to facilitate the creation, access, governance, and reuse of business services. BSRR enables centralized management of business services and interactions among SOA infrastructure elements, and it enforces standards and policies that govern interactions among service providers, users, and assets. Overall, BSRR promotes closer alignment to business objectives, reuse of IT assets, and incremental adoption of SOA.

In the market, there are Business Service Registries that answer the questions "What are the services?" and "Where are the services located?" And you can find just Business Service Repositories, which address how the services are used, how they interact, who is using the services, and why they are used. Looking at Figure 5.1, both a registry and a repository are needed to achieve the benefits of SOA—you need both capabilities to deliver the value you need.

For successful SOA deployment, as you move beyond your first discrete project, a BSRR is required for the full value of SOA. You should look for these capabilities when deciding on a BSRR:

■ **Publish and Find services**—The BSRR needs to be capable of publishing the services from different parts of the organization and offer the capability to find the services. This capability is the heart of reuse. This capability to socialize your services enables the organization to identify common services to avoid duplication and foster reuse. Make sure you are looking at a BSRR that supports not only discovery and reuse of services, but also associated services in all areas such as metadata management. If not, you will not be able to classify

services, subscribe to changes and updates, or have notifications sent to the right users when a change is made.

- **Govern**—The BSRR needs to enable the management of your SOA assets through the full production lifecycle, from development, test, production, and retirement. It should have full access control to enable your organization to manage who can access what services. This capability is needed throughout the lifecycle to control by user, by user type, and by where a service is on the governance lifecycle.

- **Enrich**—Your BSRR needs to enhance your connectivity by enabling dynamic and efficient interactions between services at runtime. By leveraging dynamic linkage, it enables your Enterprise Service Bus (ESB) to find the best-fitting endpoint when the request is received, supporting dynamic SOA and loose coupling.

- **Manage**—To help optimize service performance, the BSRR needs to enable policy enforcement and conduct impact analysis. It should enable the measurement of services metrics and enable an understanding of the performance of services. This understanding can assist the business with its service-level agreements.

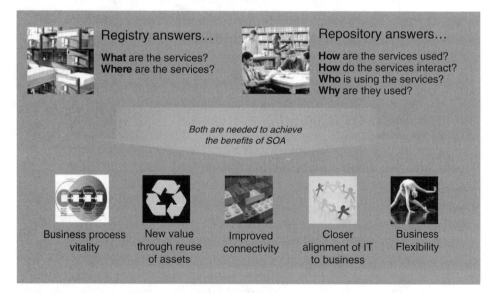

Figure 5.1 What is a registry, and what is a repository?

Overall, a BSRR should perform the functions of publishing services, finding services, enriching services, managing services, and governing services. But in addition to the functions just described, I believe that, in looking for the right BSRR, you need to make sure that services support interoperability via standards. Services standards are critical to leverage existing investments and infrastructure, such as support of WSDL, XML, XSD, BPEL, SCA, and other standards to support true interoperability. This open standards support enables integration with all standard registries and repositories. You need to ensure that your BSRR supports a unified view across the various types of information sources. Remember, the BSRR is similar to a card catalog in the library, so it needs to be able to link to sources of information across the organization.

ENTERPRISE SERVICE BUS (ESB)

Probably since the introduction of SOA, the most-written-about technology is the Enterprise Service Bus (ESB). Imagine your SOA: Everything that you need is there—but all the applications, functions, data, or services will not give you a more flexible business if they aren't connected in an efficient manner. Just because you have used web services to create new services or service-enabled an existing asset as a service, that doesn't mean your company could anticipate all possible failures that can destroy even the most elegantly written web service, adding unwanted and inflexible complexity to the implementation. Remember back to our SOA reference architecture in Chapter 4, "SOA as the DNA of a Flex-pon-sive* and Innovative Company." The ESB was at the center of that architecture.

An ESB can be described at a number of levels, depending on the level of complexity of the connection required.

1. Some parts of the business simply want to know that they can quickly, safely, and reliably move any information from one application or service to another (or, indeed, from many to many).

2. Other parts of the business wonder whether they need to make changes to their programs to handle multiple, differing data

formats that they now might be required to work with, and they are concerned about how complex their programs suddenly will become. They are imagining long nights staring at tables of differing data formats, trying to figure out how to match up the sending format to the receiving format.

3. Other parts of the business are planning to move large amounts of XML through the enterprise, and they know what impact that might have on the processor load as each server that tries to deal with these expanded datasets slows down while trying to run through varying web services security routines or process numerous large XML-based data messages.

An ESB helps to solve the problems of potential incompatibilities and maintenance hassles of application interfaces. An objective of SOA is to focus on what services can do for the business and treat its capability to connect to other parts of the environment as a given. The ESB makes this assumption a reality.

WHAT IS AN ESB?

The Enterprise Service Bus (ESB) can help you achieve the goal of SOA. It is a flexible connectivity infrastructure for integrating applications and services. The ESB is at the heart of an SOA, powering it by reducing the number, size, and complexity of interfaces. The ESB does the following five things:

1. Routes messages between services
2. Converts transport protocols between requestor and service
3. Transforms message formats between requestor and service
4. Handles business events from disparate sources
5. Ensures quality of service (security, reliability, and transacted interactions)

ESB BEST PRACTICES

Going beyond the ESB functionality, let's delve into the key best practices for ESB in the marketplace. You need an ESB without limits. Because SOA demands more than just an ESB to solve

connectivity issues, the ESB should be extended with an ecosystem of complementary products to deliver a complete integration and connectivity solution. Given that this key integration technology is critical to successful SOA implementations, make sure you have a solid plan for your connectivity and integration area.

1. **Connect all your valuable assets**—Your SOA is much more effective if you are able to tie in all assets, whether they are web service enabled or not. Why leave out a valuable asset and reduce the effectiveness and competitiveness of your business? Many businesses have valuable assets that might not be web service enabled, such as existing applications, files, databases, and other types of information-based programs and storage. The ability to discover what information and processes exist within your business applications—and including them as part of your SOA without changing them—is key to your ability to innovate on demand. In addition to accessing assets that are not service enabled, a service registry is important to describe and catalog all the services available so that the business can rapidly orchestrate new processes to support ever-changing business models.

2. **Provide service monitoring for end-to-end visibility of service interactions**—Your ESB needs to provide your business with end-to-end visibility of your resource utilization, alerts to the problems in your deployment, and the capability to drill down to find them. The facts show that 80% of time is spent figuring out what the problem is, and only 20% of the time is spent actually solving the problem. When you are evaluating ESB choices, make sure that you are looking for one that can improve business visibility and help to optimize flow of information. That means evaluating for the following characteristics:

   - Service problem identification and resolution
   - Service management automation
   - Heterogeneous SOA platform support
   - Integrated console
   - Lifecycle management

If everything is running through your ESB, you need to be sure you have effective tooling to support the tracking and management of assets as they move through the ESB.

Suppose you have been doing well in your SOA planning—you are successfully connecting all your platforms, applications, and services—and you have good linkages between your applications and your processes flowing through your ESB, connecting through your existing infrastructure and new deployments.

But now when things are up and running, you need to understand certain functions. How do you know what is going on? Can you track what is happening in your systems, or are you limited to just what your ESB can tell you? In the highly connected and interdependent environment of an SOA, it becomes critical to be alerted to any situation you define—to increase both automation and awareness of business activity—or lack of it, due to bottlenecks or failures.

For an ESB without limits, you need to be able to identify problems and resolve them quickly, drilling down from the symptom to find the real problems. This needs to be possible throughout the entire lifecycle—not just in a single environment, but across your SOA and for multiple platforms. Ideally, everything should be visible and managed through a single, powerful console, to ensure that nothing gets missed. Your ESB needs to be fully monitored and managed, including coverage for other vendor middleware products that might be deployed in the SOA.

3. **Move beyond File Transfer Protocol (FTP)**—It's astounding to know that approximately 70% of data moved around an enterprise is done using FTP protocols, according to Gartner. So FTP needs to be part of your SOA. However, on average, FTP fails 20% of the time, causing data loss and data corruption, which can lead to financial loss, if you are assuming that information has been sent correctly. Also, it is very difficult to prove what was sent, when it was sent, who actually sent it, and whether the sender was authorized to send it.

Although FTP programs are perceived as being "free," they have hidden costs and challenges. How can you automate and integrate the sending of files produced by other applications? What if the destination application needs it in a different format? How do you ensure the end-to-end process? Standard FTP programs often require a lot of manual intervention.

Regardless of size, businesses need to comply with an increasing number of financial and other regulations. Proving what was done, when it was done, and who did it is becoming increasingly important. File transfer can be particularly prone to error in meeting these requirements, and, as previously mentioned, it often fails. The new breed of managed FTP solutions integrated as part of your ESB helps provide regulatory compliance by providing the means to prove who did what, when, where, and how.

4. **Ensure quality of service**—Life would be simple if every vendor, application, and technology used the same standards and protocols to communicate and exchange information—but that is just not possible. Different services require different qualities of service to match the business need at a particular moment in time. This could depend on any number of factors: the value of the customer, the value of the transaction, security requirements, business impact, and risk—if the information is not delivered. All these differ by industry. For example, the assets in the retail industry have different requirements and priorities compared to real-time defense and weapons systems in the military.

If you stand back and take into account the vast array of formats, how data is stored and used across all your applications, and the number of ways that data can and must be handled, you start to realize that you need an ESB that can make decisions based on the business climate, business rules, and actual content of the transaction at that time.

If the value of a particular stock exceeds a threshold set by the customer, the ESB must be capable of dynamically changing the quality of service and delivery mechanism so that if your

customer is a high-value customer, that customer is notified by cellphone without delay. Other examples include these:

- Insurance field operatives can be alerted if the terms and conditions on a policy have changed (as they are serving the customer).

- Customers in a store can be notified that there is a special offer on a product or related products when they scan a product's bar code.

- A fighter plane can be notified that the target is no longer hostile, to stop weapons launch.

You can see that each example warrants a different quality of service based on situational analysis. This capability means that every asset in your business, no matter where it is or how the information is stored, can be truly integrated.

Your business runs 24×7, so your ESB should, too—it needs to be flexible not just in the data it handles, but also in the way in which it is defined, deployed, and managed. Surely one of the reasons is to enable your business to offer the quality of service that your customers are demanding. Your customers will not want to be restricted by your infrastructure, whether you need to shut down your systems to update them or whether you are making your customers jump through hoops because some of your business runs on different hardware that is inaccessible from other parts of your business. Or maybe you end up creating a headache for yourself because you need to offer a high quality of service for some customers or some business transactions, and you end up doing everything the same way because you can't tune your qualities of service according to the part of the business, the time of day, or even the contents of the transaction. Your ESB, like your business, needs to be adaptable to the changes in demand placed on it. Imagine a transportation and logistics firm. It might start out delivering everything in a local area in a small truck, but as the business scales, different logistics and different modes of transport will be needed. The same applies to your ESB.

You really need your ESB to be as flexible and responsive, delivering the highest quality of service.

5. **Ensure business continuity—high availability, scalability, and resilience**—If your business and throughput suddenly grow, how do you cope without rearchitecting your solutions? You must have a way of spreading the workload across multiple parts of your SOA so that if a server fails, the others can take over the increased workload—with no human intervention required. When it becomes available again, the server resumes its workload. All this happens dynamically without altering your existing applications. Avoiding single points of failure is also important. What if your connectivity is knocked out? Do you tell your customers to come back tomorrow? Of course not. You can't afford to drop your service levels and lose money.

An ESB must be able to exist and be managed logically as a single entity. In reality, however, it could be physically distributed across several sites and even different geographies. This means workloads and categories of processing can be distributed across several physical ESB in the "domain" with each one being aware of the other. So now you have an advanced, distributed ESB with no single point of failure, but one that is manageable and configurable from a single console.

6. **Reduce business risk through complex event processing**—On average, IT departments are aware of—or can handle—only 33% of the total events that occur in their enterprise. In some cases, a single event does not mean anything, but some combination of events can be interpreted as a "business situation" to which we need to react.

Consider three examples:

   a. A credit card transaction on an ATM in Europe is followed by a transaction with the same card in the USA within ten minutes—how quickly can you detect fraud?

   b. A customer cancels two orders in two days and fails to place a regular order—is this customer about to defect?

   c. A series of events on one side of the world leads to a disaster. A similar set of events is occurring elsewhere—can a second disaster be prevented?

Consider any single event alone, and nothing out of the ordinary stands out. But a pattern of events might indicate something more meaningful or sinister.

Within your SOA, you need to be able to handle these kinds of events and capture and learn from history so that if the event happens again, you know what action to take next time. Your SOA now becomes "aware" and acts as the "nervous system" of your business. The business analyst needs to be able to easily define patterns so that the ESB can detect situations before they actually happen. This significantly reduces business risk for your company and your customers.

As messages from any source flow through the ESB over a period of time, the ESB analyzes them based on predefined patterns. Time is a key factor. If a pattern of events occurs within 24 hours, it might be treated as business as usual and normal. If the same set of events occurs within 10 minutes or 30 seconds, it could have a totally different meaning. Detecting patterns of events enables the ESB to take the necessary action, such as sending an alert to a mobile phone, instructing a device on an oil pipeline to open or shut a valve, or even instructing a device to administer insulin to a diabetic patient.

Conclusion: When looking for an ESB, the previously described criteria are helpful in ensuring that you have an ESB without limits (see Figure 5.2) to assist you in the following:

- Globally coordinated and secure transactions
- Integration with the ESB
- SOA hardware that extends ESB
- Universal transformation to meet your needs
- Service registry to dynamically extend and govern ESB
- Service monitoring for end-to-end visibility of service
- Service orchestration to seamlessly extend your ESB to include business processes

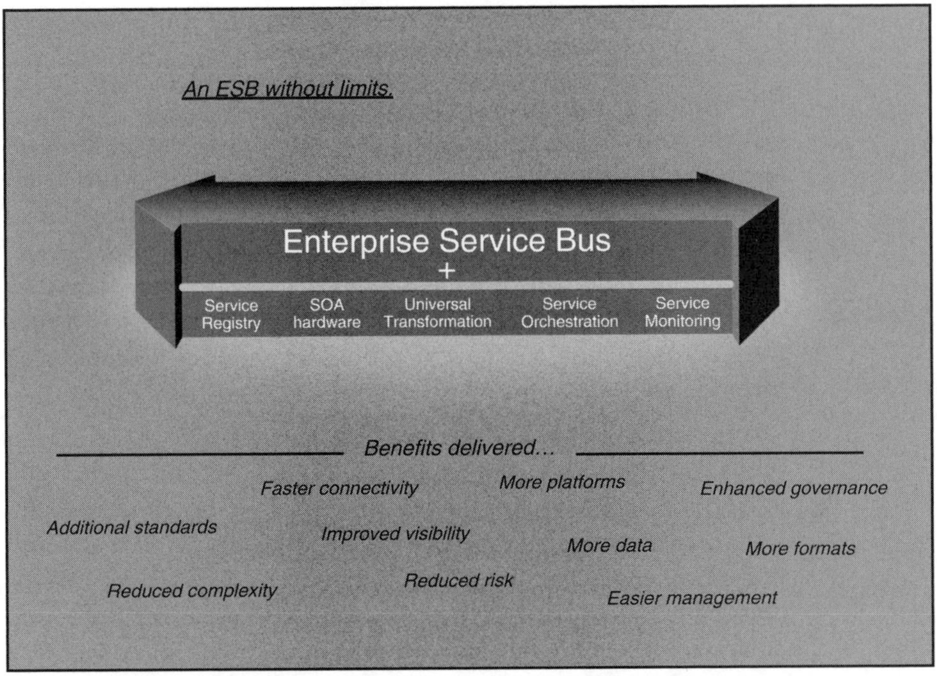

Figure 5.2   ESB without limits

CASE STUDY
XEROX CORPORATION

Best known throughout the world for replacing the blurry, messy mimeograph with the crisp, clean, and sharp photocopy, Xerox Corporation (Xerox) revolutionized office work as its name became synonymous with its flagship product, the copy machine. Xerox research is also credited with many innovations that define personal computing today, including Ethernet, the graphical user interface, and the mouse. Based in Stamford, Connecticut, Xerox (www.xerox.com) has 58,100 employees worldwide who are committed to helping people find better ways to work.

While copying has been good to Xerox, the widespread duplication of efforts to custom-code new business applications for its many product divisions became a bottleneck that hampered productivity. The multiple corporate divisions that produce Xerox's wide range of

products and services require a steady flow of new business applications to automate manual processes, serve customers better, and achieve ever-more-demanding marketing goals. But developing each new application from scratch was a waste of effort, especially because many applications shared common back-end databases and enterprise resource planning (ERP) and customer relationship management (CRM) systems. To centralize these programming efforts and bring costs under control by using more efficient methods of application development and integration, Xerox created its Integration Competency Center. This group, dedicated to integrating Xerox's business applications with back-end systems, set to work to build an information technology (IT) architecture that would enable them to reuse coding assets and leverage a common infrastructure for integrating a large number of applications.

ESB Delivers an Infrastructure for Flexible Connectivity

After several years of integrating applications using CORBA code, the group found that they were writing increasing amounts of custom code, sending costs up and slowing deployment cycles. Xerox began to evaluate middleware for a new Enterprise Service Bus (ESB) architecture—a pattern of middleware that unifies and connects services, applications, and resources within a business. The ESB pattern enables the connection of software running in parallel on different platforms and using disparate programming languages and skills, allowing Xerox to more quickly and easily introduce new applications and updates to their users.

To provide the integration business logic for its ESB framework, Xerox chose an SOA solution providing universal connectivity—an ESB with full failover capabilities using the message-oriented, event-driven, and web services capabilities. With its new ESB solution, Xerox estimates it is saving $720,000 annually in the cost of making changes to its applications, which formerly required custom coding to reintegrate with back-end systems. In addition, application changes take 25% of the time they took previously. "We achieved payback in 24 months," says Ram Sunkara, Manager, Integration Competency Center, Xerox.

continues

Open, Flexible, Available Infrastructure Powers 50 Solutions

Among the 50 applications that run on the new infrastructure are web services for looking up service providers for Xerox's customer support teams, performing credit authorizations, managing customer problem calls, fulfilling parts orders, and capturing user profiles for printers. Many of these applications require 24×7 availability. The open standards–based integration solution supports a service oriented architecture (SOA) that is compatible with multiple methods of communicating with back-end systems.

With its ESB integration solution and SOA, Xerox is moving to standardize application integration throughout its global organization. This entails creating a set of web services for leveraging some existing mainframe information and making it accessible via the Web. "Right now we're working on tying in our European operations and establishing governance practices for continuous process improvement," says Sunkara.

This ESB without limits has a set of items that I encourage you to understand before you design your plans on how you leverage connectivity with SOA.

- **Globally coordinated and secure transactions**—Transactions are critical to your business, and the secure updating of resources as part of a transactional unit of work is just as critical. An individual transaction can look small and insignificant, but your business systems need to be able to treat all your transactions as important. A transaction needs to be able to update resources and complete its unit of work, or key information will be lost if there are any problems or failures. For example, if you are moving money between accounts, you really want to ensure that both accounts are updated, or someone, somewhere, will end up losing out. And what about booking your holiday—reserving your flight, hotel, and rental car?

  If in your business you want to update a number of resources within a transaction, you need to make sure they can take place within a unit of work, or you will face a large amount of

added complexity as you try to write rollback scripts to cope with any scenario. And complexity is what we need to avoid— it's one of the reasons we want to use an ESB in the first place. The ESB had better be able to coordinate resource updates, where possible—and that means not just in its own environment, but also in your extended environment. You need to make sure your ESB can utilize what you already have in place, not rip and replace.

When you are processing transactions—any or all of which could be critical to your business—you need to know that the information is secure, and, again, you need to have that security without adding to the complexity of your environment.

- **Complete integration with the ESB**—Your ESB needs to connect everything with everything. Some ESBs in the marketplace just connect applications and web services. An ESB should be able to not only integrate applications and web services, but also provide a connection to all systems, files, and information from all parts of the business, and then extend the lifecycle and value of existing applications, systems, and data.

- **SOA hardware that extends ESB capabilities**—XML and web services create new challenges for integration because excessive XML processing can cause bottlenecks to core functions. You want to minimize the complexity and reduce the cycles of implementing SOA infrastructures, specifically those that include XML and web services, while enhancing performance, security, and management of business processes implemented under SOA principles.

In the world of SOA, services can come from anywhere and do pretty much anything—internally or externally. SOA introduces many issues, including serious security issues that most ESBs don't even think about, creating limits to the ESB that can drag down the business goals or even the business itself. This leads to understanding the need to put *some* functions that would otherwise be deemed ESB functions into specialized processors optimized for handling specific functions. Doing so enables you to extend your ESB with hardware that is directly targeted at a specific function.

This is why you need an ESB without limits that can be extended by an appliance strategy. Appliances are specialized hardware for your SOA. They minimize the complexity and reduce the cycles of implementing SOA infrastructures, while enhancing performance, security, and management of business processes implemented under SOA principles. Appliances offer many capabilities for services, including great capability for locking stuff down, accelerating key processing, and handling key integration functions—thus making sure your ESB is really efficient and bullet-proof. You need a federated ESB strategy that enables you to put the right function in the right place—appliances *and* core transactional ESB systems on multiple platforms.

■ **Universal transformation to meet your needs**—For many businesses, mapping of data and transformation of data formats as it is exchanged between services is one of the top requirements for an ESB. After all, if your SOA needs to connect applications flexibly and the data is not in the expected format, the transformation needs to happen in the application. You have not only increased complexity, but you have also pretty much sunk any prospects of reuse for that application. So if you don't want to be limited by your ESB, transformation is a highly important aspect.

For an effective SOA, you need to be able to have data transformed from any format to any other format—whether the formats are simple or complex, highly proprietary or a core industry standard–based format. However, equally important to real SOA deployments is not just whether the data can be transformed, but where the transformation takes place. If you have transformation needs between two local applications or services, you don't want to route the message to a remote hub to do the transform; you need to have mapping capable of running everywhere you need it, even in third-party integration products, but without adding complexity to your applications or instability to your environment. That means transformation not just of any data format, but anywhere in your ESB. Transformation can be provided as a core capability of the ESB itself, or it can be deployed anywhere within the enterprise and accessed across the ESB.

- **Service registry to dynamically extend and govern ESB—**
  Earlier I discussed the critical role of the Business Service
  Registry and Repository. Your ESB selection needs to do more
  than simply connecting; it needs to be able to find and access
  resources dynamically that are in a registry and repository. It
  needs to be managed through policies across the enterprise.
  And it gets extra credit for dynamic service definition and location, and for defining use and reuse of assets through policies.

- **Service monitoring for end-to-end visibility of service interactions—**If everything is running through your ESB, you need
  to be sure you have effective tooling to support the tracking
  and management of assets as they move through the ESB.

  Suppose you have been doing well in your SOA planning, and
  you are successfully connecting all your platforms, applications, and services, including good linkages between your
  applications and your processes flowing through your ESB.
  But now when things are up and running, everything seems
  out of control. How do you know what is going on? Can you
  track what is happening in your systems, or are you limited to
  just what your ESB can tell you? In the highly connected and
  interdependent environment of an SOA, it becomes critical to
  be alerted to any situation you define, to increase both
  automation and awareness of business activity—or lack of it,
  due to bottlenecks or failures.

  For an ESB without limits, you need to be able to identify
  problems and resolve them quickly, drilling down from the
  symptom to find the real problems. This needs to be possible
  throughout the entire lifecycle—not just in a single environment, but across your SOA and for multiple platforms. Ideally,
  everything should be visible and managed through a single,
  powerful console, to ensure that nothing gets missed. Your
  ESB needs to be fully monitored and managed, including coverage for other vendor middleware products that might be
  deployed in the SOA.

- **Service orchestration to seamlessly extend your ESB to
  include business processes—**As you learned early on, process
  is a key part of SOA. To deliver an ESB without limits that provides real SOA, there must be strong integration with business

process flows. You need to solve your connectivity issues along with and as a part of your process plans. If you are looking to streamline your business through effective and optimized processes, you need to ensure that your processes are efficiently orchestrated and effectively linked to the underlying applications and services. To do this, you need to make sure you do not complicate your processes with connectivity interfaces. You need to ensure that your ESB works seamlessly with your process layer, but also ensure that process and connectivity are effectively decoupled. You need to make sure that your ESB without limits can deliver a robust, scalable environment that integrates with the way you deploy your processes.

The conclusion is that complex event processing helps your business to react more quickly to (and detect) more situations that might otherwise remain invisible until it is too late. The ability to be proactive can save your business a lot of money.

YOUR ESB UNDERPINNING THE BUSINESS

If your ESB can handle all the issues raised in the previous section on best practices—and more—then business flexibility, agility, and innovation flourish. All the complexities of the technology and interdependencies are abstracted so that the business can see a set of well-defined services that can be orchestrated into higher-level business processes. The business can then request new services to be built and catalogued, secure in the knowledge that they are independent of technology changes. Vendors, products, and applications could be changed or even swapped out over time, but the business processes can remain stable for as long as the business sees fit. This is how SOA really differs from previous forms of integration, by separating *what* needs to be done from *how* it gets implemented.

CASE STUDY
STANDARD LIFE GROUP OF COMPANIES

Standard Life group of companies Plc, headquartered in Edinburgh in the U.K., has become one of the world's leading financial services companies. The majority of Standard Life group of companies' business and revenue is generated through independent financial advisors (IFAs) that help their customers select financial and insurance products from a number of different assurance companies. Many IFAs utilize industry-sponsored portals to obtain product information, compare prices from multiple providers, and provide a single view of a customer's holdings.

Standard Life group of companies realized that, to remain competitive, it needed to offer its IFAs easier, more flexible, and quicker online access to its to financial information. Standard Life group of companies also needed to reduce the cost of doing business with multiple business channels. By reducing its costs, not only could it improve its bottom line, but it also could improve its competitive standing and its relationships with its IFAs; more self-service and quicker processes via automation could help the IFAs improve their margins. Standard Life group of companies wanted to provide the data the IFAs needed through portals and its own online channels, consistent with the excellent service they provided through traditional channels, thus helping them to exceed their competitors. They sought to establish a new, more flexible information technology (IT) architecture that would allow them to quickly and easily deploy new services by leveraging reusable web services in portals and in other new channels. The new IT platform also needed to leverage and reuse the company's existing processes and technology assets. They wanted to implement an SOA that would componentize the IT functions and associated business processes into self-contained, modular applications to work together without relying on custom-coded connections. The modular components could

continues

then be reused to meet the IFAs and new strategic distribution partners' changing business needs, and to help shorten development cycles and lower costs.

The SOA enables IFAs, agents, and customers to access more than 550 business services, including providing pension valuations, producing customer statements, and maintaining customer information.

The SOA also allows Standard Life group of companies to easily deploy new services by combining web services, thereby simplifying the process of working across its various business channels. Instead of custom-designing an application for only one channel, Standard Life group of companies can reuse web services across its various operations, resulting in a significant decrease in customer application development times. Because the company can reuse nearly 51% of its web services, it has saved more than £10 million in development costs. The flexible, modular design of the SOA enables Standard Life group of companies to be more agile and respond to new business opportunities with greater speed.

Since implementing its new SOA, Standard Life group of companies' transaction rates on its SOA have increased year on year. Today more than 50% of its eight million daily mainframe transactions are generated through applications in its SOA. This has been done without requiring an increase in IT staff and, in fact, has been achieved in a period where IT staff head count overall was reduced by a third. In this period, productivity and delivery on the SOA has increased such that over 150 applications are now running on it. By making its web services available to business partners, the company ensures that customer information is consistent. IFAs, agents, and customers receive the same information, whether that data comes from an IFA portal, the company's website, or a customer service representative. By providing easy, consistent access to data, Standard Life group of companies has differentiated itself from competitors and gained a competitive edge with IFAs and

customers. It was voted "Company of the Year" by the U.K. IFAs for the past six out of the past seven years and receives consistent accolades for its quality of service.

TYING IT ALL TOGETHER: SERVICES, CONNECTIVITY THROUGH YOUR ESB, AND THE BSRR

Now that we have walked through the concepts of reuse and connectivity through the technologies of web services, ESB, and BSRR, let's see it all in action.

In Figure 5.3, a service is first called by some application and triggers a message to be received and acted upon by the ESB. Next, the BSRR is accessed to determine which services are to be monitored and to acquire any monitoring requirements, such as filters to apply. For example, monitor the submission of orders if the submission comes from a foreign partner. This act enables different services—say, from a new external partner—to be monitored differently from those of more established partners.

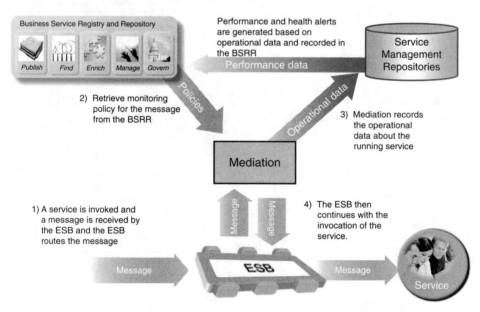

Figure 5.3   Operational monitoring interactions

Then the service-management tools capture and assess the performance of services against business and operational performance objectives. This information will be linked to service descriptions in the BSRR and accessed by mediations at runtime to affect dynamic routing, filtering, and other kinds of decisions, providing operational flexibility on demand.

As you can see from this example, these key technologies and their usage are critical to successful deployments and implementations.

THE SOA LIFECYCLE DRIVES IT FLEXIBILITY

This section brings up a great point about how these areas are working together. SOA is best considered in terms of a lifecycle. Think of this lifecycle comprehensively and approach it tactically, focusing on the sections that provide the most value for you (see Figure 5.4).

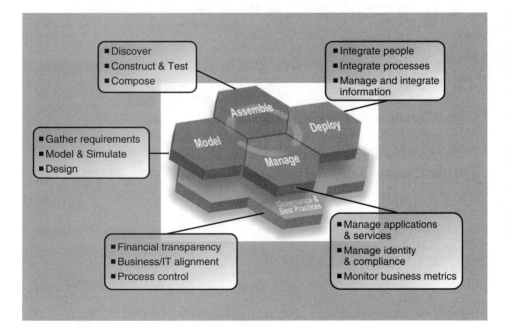

Figure 5.4 SOA Service Lifecycle.

Our customers have told us that they take a lifecycle approach to SOA. They start in what we are calling the **Model** phase by gathering business requirements, designing, simulating, and optimizing their desired business processes. That way, they can make sure they are setting the right steps in motion before further action is taken. When they have optimized the business processes, they implement it by combining newly created and existing services to form composite applications. This is the **Assembly** step. The assets are then **deployed** into a secure and integrated environment, taking advantage of specialized services that provide support for integrating people, processes, and information. This level of integration helps ensure that all the key elements of your company are connected and working together. Once composite applications are deployed, customers **manage** and monitor applications and underlying resources from both an IT and a business perspective. Information gathered during the Manage phase is used to gain real-time insight into business processes, enabling better business decisions and feeding information back into the lifecycle for continuous process improvement. Underpinning all these lifecycle stages is governance, which provides guidance and oversight for the SOA project.

This SOA service lifecycle shows the continuous improvement approach that SOA drives into the business. Again, the focus on business services and connecting these services throughout the business for better reuse of best practices drives flexibility and innovation throughout your company.

SUMMARY

To begin the journey of becoming a business that is flex-pon-sive* requires a focus on the SOA lifecycle and key elements of technology. Business flexibility requires flexible IT because virtually every business today is dependent on IT. Service oriented architecture is the key to flexible IT. The average Fortune 500 company has more than 48 different financial systems and 3 enterprise resource planning systems, so success today requires that IT flexibly leverage what currently exists in your environment.

Service oriented architecture is built on the value proposition of reuse that enables companies to leverage what is currently in their environment.

You must think through some of these best practices:

- Strategy around services (web services)
- How you store and leverage the reusability of services (BSSR)
- The strategy for connecting services at all levels of your organization (ESB)
- How to leverage the SOA lifecycle as a tactical approach to provide the most value

These IT best practices are fundamental for a successful company, but let's explore the business-centric side of SOA through the eyes of a business leader.

6

SOA Governance and Service Lifecycle

Analysts and industry specialists have talked about aligning business and IT for a long time. If a company's business structure and IT architecture are not in sync, the company cannot perform at its peak or drive the desired innovation. Today this alignment has become not only a reality, but also a source of competitive advantage. Governance is the policy, clarity, and measurements that drive the alignment of business and IT. Governance needs to be one of the first thoughts in moving toward business innovation and flexibility because it ensures a foundation for growth and a foundation for flex-pon-sive* companies. In every SOA example that we go through, governance is the secret sauce that really brought forward the results. In *Service-Oriented Architecture Craves Governance* (Gartner, Inc.: January 20, 2006), Paolo Malinverno writes:

> SOA projects are emerging. SOA governance isn't optional—it's imperative. Without it, return on investment will be low and every SOA project out of pilot phase will be at risk.

This chapter focuses first on governance overall and then how IT governance and SOA governance are linked. An important part of this journey is understanding that there is an SOA governance process and that it is a crucial element to success. We also discuss how SOA governance and lifecycle management are interrelated.

Aberdeen Group has a benchmark study that published in January of 2007. The study titled, "Management and Governance: Planning for an Optimized SOA Application Lifecycle," states that the Best in Class companies realize that enterprise service-oriented architecture (SOA) excellence requires IT operations management and governance along with a ruthless focus on controlling SOA application lifecycle costs. The report documents the challenges that early adopters have succeeded in overcoming, the value they are generating, and lessons learned. The findings at this time from over 130 companies include:

- The majority of companies are having trouble obtaining a positive ROI payback on their SOA management or governance investment.
- Best in Class companies are using SOA management and governance software now.
- Best in Class companies are achieving a decrease in development costs under an SOA, while Industry Average and Laggard companies are seeing an increase in development costs under an SOA.

WHAT IS GOVERNANCE?

"A poorly conceived [corporate governance] system can wreak havoc on the economy by misallocating resources or failing to check opportunistic behaviors," states Wharton management professor Mauro Guillen in his paper "Corporate Governance and Globalization: Is There Convergence Across Countries?" Corporate governance is the method by which a corporation is directed, administered, or controlled. It includes the policies and rules that guide their goals and directions. The stakeholders for corporate governance are typically at the highest level of the company, usually major shareholders, senior executives, and the board of directors. The most successful companies include employees,

customers, suppliers, and partners in elements of governance as well. Increasing industry regulations such as Sarbanes-Oxley (SOX) or industry-specific regulations such as BASIL II or HIPAA require governance oversight as well. Corporate governance is about establishing chains of responsibility, authority, and communication to empower people. It is more than just the proper level of disclosure, but also setting the goals of the corporation—the rules by which the company will operate—such as those around customer. Some examples of best-practice corporate governance include confidentiality and use of customer information, public disclosure of its policies, and how it views audits of its results.

In addition to the policy aspects, corporate governance is about establishing measurement and control mechanisms to enable people to carry out their roles and responsibilities. In its "Global Investor Opinion Survey," McKinsey & Company (2002) looked at how the market rewards good governance. Investors stated that they put corporate governance on a par with financial indicators when evaluating investment decisions. They were prepared to pay a premium for companies displaying good governance, ranging from 12% in North America and Western Europe to more than 30% in Eastern Europe and Africa.

For alignment to occur, not only does corporate governance need to be clear on its goals and directions for the business, but corporations must also align those business goals with IT to succeed. IT has become a source of competitive advantage for most businesses today. In fact, MIT Sloan School of Management states that "effective IT governance is the single most important predictor of value an organization generates from IT."

So what is IT governance? IT governance is the decision-making rights associated with IT, and the mandates and policies used to measure and control the way IT decisions are made and carried out in concert with the business (see Figure 6.1). Its goals are to help with the strategic alignment of business and IT to increase the value realization from business strategies and objectives. In addition, it assists with risk reduction in helping companies to understand and mitigate risks associated with initiatives and operations. Management technology enables people to achieve governance goals.

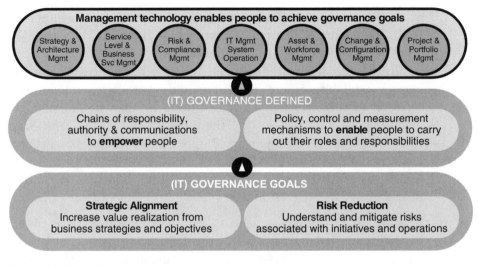

Figure 6.1   What is (IT) governance?

Because corporate governance is the overarching structure for the business, IT governance is the corresponding IT vision of the IT mandates to support the business goals. It is the set of mandates that drives an IT organization's decisions—for example, the goal to use open source or to have a certain directive around change management. It consists not only of the decisions that drive IT, but also the policies and practices that companies use to achieve the desired behavior. The way these decisions are actually made in companies today and the metrics used to ensure the alignment are all part of IT governance.

IT governance concepts have been around and documented by such industry groups as Information Technology Infrastructure Library (ITIL), a process-based methodology that delivers a set of IT service management best practices that can help you align your IT with your business requirements, improve service quality, and lower the long-term cost of IT service provision. These best practices are applicable to all IT organizations, no matter what their size or what technology they use. Originally developed by the British government in the late 1980s, today ITIL is the world's most widely accepted approach to IT service management.

In today's world of focus on growth through business flexibility and innovation, there is now a third type of governance: service oriented architecture (SOA) governance, which is an extension of IT governance. SOA governance focuses on the flexibility and reuse driven by the lifecycle of services nature of the new technology. Done correctly, and given that more than 63% of today's SOA projects are driven through line of business projects, SOA governance is driving tighter alignment of IT and business around a set of goals. For instance, how do you develop IT skills that are linked to what the business needs to drive its goals, to commit to nonstop process improvement, and to have a way to measure real value back to the business?

These three types are governance are all critical. Of course, you begin by documenting and validating the business strategy and IT strategy in Corporate and IT governance. Of most importance to us in this book is SOA governance. With SOA being a combined IT and Business environment, SOA Governance as an extension of IT governance, performs two key functions. One is to define the decision rights for the new services within IT and also to define the new decision rights that now exist between the business and IT organizations. SOA Governance is intended to improve the ability to make better decisions, faster. It gives everyone in the organization a clear understanding to what decisions need to be made and who can make them, eliminating confusion and uncertainty. With SOA being at this crucial crossroads of IT and Business, this is a crucial aspect of a successful SOA implementation. My view of SOA Governance includes the extension of IT governance focused on the lifecycle of services to ensure the business value of SOA, establishing decision rights to empower people, establishing policies and measurement and control mechanisms to enable people. In addition, in this new world of SOA, it encompasses a focus on the organizational change required. And of course all of this begins with the challenge we have been faced with for a while: the IT and business alignment challenge.

THE ALIGNMENT CHALLENGE MADE REAL

Almost any company's success story that achieves great results begins with the standard "In the beginning, there was business and IT alignment." For example, take Standard Life group of companies. The first step in their success was aligning IT and Business around a business project for enhancing their customer service and satisfaction. They implemented the solution with IT fully supporting the business goals and designs. The only way they got such tight alignment was through a governance model that was driven from the top. They could not have been successful without that strong alignment. Business and IT alignment does not happen by accident, but by hard work and an appropriate governance model to ensure that the alignment continues throughout any major projects or missions. Let's go through an example.

Take, for instance, a large insurer offering a variety of services (such as home, life, auto) running on a business model in which each business unit operates autonomously and is supported by its own IT organization and infrastructure. It has the same business process and supporting applications implemented in many ways. It doesn't have strong IT governance, so it has a minimal technology standard, which has created very diverse environments that don't interoperate. Because the company is facing increased competitive pressure and looking for ways to remain competitive, the problem is typical: Everyone is responsible and no one is responsible. The CEO knows that to compete, the company must have a consistent customer experience, so the project begins with some challenges:

- Funding and ownership of shared projects
- Lack of governance model
- Existing organizational design

The next section discusses the alignment steps for addressing this scenario.

ALIGNMENT VISION FOR THE FUTURE

In today's world, most companies don't drive the business opportunity through both business and IT strategy. You need to ensure that the business architecture and the IT architecture are driving toward the same business outcome. For a company's future success, governance needs to drive this synergy.

Let's go back to our sample challenge. Governance can help if the mechanisms are set up appropriately (see Figure 6.2). This large insurer today is similar to the left side of this figure. The corporate governance and organization are not completely in line with the IT governance structure. In fact, because the mechanisms are so disjointed, the CEO doesn't even know who is responsible for solving the customer service problem across the organization. The recommendation is that corporate governance be the overarching business value mechanism. See the right side of Figure 6.2. When all is driven by the business, IT and SOA goals and directions line up under the business goals. By aligning the organizational design with a governance structure, the CIOs have a view of the funding, ownership, responsibilities, and control that enables them to support the overarching goal.

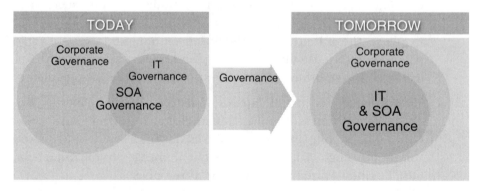

Figure 6.2 Aligning corporate, IT, and SOA governance

The future I envision is one in which corporate governance, IT governance, and SOA governance do not run separately, but instead work together to drive innovation and competitive

advantage that most companies seek. To achieve alignment between business and IT, corporate governance must be the overarching governance model focused on the business's outcomes. SOA governance needs to be part of IT governance, and IT governance needs to drive IT toward business goals.

Let's go back to our example of the large insurer. With the aligned governance model, the CEO would set the goal of better customer service and ask the question of how much it will cost and how quickly it can be done through corporate governance principles. With IT governance in place, the CIO would then ask who has the best data and who could lead the IT project across the organization. Because it is a shared view of the data, SOA governance would help address the funding, the ownership, and who has change-management responsibility. The project would move forward with clear direction and goals around the set business outcome.

The chief driver for success is to focus on the business outcome. There won't be any tolerance to support or fund an IT or SOA project without demonstrable business outcomes over a short time frame (less than 12 months). IT leaders must help bridge the business gap. In my experience, it takes an innovative IT leader with existing respect of business and a centralized IT organization to drive IT and SOA forward. If any of these three elements are not in place, the initiative will likely fail or not progress at a rapid pace. Therefore, thought leadership and tools must support the IT leader to bring, bridge, or resolve any of those three elements.

My colleague was just in Japan and listened to the team's experience with a company called Mitsui-Soko, a leading warehouse-management company looking to transform its business to logistic services through IT and SOA. The client engaged to roll out a business flexibility project with SOA in three phases:

- Assessment and vision
- Governance
- Focus on a custom warehouse-management application

I think this is an important case to understand the value of an SOA governance program. It didn't start with a tool or product license. It started with a business goal, a framework for discussion, a plan, and only then implementation.

CASE STUDY
Mitsui-Soko Co.

From Gartner's report titled "Mitsui-Soko Drives Service-Oriented Architecture for Business Agility," by Michael Barnes, 27 September 2005.

Established in 1909, Mitsui-Soko Co. (MSC) provides a diverse range of logistics services in Japan and overseas, including warehousing, port terminal operations and overland transportation. MSC currently employs 842 people with annual revenue of approximately US$872 million.

Beyond its primary focus on warehousing and logistics services, the company has expanded to include integrated logistics management for all stages of business operations, from customer production to sales, as well as the accompanying flow of information. Core to this service is the effective use of information systems to deliver relevant logistics information to customers. This also requires access to core internal systems in areas such as financials and accounting, as well as other administrative systems.

The core challenge facing MSC is to improve overall corporate agility and responsiveness to customer needs, while simultaneously improving consistency of operations and information. Moreover, Global Network Systems (GNS) is MSC's corporate vision for SOA-enabling its core IT systems. The GNS project goal is to unify all internal IT infrastructure and rationalize information assets. As a first step toward meeting the key strategic objectives of GNS, MSC identified three initial projects.

MSC broke the project down into three distinct phases.

continues

- Phase 1 of GNS was completed in June 2005. It focused on establishing realistic expectations for the SOA (in business and technical terms) and providing a foundation on which all future SOA initiatives would rest. Phase 1 enabled MSC to illustrate and document the "to-be" application architecture within MSC, and the associated infrastructure necessary to support an SOA approach by defining a common system architecture to standardize functionality, "componentize" established systems and eliminate redundancies within IT.

- Phase 2 of MSC's SOA initiative is currently under way. Leveraging the output of Phase 1, Phase 2 is an eight-week process focused on more-detailed and technical migration planning. Deliverables include a detailed system and application development plan (including a development methodology), an IT infrastructure plan, and a system development prototype. No specific reward structure was implemented to help encourage reuse among developers. However, Phase 2 is led by key architects within MSC's development team, thereby ensuring buy-in to the agreed-on project approach.

- Phase 3 of GNS includes the first stage of IT development, based on SOA principles. The nine-month project will focus on the reconstruction of MSC's warehousing and logistics applications, including the underlying data architecture.

THE SOA GOVERNANCE CHALLENGE

So IT governance is about the decision rights structure of the IT organization. With SOA being a joint business/IT environment, SOA governance is an extension of IT governance to perform two functions. One function is to define the decision rights for the new services within IT, and the second is to define the new decision rights that now exist between the business and IT organizations. SOA governance is intended to improve the ability to make better decisions, faster. It gives everyone in the organization a clear

understanding of what decisions need to be made and who can make them, eliminating confusion and uncertainty. With SOA usually driving cross-business projects, this is a crucial aspect of a successful SOA implementation. SOA governance is an extension of IT governance to support the service environment.

Two components should be taken into consideration when understanding the SOA governance environment: development of the SOA governance processes, and service lifecycle management using the governance process. When the governance decision making has been established, it is then about executing the process and managing and monitoring the results. Two types of results emerge: the services that come out of the development process, and the decisions that are made related to the service. The SOA governance processes are monitored via the SOA governance framework (see Figure 6.3), and the released services are managed via the manage component of the SOA lifecycle.

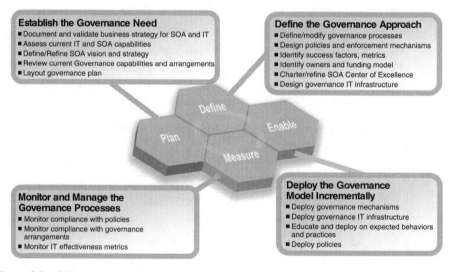

Establish the Governance Need
- Document and validate business strategy for SOA and IT
- Assess current IT and SOA capabilities
- Define/Refine SOA vision and strategy
- Review current Governance capabilities and arrangements
- Layout governance plan

Define the Governance Approach
- Define/modify governance processes
- Design policies and enforcement mechanisms
- Identify success factors, metrics
- Identify owners and funding model
- Charter/refine SOA Center of Excellence
- Design governance IT infrastructure

Monitor and Manage the Governance Processes
- Monitor compliance with policies
- Monitor compliance with governance arrangements
- Monitor IT effectiveness metrics

Deploy the Governance Model Incrementally
- Deploy governance mechanisms
- Deploy governance IT infrastructure
- Educate and deploy on expected behaviors and practices
- Deploy policies

Figure 6.3 SOA governance lifecycle

In Figure 6.3, we see this SOA governance framework of plan, define, enable, and measure.

In the Plan stage, you establish the governance need. This is where you document and validate business strategy for SOA and IT,

assess current IT and SOA capabilities, and define and refine SOA vision and strategy. This is where the overall governance plan should be laid out.

The approach is mapped out in the Define stage. This includes the governance processes, the design of the policies and enforcement mechanisms, and the identification of the success factors and metrics. Also in the Define step, you identify owners and a funding model, and charter a SOA center of excellence to develop the right skills to both design the governance IT infrastructure and set the right business linkages in place

In the enable stage, you deploy the governance model incrementally. This includes the governance mechanisms and the deployment of the governance IT infrastructure that you laid out the plans for in the Define step. In addition, you think through the education on expected behaviors, practices, and policies in this stage.

The Measure stage sets up the monitoring and management of the governance process. It is important to ensure compliance with policies and governance arrangements, and to monitor the IT effectiveness metrics. This framework is about establishing the end-to-end SOA governance processes—how decisions are made and the policies for the SOA lifecycle.

The challenges that SOA governance addresses can be classified into four critical areas:

- Establishing decision rights
- Defining high-value business services
- Managing the lifecycle of assets
- Measuring effectiveness

ESTABLISHING DECISION RIGHTS

One major challenge that SOA governance helps a company to address is establishing decision rights. An example at this stage adds perspective. Let's consider a business in the insurance industry that has separate groups or business units that focus on their

own individual areas, such as home, life, and auto insurance. Similar to most of my customers that I work with today, let's assume that one of this company's challenges is that each of these groups is working with the customer separately. Now the fun begins. The company recognizes the need to implement a common customer-service process—a one-stop-shopping experience for customers to fulfill all their insurance needs. Because the company is currently operating as siloed business units, with each unit operating separately with its own IT staff and infrastructure, the systems between the units don't talk to each other. SOA governance can assist with this challenge by framing the key issues:

- Who decides which existing unit has the best customer data for the new shared process to be used by the company?

- Who owns the shared service(s)? Who should fund it? Who is responsible for upgrades?

- How do you motivate each unit to reuse the service (instead of each using its own unique version because they all feel they have unique needs)?

- Who decides who can use the service and how often?

SOA governance helps with funding and ownership of shared services, executive commitment to the governance model, and the organizational design—all critical items in helping companies have successful SOA deployments.

DEFINING HIGH-VALUE BUSINESS SERVICES

The next challenge that SOA governance can assist with is defining high-value business services. Now let's take an example in the banking industry. As with many banks, our example bank is one that is expanding into new geographies with differing regulatory requirements. This company wants to roll out a new customer service solution into different countries. To lower total cost of ownership, it wants a flexible implementation that can be tailored to local requirements. The company has selected SOA as its enabling technology and needs it to support the sharing of reusable business services that can dynamically be bundled or unbundled as

required to enable compliance in each geographical area. Effective SOA governance can assist with this task in multiple ways:

- What common business services are needed?

- What potential applications will reuse the service(s)?

- Which policies are common and which are unique? Can the differences be isolated to maximize consistency?

- What services already exist and are candidates for reuse?

SOA governance can help by establishing a process for shared services, facilitating communications, and enforcing standards, platforms, and policies. In addition, it adds value by identifying and implementing shareable services. A key to good SOA governance is the ability to classify services into logical domains and assign owners to each domain, to simplify the management and implementation of an SOA.

Two domains require attention. First is the business service domain. This is the domain in which services provide business value (for example, request for information) and contain business logic. The second domain is the infrastructure service domain in which services provide indirect business value and do not contain business logic (such as authenticate users). The domain owners monitor, define, and authorize changes to existing services and decide when a new service in their domain is required.

This is one of the reasons why governance is such a key to success in all the deployments that I've seen. Because of the importance of the method for defining business processes, services, and metrics, and of taking an enterprise view of services and data (horizontal— not siloed), SOA governance enables you to find best practices in identifying and defining shared services. This is the heart of the value proposition of enhancing business models.

MANAGING THE LIFECYCLE OF ASSETS

SOA governance also helps address a core area around the lifecycle of assets. This time, let's look at an example of a retailer. This retailer is seeing a more competitive marketplace and a drop in its customer satisfaction. To address this business challenge, the

company wants to fix its billing policy. This seems easy enough; however, the IT team finds it hard to identify which applications and services are impacted by the new billing policy. They try to understand all the impacts, but because of a strong business deadline, they implement the changes and go into production without realizing that another unit was using the billing system as well. The result is customer complaints and outages. It is not uncommon for businesses to not fully understand how all their pieces and parts are shared throughout the company. And although the company had an SOA environment, it had not instituted a way to manage changes and determine who was using the shared services.

Effective SOA governance would have assisted this retailer by addressing the following questions:

- How can the shared services/assets be organized so they can be effectively reused later?

- Who is allowed to change a service that is reused by others?

- Who is using a service, and what will be impacted by changes to that service?

- Who needs to approve any changes?

- Who will be responsible for funding upgrades to meet a specific user's requirements?

If set up correctly, SOA governance could have helped with change management to ensure that the other unit was not affected by the changes. It would have set policies for publishing, using, and retiring services, and would have created an infrastructure to help organize and discover services' assets, govern access, and monitor service vitality. (Remember back to our discussion about the registry and repository.)

MEASURING EFFECTIVENESS

The final challenge for SOA governance to tackle is the measurement of effectiveness. As my father taught me early on, if you can't measure it, you will not pay attention to it. No industry is immune to these challenges, so this time, let's focus on telecommunications. This company is ahead of the curve and has embraced an

SOA strategy to improve staff productivity and lower costs. Two major divisions exist—a commercial group and a residential group, each with differing needs. The residential division in the telecommunications organization wants to launch a new offering that requires changes to the billing system. (There's that billing system again.) Because the commercial division development team made existing functionality available as services, the residential group leveraged it, which is good. However, difficulties appeared when the residential division launched a heavily used new offering that involved one of the commercial division's services. The increased usage slowed response times for every application using the service. It also increased the commercial division's costs. Unfortunately, a service-level agreement (SLA) had not been implemented, which would have generated a plan to handle the additional workload. In addition, because appropriate monitoring tools were never deployed, the commercial division was unable to charge any other division for the service usage.

Effective SOA governance would have assisted in the following areas:

- What are the performance goals of a service?
- What IT standards are needed for performance metric gathering and monitoring capability?
- What service-level agreements are needed?
- How should performance metrics be gathered and monitored?

Good governance would have established a way to measure service utilization and cost, project cost, and the business benefit of the actions taken. In addition, it would have provided access and visibility to information. The residential group would have known about the commercial group's intentions ahead of time, and the commercial group could have considered the performance issues that might have arisen due to its usage.

The best way to handle these challenges is to establish an SOA Center of Excellence (see Figure 6.4), which combines the expertise and assets from across your company. An SOA CoE helps companies that have made an enterprise-wide commitment to architectural change speed the adoption of that change, mitigate risk, and align the transformation with industry best practices.

The SOA CoE accomplishes these goals by leveraging assets and best practices developed from experience across the company with similar enterprise transformations. In essence, the CoE is designed to supply assistance in implementing an SOA in concert with the business design and goals.

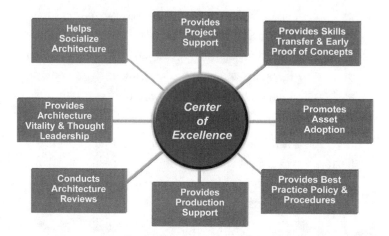

Figure 6.4 SOA Center of Excellence (CoE): a proven organizational model for governance and management

CASE STUDY
A LARGE PROPERTY AND CASUALTY INSURANCE COMPANY

A premier property and casualty insurance company providing personal, commercial, marine, agribusiness, and excess and surplus insurance products across the United States faced a business challenge of improving partner relationships. Building strong relationships with a national network of several thousand independent agents is an important cornerstone of the insurer's market leadership strategy. The company has recently faced challenges from increased competition and new market demands for faster and more personalized service. In today's marketplace, independent agents and their customers are placing more demands on the company. The property and casualty insurer can deliver outstanding support to agents with an industry-focused, SOA platform.

continues

The insurance carrier recognized the need to become more agile to bring new products to market faster and differentiate its services. The company began to explore how it could better deliver outstanding service and support to agents—including new business acquisition, policy management, and claims management—across its core business functions, while reducing manual touch points and operating costs. However, the company's broad assortment of inflexible legacy IT systems made it difficult and expensive to introduce new business processes and services. The company's large and continually changing product line added to the challenge, as did the need to comply with multiple regulatory requirements.

In keeping with the value proposition of SOA to provide the needed flexibility in business process and IT systems, the large insurer decided to implement its solution using SOA solutions linked to industry standards and best practices. The SOA solution enables the company to compose loosely coupled, insurer-specific business processes from prebuilt and custom business services that are published, managed, and governed across the enterprise using Association for Corporate Operations Research and Development (ACORD) and Insurance Application Architecture (IAA) industry standards. The SOA solution helps the insurer integrate and connect a wide variety of legacy IT assets, including mainframe applications, IMS billing software, single sign-on user authentication systems, and agent authorization software. But one of the secrets to its success is the focus on governance. The company has created an SOA Center of Excellence to prioritize business needs and evaluate which IT assets to extend or replace.

While the insurance carrier recognized that it could dramatically improve business agility by deploying composite business services, to deploy these business-critical solutions, the company needed to manage the technology, security, governance, and interoperability issues, which was not possible under its existing IT infrastructure. The CoE provided a vehicle to incrementally transform core business processes, while providing the semantic interoperability and

SOA governance foundation to deploy solutions across multiple lines of business, end users, and business partners. Success from initial service-realization projects, with the leadership provided by the CoE, allowed an evolution over time into an enterprise-wide, multiyear business transformation initiative to create an on demand IT infrastructure capable of automating and outsourcing several key business functions. The resulting operational advances will help the insurance carrier become more agile, improve service levels, and reduce operating costs. The CoE pursued an incremental path to SOA, starting with billing solutions, followed by a new business acquisition solution focused initially on three products within personal property. These solutions leveraged existing IT systems and used industry and Web-service standards including ACORD, IAA, and those from the Web Services Interoperability (WS-I) organization. The incremental approach mitigated deployment risk and demonstrated the business value and rapid revenue generation capabilities of SOA-based solutions.

The insurance carrier expects to improve its financial performance and market share by transforming additional siloed applications to composite business services. The company has already embarked on major initiatives to change its core processes around policy administration. With a focus on responding to new market needs through better service and greater business agility, the company is further establishing itself as a leading innovator of products and services in the insurance industry, and SOA governance is a key to its success.

THE SOA GOVERNANCE LINK TO SERVICE LIFECYCLE MANAGEMENT

Governance is not management. Governance determines who makes the decisions. Management is the process of making and implementing the decisions. In Figure 6.5, we see the linkage point with the service lifecycle. As a reminder, the Service Lifecycle was defined in Chapter 5, "SOA Key Concepts," around Model,

Assemble, Deploy, and Manage. Services are created with the Model, Assemble, and Deploy sections of the SOA lifecycle (see Chapter 5 for more information on the SOA lifecycle); once deployed, they are controlled in the Manage section of the SOA lifecycle. The overall process is a closed loop because services can be updated during their life and would, therefore, go back into the model phase again.

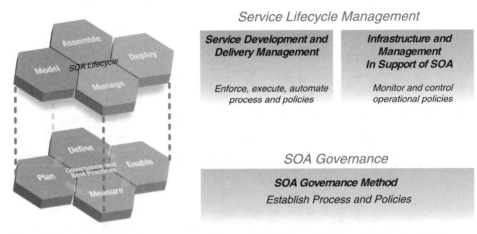

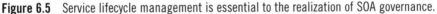

Figure 6.5 Service lifecycle management is essential to the realization of SOA governance.

Governance is involved in making sure that the process is enforced when services are developed and/or delivered. After a service has been deployed and is in the Manage phase, governance is about monitoring the operational policies established by the SOA governance and management method.

That the key component of the governance framework is the governance of the Model, Assemble, and Deploy phases of the SOA lifecycle. In realizing SOA governance, the management of the Model, Assemble, and Deploy phases is essential and referred to as service lifecycle management in this figure.

Service lifecycle management is broken into two facets: service development and delivery management, and infrastructure and management in support of SOA. In Figure 6.6, we focus on service development and delivery management; it addresses the essential need to govern the development of services process through the

established governance framework and management dashboards. The following are the key areas in service development and delivery management, and their associated SOA governance concerns:

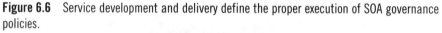

Figure 6.6   Service development and delivery define the proper execution of SOA governance policies.

- **Change and release management**—Determine when, what, and by whom services can be changed
  - Establish policies for controlling risk of change
  - Automate and enforce policies to reduce risk
- **Requirements and quality management**—Ensure that services are developed in alignment with business requirements, and ensure functional and performance compliance
  - Ensure that business needs drive IT investment
  - Validate that deployed solutions meet quality measures
- **Design, analysis, and construction**—Ensure that sound design and development principles are adhered to, for maximum asset reuse and reliability
  - Define accepted reuse, architectural, construction policies
  - Enforce policies through integrated solution
- **Process and portfolio management**—Ensure that projects follow the established governance policies through project frameworks and monitor performance across all projects
  - Document and maintain governance process
  - Optimize/manage services portfolio

Now we've set up SOA governance and discussed the services life-cycle management portion of service development and management. Next, we talk about the other half of service lifecycle management: infrastructure and management in support of SOA (as shown in Figure 6.7).

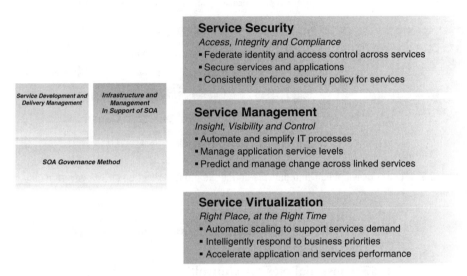

Figure 6.7   Infrastructure and management in support of SOA

SOA project characteristics cause new infrastructure and management considerations. Some of the key pains customers face in an SOA environment are listed here:

- The distributed, cross-boundary nature of services and access to them presents new security risks that need to be managed.

- The rapid deployment and loose coupling of services along with their virtualized application flows present new complexities in key IT process that need to be managed.

- The performance and prioritization of virtualized services needs to be effectively handled while efficiently utilizing available resources.

To address these challenges companies face, we need a number of capabilities that can be broadly categorized into three areas:

1. Security for the SOA-based applications and services
2. Management of the SOA-based applications and services
3. Underlying infrastructure in which virtualization is an increasingly popular and effective technique

SERVICE SECURITY

To secure SOA-based applications and services, companies should address these issues:

- The need to manage identities and access control across multiple applications, platforms, business partners, and business entities

- The need for an end-to-end security architecture that can be deployed and integrated with existing, disparate security models already deployed in the enterprise

- The need to consistently enforce security policies across the environment

SERVICE MANAGEMENT

The dynamically assembled SOA applications and the inherent interdependence that comes from application reuse can overwhelm IT operations managers.

To ensure that these dynamic SOA-based services are deployed properly in the production environment, as well as managed and maintained, the following must be addressed:

- Manage and automate processes
- Manage application service levels
- Predict and manage change that is inherent in SOA environments

The challenge in service management for SOA is that the same qualities for management from initial release to ongoing updates to change management are required. IT executives need to be able to maintain the integrity of the existing services and their relationships and most importantly maintain the service levels of the

existing and new applications. Because SOA drives the focus on horizontal processes, service management of SOA requires that the automation and execution of those processes be done in such a way that maintains the integrity of the existing services and their relationships. Similarly there needs to be ongoing management of the availability and performance of these services. Given that services are shared, a service may be used in a so many different ways that these items are of particular focus. You will also need end-to-end visibility into SOA services and their interaction with shared resources. Visibility into message content, transaction workflows and flow patterns and the ability to identify and isolate performance bottlenecks across technology and platform boundaries are essential to monitoring and delivering the specified service levels for each SOA-based service.

Since SOA services are assembled from existing applications and services, they share the underlying applications and IT resources. Any change made to one service could impact other services in unforeseen and unexpected ways. And while the best SOA governance tries to provide headlights into the usage, to maintain control and create a map of these dependencies and relationships, technology is required. You should consider a Configuration Management Database (CMDB). This CMDB can serve as a single version of truth to facilitate the introduction of any change in the environment so as to ensure that the services continue to deliver to their SLAs. The CMDB can provide a consistent view of the SOA services deployed in the environment and its mapping to other services, applications, and IT resources. It can help discover relationship and interdependencies of various SOA services and when any change is introduced into the environment it can help clients predict the IT and the business impact of that change.

SERVICE VIRTUALIZATION

Implementing specific infrastructure techniques that can respond dynamically to an increased number of services (used in dynamic and new ways) is an important consideration. In SOA, applications are broken up into constituent services. The services are used in

new ways, which makes it difficult to effectively plan infrastructure capacity. Thus, infrastructure responsiveness is important. Virtualization is an effective technique to help by doing the following:

- Support scaling infrastructure resources for services that become popular

- Prioritize infrastructure across multiple services and/or business processes (composite/dynamic applications)

- Accelerate application performance by distributing composite/dynamic applications across infrastructure resources

The key operative thought with service virtualization is to make sure that the services are at the right place at the right time—with the right quantity. Services can be placed for execution on an infrastructure resource (by middleware). Their lifecycle (starting and stopping them) can be managed (by middleware). Finally, services can be mobile, meaning that they can be moved around (by middleware across infrastructure resources).

CASE STUDY
University of Pittsburg Medical Center

University of Pittsburgh Medical Center (UPMC) is Pennsylvania's largest integrated healthcare delivery system—with revenues of $5.8 billion—and one of the nation's most influential healthcare institutions. In addition to operating the nation's largest transplant program and an array of highly specialized clinical services that draw patients from across the nation and around the world, UPMC acts as the major source of routine healthcare services for residents of western Pennsylvania.

With UPMC's rapid growth and large investments in advanced IT initiatives, being integrated hasn't always been easy. Each new hospital added to the network increased the complexity of the organization; each new system added to the complexity of its IT

continues

infrastructure. In the big picture, this created a tremendous challenge—finding an effective way to leverage integrated information across its large and diverse system.

UPMC is working to transform its IT infrastructure through consolidation and standardization across the entire enterprise. Over time, UPMC's 931 servers will be reduced to 319, 9 operating systems will be reduced to 4, and 40 storage databases will be reduced to just 2. To manage the infrastructure centrally and efficiently, the solution will employ a common toolset. UPMC's reliance on standard technology enables a high degree of virtualization within the infrastructure, further driving efficiency and leading to overall IT cost savings of up to 20%.

In the final analysis, though, the true value of the solution can be measured by the way UPMC cares for its patients. The new infrastructure will enable the seamless and secure sharing of patient data across applications and multiple locations, thus providing caregivers with instant access to the information they need to deliver the best possible patient care. At the core, infrastructure simplification—characterized by the flexibility, adherence to standards, and data model consistency of IBM's service-oriented architecture approach—is what makes it possible. These same infrastructure properties will enable UPMC to add new capabilities rapidly and seamlessly. And as UPMC develops new solutions for the broader market, its open infrastructure, combined with IBM's go-to-market expertise, will speed its fruition.

GOVERNANCE AND LIFECYCLE MANAGEMENT LINKED THROUGH THE SERVICE REGISTRY AND REPOSITORY

Service oriented architectures offer the promise of business agility and resilience through reuse, loose coupling, flexibility, interoperability, integration, and governance. To achieve these benefits, services need to be governed and managed throughout

their lifecycle: Model, Assemble, Deploy, and Manage. The lifecycle of a service is similar to the lifecycle of an application, with one new major addition. Because services are used across many lines of business, and because the need to reuse services is a major value of SOA, there is a new requirement to be able to quickly and easily discover services as new subsystems are being created. Services might be located in different places—internally, externally—and in different lifecycle states: under development, in-plan, deployed, or retired. Discovery of the service, its owner, and its status will be critical to achieving the reuse benefits of SOA.

To be able to successfully provide visibility of services across an enterprise, there is a requirement for a central place to publish and find services and information about services. As we discussed in Chapter 5, this is called a repository and/or registry in SOA. A registry is someplace where you can register that you have a service and a pointer to that service. Think of it as a services phonebook. A repository is where metadata about services and related SOA artifacts, such as policies, can be stored. These artifacts are useful in describing the nature of service usage, such as how a service is used and how it interacts with other services. Service metadata artifacts provide information about a service tailored to specific phases of the SOA lifecycle. By managing the service metadata, a registry/repository can manage the lifecycle of services.

Figure 6.8 shows a view of this link across service development and delivery management to infrastructure and management. A registry and repository plays a major role in the four phases of the SOA lifecycle. During service modeling, a registry and repository can be used to create or reuse service taxonomies, vocabularies, and XML schemas. During service development or assembly, a registry and repository can be used to locate services for reuse and to enable service composition—that is, the creation of new applications and services from existing ones. During service deployment, service descriptions stored in a registry and repository are used by runtimes such as an Enterprise Service Bus to enable dynamic interaction between services.

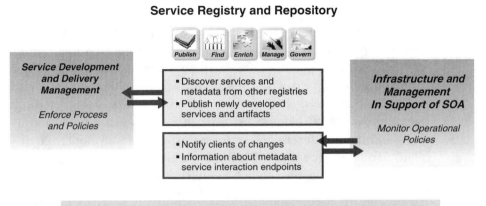

Figure 6.8   Service registry and repository completes the service lifecycle management.

Spanning the SOA lifecycle, a registry and repository is an enabler of SOA governance. Typically, an enterprise architect defines the governance policies and processes that the IT organization uses to develop, run, and maintain services. A registry and repository is then deployed to enable the execution of these governance policies and processes. It stores policies that govern service usage and interactions. It helps perform impact analysis of changes to service. It maintains versioning of service. A registry and repository also classifies services by lifecycle phase so that policies and processes are applied as required.

HOW TO GET STARTED

The steps to aligning business and IT through governance and enforcing many of the policies through Lifecycle management are as follows:

1. Establish the need and the team. The need is usually captured by documenting and validating the business strategy and IT strategy. This should be done by a set of co-owners: one from the business and one from IT who will drive the business architecture and the IT architecture. The goal of this leadership team is to drive maximum value and rapidly respond to

changes in the business. They should be looking to enable the business to make conscious decisions about IT and to shape the principles, practices, and roles that will be needed to drive consistency across business and IT. Bottom line is that these leaders set the priorities for the business. Next enlist the team—this could be virtual—who will be the champions and evangelists for the new model and will help decide on the focus areas of process and services required. This team will do the communications and checkpoints to ensure success.

2. Define the approach. This should be a focus on the governance processes, the design of the policies and thoughtful work on how these are enforced. Just by having policies in place does not mean that they will be used if you don't think through how you will measure the success of them. It is in this step that I would advise you to charter or refine your SOA Center of Excellence. I can't say enough about how important this step is.

3. Deploy the model incrementally. SOA is a journey. There will be organizational change that will be required. Just in thinking horizontally requires a cultural shift so do not underestimate this work. Make sure you plan for education as you deploy your defined policies. And make sure you deploy on expected behaviors and practices.

4. Monitor and manage the processes. Make sure you have compliance with your set policies and with governance arrangements. Since you get what you measure, keep a close eye on your IT and SOA effectiveness metrics.

SUMMARY

IT and business alignment is a critical step in driving growth through innovation and flexibility. Governance is the alignment, clarity, and measurements that drive synchronization between business and IT. This alignment is crucial for companies striving to be flex-pon-sive*. Three perspectives of governance exist: corporate governance, IT governance, and SOA governance. The governance process starts with a strong team of leaders to drive changes

throughout the organization. Because business and IT alignment begins with desired business outcomes, it builds on a concept from Chapter 4, "SOA as the DNA of a Flex-pon-sive* and Innovative Company," of ensuring that you focus on breaking apart your business into your areas of focus. Because governance and lifecycle management are part of the IT flexibility plan in a flex-pon-sive* company, let's next focus on the business flexibility starting points that can enable competitiveness in the marketplace.

7

Three Business-Centric SOA Entry Points

Everyone wants to be successful. In today's marketplace and, more important, in the future, businesses must become more flexible to survive. Businesses today need to be able to change at the speed of the market; therefore, understanding and being able to change business processes quickly is crucial to remaining competitive. Historically, some roadblocks have arisen to achieving this goal. Unfortunately, many business leaders do not have a clear understanding of their business and IT processes. Symptoms of a lack of process knowledge include these:

- Multiple, redundant processes that perform the same task
- Simple processes that are still performed manually
- Inflexible processes and systems that are "hard-wired" together

It is not a surprise that one of the top projects that companies start with is based on leveraging Business Process Management (BPM) and streamlining processes across the company.

The other two major projects that companies start with are extending the ability to collaborate across the business and creating a single view of customer or product information.

This chapter delves into the intricacies of each of the three entry points and helps point you in the direction that is most suitable for your business needs. Without this focus on these business-centric entry points of BPM, collaboration, and information, a company cannot become flex-pon-sive*.

BUSINESS PROCESS MANAGEMENT AS AN ENTRY POINT

BPM is a top-of-mind item for most executives today. According to Gartner's recent white paper "Business Process Management Suites Will Be the Next Big Thing," many customers are exploring this area with growing interest.

Why? Because all business leaders want to know what is happening in their business. They need to be able to improve and grow their business, but they cannot achieve these goals if they don't understand how their company is operating and why things happen. Most business leaders today cannot articulate their processes, so they can't optimize them, deploy them on-the-fly, or monitor how effective their processes are.

A recent study by Aberdeen Research noted "greater visibility into operations management" ranked as one of the highest focus areas for companies today. Not only that, but across five different industries, the survey results revealed the same priority (see Figure 7.1). BPM directly addresses the flexibility strategy by emphasizing continuous improvement to both business and IT processes. Those who master BPM are better able to align IT resources to meet business priorities. BPM enabled by SOA is required for a flex-pon-sive* company to be innovative.

But before we discuss the benefits of BPM, what is BPM? BPM is a discipline combining software capabilities and business expertise through people, systems, and information to accelerate time between process improvements, facilitating business innovation. It is how you view your processes for continuous improvement

through the design, automation, and management of them. And then after the processes are in place, it is answering the key question: How do you evolve those processes at the pace required to keep up with changing market conditions and business priorities, aligned with strategic and operational goals? BPM provides the discipline to improve an organization's ability to adapt quickly and cost-effectively, whether it is through creating new revenue streams or by enhancing current ones.

Top priority	Industry				
	Discrete	Process	Consumer	Services	Public
Better real-time visibility into business operations	65%	67%	65%	80%	75%
Streamlining of order fulfillment processes	26%	42%	6%	24%	13%
Regulatory an (e.g., Sarbane					26%
Linking of dis					25%
Standardizatio manufacturing					
Reduction of					
Easier connections with external partners/supply chain partners	10%	8%	12%		26%
Shorter product lifecycles	3%		6%	8%	13%

Source: Aberdeen Group, Mar, 2006

Figure 7.1   Aberdeen Group Study: Real-time visibility into business operations is the top concern out of 11 categories for all five industries polled.

How does BPM accomplish this? It focuses on achieving strategic business objectives by directing the deployment of resources from across the organization into efficient processes that create customer value. This focus on driving overall top- and bottom-line success is addressed by integrating verticals and optimizing core work (for example, order-to-cash, integrated product development, integrated supply chain). In addition, intrinsic to BPM is the principle of continuous improvement, perpetually increasing value generation and sustaining the market competitiveness (or dominance) of the company.

BPM is not a new concept. However, the technology underpinnings now provide a flexible IT framework (SOA) that was not available in the past. As your company adopts greater process-management disciplines, there are phases of organizational maturity, and, in

turn, competencies that must be mastered. Gartner developed the Business Process Management Maturity and Adoption Model that identifies the evolutionary phase of maturity that your organization must master on its quest to be process driven.

Gartner identified the critical phases an organization transcends as it gains greater process competencies (see Figure 7.2).

0. **Acknowledge operational inefficiencies**—You know what your problems are.

1. **Process aware**—Your organization becomes aware of the need for a discipline around business processes.

2. **Intraprocess automation and control**—Your organization begins to see the value of software to automate your core business processes inside the organization.

3. **Interprocess automation and control**—Your organization begins to see the value of software to automate your core business processes outside the organization.

4. **Enterprise valuation control**—Your organization links business valuation to process execution.

5. **Agile business structure**—Your organization innovates new businesses, products, and services through an agile business structure.

In reviewing these main phases, I want to share the top lessons learned around BPM from more than eight years of customer engagements and, for the last two years, seeing hundreds of customers design and deploy BPM supported by SOA. Based on these collective experiences, some of the best practices around BPM can be grouped into these key areas:

- Having business and IT work together to select the right business processes to drive improvement

- Leveraging IT tools such as modeling and simulation

- Basing the deployment on SOA

- Establishing a business process domain

- Using executive dashboards and scorecards to manage business

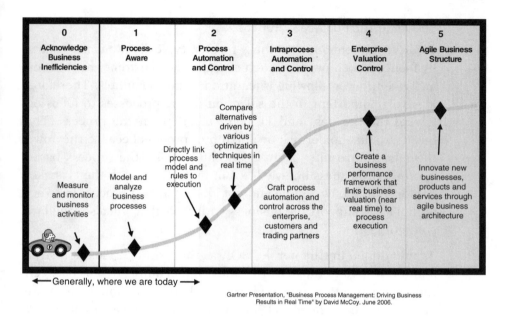

Gartner Presentation, "Business Process Management: Driving Business Results in Real Time" by David McCoy. June 2006.

Figure 7.2 Business Process Management Maturity and Adoption Model

The following sections delve into greater detail on each of these five key areas and how your organization can use them to become a flex-pon-sive* company.

BUSINESS AND IT STAKEHOLDERS WORKING TOGETHER TO SELECT THE RIGHT BUSINESS PROCESSES TO DRIVE IMPROVEMENT

Not only must you understand business processes, but you also must know how they will impact the business. According to Omar El Sawy in his book *Redesigning Enterprise Processes for E-business* (McGraw-Hill/Irwin, 2000; ISBN 0072426756), 67% of companies produced marginal or failed results in their process re-engineering efforts. This could be because the business leaders did not know what the impact of the changes would be to the company.

CHOOSING THE BUSINESS PROCESS

To drive and enhance business results, typically a business starts by focusing on a process, such as improving customer acquisition and retention or allowing integration of new channels. Therefore, it is very important in the selection of the processes to focus on having the business and IT team together on the process. The business stakeholder has ownership of process because they own the business results. They define and design the process based upon their business knowledge. But by teaming with the IT stakeholder from the beginning and not looking at that process in a vacuum, IT can support the business with tools that will also facilitate communications.

As mentioned in Chapter 4, "SOA as the DNA of a Flex-pon-sive* and Innovative Company," the lines are beginning to blur between the IT organization and the business. It is impossible to separate IT and business strategy. IT doesn't support the business; it *is part of* the business. So it is more important than ever to bridge the gap that exists today between the business and IT.

The best way to bridge that gap is to create a process design team. The team should have clear roles established and ownership assigned to the processes. Members should be from both the IT and business organizations. Having a team that is aligned ensures that IT will correctly implement what the business designs; the team will be on the same page.

After the team is established, the key for the team is to find the process that will differentiate the business and to match the scope and visibility of that project with the level of maturity of the company. For instance, depending on your company's maturity, you might want to start with a single siloed process. Or if your company is more mature, perhaps you will start with a horizontal process, such as a supply chain that goes across many boundaries. Remember back to Chapter 3, "Deconstructing Your Business: Component Business Model," on the view of the Component Business Model. This could be one of the tools that you leverage to determine that key focus process. In fact, the Component Business Model is the best practice in this area.

According to Forrester Research, you'll want to explore four major areas of business processes to improve your business:

■ **People-intensive processes**—A strong focus on automating people-intensive activities such as servicing customers, operating call centers, managing sales operations, supporting field-based agents, and routing internal requests by employees might be a good place to focus on.

■ **Decision-intensive processes**—These involve decision making, often by highly trained individuals, using tools such as business rules and business intelligence (BI) for analyzing business information. Examples of decision-intensive processes include underwriting and mortgage origination.

■ **Document-intensive processes**—These involve a strong focus on processes that make extensive use of scanned images for back-office processes and processes that require people to use documents extensively.

■ **System-intensive processes**—These focus on automating processes that integrate systems and applications that typically involve few exceptions and limited human participation, handle high transaction rates, and are used for externally focused processes linking two or more enterprises.

Regardless of your organization's maturity, it is important to understand what differentiates your business from your competition. You must identify those core processes. By using the techniques discussed in Chapter 4, such as CBM, you can logically determine which process to start with and actively involve both businesses in IT.

As an example of a customer that had business and IT as equal partners, consider a leading financial services provider in Germany. The company had a postal mail-delivery cycle that took too long. It extended the time it took to accomplish simple business transactions, resulting in poor service that left dissatisfied customers and high administration costs. Business and IT partnered to tackle this major process issue. They created a work council to restructure the departments and to reorganize the processes. They involved all the key stakeholders to define the

new processes and make enhancements to current ones. They followed the basic tenet of partnering and ensuring that they selected the right business process. Then they moved on to the next step.

MODEL AND SIMULATE THE CHOSEN PROCESS

After you have selected the right area of focus, the IT organization can introduce tools to assist in the speed and flexibility of executing on the business process. The two areas we will now focus on are modeling and simulation. Modeling is simply a way to document your process. You may use a white board today or a simple tool like Microsoft Visio or even PowerPoint. The issue with those tools to document your processes is that they do not easily allow you to demonstrate change in the process. The power of more BPM-focused tools combine the power of modeling for easy change and simulation (which we will discuss in a minute). Modeling helps organizations fully visualize, understand, and document business processes to close the gap that exists between a company's lines of business and IT's understanding of the business drivers. Given that a business process is a defined set of activities leading to specific results, modeling provides the added assurance that best practices are well documented and communicated throughout the organization before deployment.

For example, business analysts can use modeling to define alternative scenarios, differing in resource allocation, branching assumptions at decision points in the flow, and other parameters, to see which alternative results in the lowest cost, fastest average cycle time, lowest percentage of service-level agreement violations, or other optimum business measure.

Simulation is our second area of focus. Simulation allows you to test drive your proposed process changes and determine the results. Since most process failures occur because companies can't determine the outcome of the process change on the organization before putting it in production, simulation is a core function that flex-pon-sive* companies dn't want to be without.

By using a modeling tool that includes simulation capabilities, the simulation can help you identify bottlenecks in the process,

enabling you to analyze new alternative scenarios, resulting in significant time and cost savings before they are implemented throughout the company (see Figure 7.3). When the analyst has the model of the business process, she needs to identify the tasks that will have the greatest impact to the company's performance. This can be done by running a simulation based on the selected criteria that reflects her processes environment. If she believes that this process is not running at an optimal level, or if she finds bottlenecks or workload imbalances, she can modify the model to create "what if" or "to-be" scenarios.

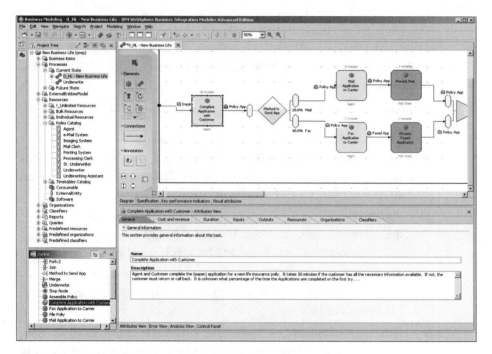

Figure 7.3   Example modeling and simulation tool

Business process simulation and analysis is a critical component of BPM. Predicting business outcomes is invaluable; it can determine the "go" or "no go" of a project, justify resource investments, and help determine what will yield the best bang for the buck. When the business outcomes are analyzed and the project investment is

justified, you can confidently plan and budget for the project. After deployment, you can continue to optimize your business by examining bottlenecks or workload imbalances, and you can stop any issues while the process executes in production and before problems arise.

In contrast to using these best practices software tools, in some companies' business analysts get together to define their newly enhanced processes. They spend hours documenting it in PowerPoint or another nonprogrammatic tool. Then, without communication, they pass over a document of more than 100 pages to IT to implement. It is no surprise that, in most causes, they do not get what they thought they asked for and cannot articulate the expected results. By partnering from the beginning, IT can apply tools that can ease that handoff but also can understand the logic of the improvement.

Additional benefits of modeling and simulation include the following:

- **Clarity**—Through a visibly mapped approach, organizations can optimize those business processes that drive maximum ROI and competitive differentiation.

- **Productivity**—After proven best practices have been modeled and documented, they can be made available for reuse throughout the organization, resulting in accelerated productivity.

- **Responsiveness**—BPM enables organizations to quickly modify applications to immediately respond to time-sensitive business challenges.

- **Business flexibility**—Modeling provides the business user with the tools to modify and simulate business processes and see how a new business process will affect the business.

- **Measurable metrics**—Modeling enables business analysts to define concrete performance metrics, aligned with strategic business goals, and link them to specific process activities and parameters. Those metrics could be anything related to revenue, margin, costs, timeliness, throughput, productivity, customer satisfaction, and so on.

- **Tighter integration of IT with business goals**—Modeling permits business analysts to perform the precise modeling of processes based on resources, roles, organization, information, and business metric perspectives. It also enables business analysts to perform simulation studies of process models under various conditions to assess process performance, generate performance statistics, and conduct what-if analysis. Furthermore, business analysts can perform break-even, internal rate-of-return, and other project-justification analyses.

Clearly, modeling and simulating the process make up a critical step in choosing business processes because they help both IT and business leaders gain a better understanding of the impact of their roles on their organization and the value their collaborative efforts will deliver. They also enable IT and business leaders to fully understand the impact of streamlining business processes and testing scenarios before additional time and resources are allocated.

However, remember our definition of BPM—BPM is both a management discipline and a technology platform. Modeling and simulation are complementary and critical aspects within a larger BPM strategy. As a management discipline, BPM replaces traditional views of business based on discrete functional organizations, systems, and metrics with those based on cross-functional core processes aligned with high-level business objectives. As a technology platform, BPM provides the set of software tools needed to optimize performance, make abstract performance goals concrete, connect them to process data, automate and monitor process activities, and provide a platform for agile performance improvement.

The end game of BPM is unprecedented process flexibility, with processes determined in real time by the events or outcomes. When you realize this, you gain a greater understanding of how modeling and simulation complement the management and technology views of BPM while helping to drive greater business results.

BPM DEPLOYMENT USING A SERVICE ORIENTED ARCHITECTURE

After the business process model has been defined and simulated, the next best practice is to make sure you deploy your processes using SOA. If you remember back to our definitions, processes can be a set of business services. Those business services can be assembled together based on what is happening in the environment.

For example, the U.S. Open Tennis Association achieves outstanding flexibility by accomplishing the repeatable business tasks that make up its scoreboard processes with modular, interchangeable software services. This is a hallmark of SOA. When a match begins or ends, when a game is won, or when a point is scored, these are examples of "events." SOA gives the U.S. Open the ability to sense and detect events such as these and trigger an appropriate reaction or response based on business rules. Without the flexibility that comes from SOA, the U.S. Open would have had to custom-code the system and then suffer the cost, risk, and expense of recoding it every time they wanted to make a change.

Leveraging SOA as the underpinning technology for deployment dramatically reduces process times and deployment costs. If the business model has been done right, when business processes or business rules change, they change in only one place, and the results are seen everywhere as needed. This means that IT can implement solutions faster, with better communication and fewer errors.

BPM can be implemented without SOA, but it might not give you the competitive advantage that you had hoped for. Together, BPM and SOA help facilitate the next phase of the business process evolution. The evolution is occurring now because of the heightened need for enterprises to compete more effectively by adapting to market changes faster, continuously improving efficiencies and streamlining collaboration across traditionally siloed departments. SOA supports the inevitable change that occurs in the business processes, change driven by regulatory pressures, a competitor move, or changes to customer behavior. SOA allows you to flexibly treat elements of business processes and the underlying IT infrastructure as standardized components (services) that can be

reused and combined to address changing business priorities. SOA allows you to separate "what you do" from "how you do it." Abstracting the definition of the business processes from how those processes are executed gives businesses greater responsiveness and flexibility. This "abstraction" allows for changes to the business process without significant reengineering of the underlying technology and, conversely, allows for changes to the technology infrastructure without impacting the business process.

In reviewing the Gartner maturity model, shown in Figure 7.2, you see that getting to higher levels of value and maturity with BPM requires an underpinning of SOA. That is because of the flexibility and reuse that SOA brings to the table. SOA brings a mandate of reuse that supports this business process evolution. For example, when a company shares business processes beyond a team or even a department, the processes improve because a greater number of parties are focused on overall productivity and organizational excellence. In addition, SOA speeds the process of changes and reduces ongoing maintenance and support costs.

Until now, customers have been using various technologies and products to integrate business processes that span different aspects of the enterprise—for example, people, systems, customers, and business partners. These invariably result in a complex, inflexible operating environment, and usually require different skills and resources for each type of process. This results in high costs and slow solution building. An SOA-based architecture delivers one common model to connect, map, and execute underlying services.

ESTABLISH A BUSINESS PROCESS DOMAIN

Until now, the discussion has centered on the right process, team, and technology to make BPM successful. Now I turn the discussion to the area of discipline. For this lesson learned, our data shows that customers who establish a Center of Excellence (CoE) as a way to share best practices have greater success. This CoE mission involves several steps.

First, establish the governance practice on how decisions would be made on BPM. Refer to Chapter 6, "SOA Governance and Service Lifecycle," on the governance model that the BPM CoE would need to fit into. Because this involves a process, the process design team should play a critical role in this discussion. Part of that role as defined in Chapter 6 is to educate all stakeholders on the best practices for building business processes with SOA.

The next role of the CoE is to use a central repository to manage all the services that might be reused. A key to shortened time to value is guaranteed if an organization uses pre-existing business models and frameworks for parts of business that are not unique. For instance, currency conversion as a process service could be leveraged in a central location as a best practice. Other examples include these:

- In banking, a reusable best practice could be a mortgage application process that documents completion and review of a customer mortgage application through the mortgage lending decision.

- In insurance, a reusable best-practice process could be a new business life process that documents completion, routing, underwriting, and creation of a policy.

- In retail, a reusable best-practice process could be a product invoice payment process that documents receiving an invoice and comparing it to the original purchase order, and reviewing a damage report through the payment path.

- In telecommunications, a reusable best-practice process could be a DSL provisioning process that documents a prequalification of customers and entering/releasing of the DSL order.

- In industry, a reusable best-practice process could be a supplier forecasting process that documents a supplier request, review of the responses, and generation of the purchase order.

For IT, this central repository is critical to building and leveraging reusable assets. The CoE should help define who will build the shared best practices but also should define up front how they will be funded, who owns them, who will maintain them, and how they

will be hosted. For more information on the attributes of a great registry and repository, see Chapter 4.

A final and most important role for the CoE is facilitating an ongoing, iterative loop of improvement and optimization. This should lead the total cost of ownership discussion on processes and address ways to make improvements in cost-effectiveness and process quality.

For a solid CoE, leveraging best practices is crucial element. A key element in successful BPM engagements is the ability to identify what solutions should be applied to top problems and how those solutions should be implemented. Methodologies from Six Sigma, Rummler Brache, and LOVEM are frequently used as guiding principles in BPM projects. Add to the equation the advancement of software based on the latest in SOA, and the current BPM story promises to deliver extensive returns. However, with higher value sometimes come greater complexity and risk. A new BPM methodology offers tremendous value and structure here.

A twenty-first-century BPM methodology based on best practices and SOA-enabled software is a good place to start. A guiding roadmap can align the rollout of a BPM engagement in context of a logical project lifecycle, to help clients prioritize and understand where to focus and which software to use. Core assets of a methodology could include an assessment in the form of a questionnaire to provide guidelines on how to frame the engagement, including risk and strategy analysis, adoption-level insight, and starting points, resulting in appropriate software solutions, timeframes, and milestones. A corresponding set of "service engagement points" based on best practices that offer proven value in tackling BPM projects is also needed. These services map to the specific software tools necessary to tackle the problems identified by the assessment. Examples include process-documentation techniques, process benchmarking, dashboard design, and process change management. Combining the assessment and the service engagement points and applying it to a logical BPM lifecycle from strategy through measurement, all while driving to continuous improvement, ensures that a BPM methodology will help companies achieve the promised value.

EXECUTIVE DASHBOARDS AND SCORECARDS HELP YOU MANAGE YOUR BUSINESS OPERATIONS

One of the highest priorities for many businesses is gaining visibility into business operations as the business runs. Defining business process measures in a modeling tool enables you to monitor the processes by capturing data to compute those measures and deliver them to business end users via role-based business dashboards. Key performance indicators (KPIs) enable you to track and modify business process flows as they run. This means that you can watch for bottlenecks and other delays, and make decisions about rebalancing workloads to eliminate problems in real time. These KPIs should be unique by industry. Table 7.1 shows an example of KPIs for various industries.

At the same time, you should be able to view derived information from runtime process data and histories in custom dashboard formats for effective information delivery. Software tools enable you to show trend information so that problems can be proactively avoided rather than reactively fought. KPIs can also be used to build scorecard views for all levels of the business so that concerned parties have a clear view of the state of the business. By setting "triggers," process monitoring can be automated so that specific actions are launched when certain events occur in currently running processes. For example, in an order-management process, large orders might be flagged for extra care and attention, resulting in higher customer satisfaction and future business. In another business, service-level agreements can be tracked to ensure that you are meeting the commitments; in a distribution business, inventory levels can be tracked and stock reorders initiated to ensure satisfactory customer order fulfillment. The results: Lower costs equal higher profits.

Table 7.1 KPI Examples

Type of Process	Key Performance Indictors
Distribution processes	Percentage of deliveries on time
	Delivery days late vs. early
	Delivery days late vs. early by location
	Incomplete deliveries
	Freight price percentage of revenue
Credit processes	Customer credit exposure
	Customer average arrears analysis
	Customer credit limit exceeded
	Credit risk vs. capital reserves
Tracking customers by segment	Change in customer retention rate
	Customer costs to serve trend by quarter
	Segments with lower-than-expected profits
	Net change in customer satisfaction
Inventory processes	Average stock level and value
	Zero stock days
	Inventory stock outs
	Reserved quantities and values
	Withdrawn quantities and values
	Book and physical stock group currency value
	Full year moving average of top 50 stock item levels
Procurement processes	Open days for request for price quotation, purchase order, and requisitions
	Average purchase order and contract value
	Days from requisition to purchase order
	Supplier scorecard of on-time deliveries
	Supplier scorecard of percentage of goods delivered broken

The right KPI metrics enable you to take BPM to a new level: This capability can lead to real competitive advantage and ensure that business-critical operations remain operational and effective at all times. Figure 7.4 shows a sample business dashboard.

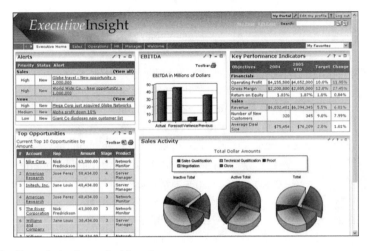

Figure 7.4   Example business dashboard

FINAL INSIGHT INTO BPM

BPM as a stand-alone solution is nothing new. But BPM enabled by SOA is new and is real. Companies are seeing real benefits in the ability to address change quickly and flexibly. Business leaders know that the ability to change is manifested within their company in the form of the business processes that deliver their company's goods and services each day. Business processes are the circulatory system of a company. Either improve the processes to remain competitive or lose. This is a common business challenge every company faces. BPM enabled by SOA provides not only process redesign and improvement, but also the latest software technology, to provide differentiated and sustaining process innovation. SOA makes becoming a flex-pon-sive* company a reality.

CASE STUDY
DELAWARE ELECTRIC COOPERATIVE

Delaware Electric Cooperative (DEC) is a $110-million-revenue electric Coop in Kent and Sussex counties, Delaware. Today Delaware Electric Cooperative is a progressive member-owned electric utility serving over 60,000 member-owners with over 75,000 meters. DEC's expected growth rate is 5–7% annually. Talking to Gary Cripps, CFO DEC, their goals were to improve customer satisfaction and service while reducing customer service calls. In addition, Gary needs to facilitate 24×7 operation, eliminate outdated customer information, and improve call center processes to achieve performance metrics.

Gary faced a set of challenges common in today's environment.

- Processes dictated by proprietary application vendors

- A diversity of proprietary applications

- Many point-to-point solutions

- No industry standardization

- A risk in to their existing business by changing technology

Delaware Electric Cooperative started its journey to fix these business process challenges by focusing on the business outcomes first. Needing flexibility and a reduced cost model, they selected SOA as the enabling technology. Given their focus on several key processes, like improving call center processes and customer information, they began their journey combining the SOA entry points of BPM with SOA. To drive its business, DEC is using SOA-enabled software to connect its various legacy sources of information located in proprietary applications as part of a larger SOA strategy.

continues

Specifically, the company needed to quickly and efficiently link multiple interfaces consisting of home-grown and various proprietary-based applications, including geospatial, system data acquisition, and smart metering, for example.

Realizing that the company did not have enough resources or, in many cases, source code authorization to connect existing applications point to point within a reasonable amount of time, DEC selected SOA-enabled software to provide a standard interface to the company's existing proprietary applications and to simplify the integration of DEC's information technology assets.

In Cripps's words, "SOA helps my customer." SOA provides real-time visibility into processes and allows DEC to be able to better optimize their business processes based on a load profile and price. Ultimately, this real-time visibility translates into actionable decisions for DEC customers. For example, their customers can prioritize when to operate at peak capacity when rates are optimal and when to scale back operations when rates begin to rise.

CASE STUDY
CASHCALL, INC.

CashCall, Inc., is an automated online lending company. Operating 24 hours per day, 365 days per year, the company provides its customers with fast access to loans in amounts up to $20,000. Once the company approves a customer's loan, it then wire transfers the funds directly into the customer's bank account in as little as 15 minutes. CashCall currently employs 450 people and is based in Fountain Valley, California.

CashCall wanted to be the first company to offer personal loans via the Internet for up to $20,000 that could be deposited into a customer's account within minutes. Yet defining its customer base,

designing its business processes, and anticipating the level of demand in an undefined business space challenged the startup company. CashCall realized that it would need to be flexible enough to adapt to business needs and market variations on-the-fly while still functioning efficiently. By leveraging streamlined processes, it hoped to deliver high levels of service that would draw in customers and keep them loyal before competition emerged. The company's developers knew that traditional technologies would be too rigid to support this mission, since changes to business processes frequently required intensive application coding, wiring, and reconfiguring of systems. CashCall needed a flexible and robust platform through which to launch its innovative business.

CashCall is successfully forging ahead with a first-of-its-kind business enabled by its foundation in an SOA. The solution establishes a flexible layer of business logic, allowing CashCall to quickly translate business-level decisions into process-level changes without low-level translation and coding. Web services created using SOA-enabled software seamlessly integrate the changes with the company's other applications so the client can quickly implement a process change company-wide. And since the SOA technology is fully reusable, the company's flexibility doesn't degrade over time. The singular provider in the industry bolsters its position by continually rolling out improvements and reacting to real-world pressures. Since its inception, the company has automated its formerly manual underwriting process, speeding processing time and reducing the risk of human error.

CashCall can make business process changes an estimated 90% more quickly than under traditional business architectures, which will help it maintain its front-runner status even when competition emerges. The flexibility and efficiency supported CashCall's growth into a $500-million company within two years of its launch.

CASE STUDY
A RETAIL AND MANUFACTURING COMPANY

A large retail and manufacturing company in the U.S. with a large dealer network wanted to improve customer service and employee productivity. However, the company was faced with a flexibility problem that was hindering these business goals. They had a myriad of internal applications for coordinating information among credit applications, credit approvals, and loan origination. Although there is nothing unusual or wrong about this, these applications were highly autonomous and did not easily "talk" to each other. As a result, connections among the applications were accomplished through rigid, custom-developed coding, and a change to any one application would require a considerable amount of time and effort to fix the brittle linkages that no longer worked after the change. Additionally, external collaboration was very cumbersome. So not only was it difficult to share information among applications and throughout the company, but it didn't enable dealers to maximize marketing campaigns and develop customized financing strategies for customers because financing and loan options were buried too deep in the information.

To overcome these problems that restricted their growth, this company leveraged the principles of SOA by taking incremental steps to increase the flexibility of the linkages among their various systems. Their first project is designed to tackle the credit approval process and is integrating the various stages associated with loans, including credit applications, credit rating scores, and loan origination. They "uncoupled" their hard-wired connections and treated the functions performed by its applications as independent "services." This will allow their dealers to improve customer service by more quickly and easily developing financing strategies based on customers' unique needs. While this large company expects great returns from their initial SOA projects, it has plans for expansion in the future.

This company is following a best practice by incrementally building an SOA that will eventually connect its entire global organization, dealerships, and manufacturing partners' processes. This "linking" of the company through BPM enabled by SOA will enable customers, partners, and employees to more effectively communicate, streamline business processes, and boost productivity. This first project is designed to tackle the credit approval process and is integrating the various stages associated with auto loans, including credit applications, credit rating scores, and loan origination. They "uncoupled" their hard-wired integrations, making them "services" that are independent of each other. This will allow their dealers to improve customer service by more quickly and easily developing financing strategies based on customers' unique needs.

The benefits of this new BPM through SOA strategy include the following:

- No need to touch every component when changes need to be made.

- Cycle time is reduced internally to deliver different financial offering for dealers and deliver them efficiently.

- New offerings are brought to the market faster.

- Financial programs that map to marketing promotions can be done faster and cheaper.

- Customer services can be improved by more quickly and easily developing financing strategies based on the customers' unique needs.

INFORMATION AS AN ENTRY POINT

Information is king, or maybe queen! For a company to be flex-pon-sive*, it must know its customers, employees, partners—and the list goes on. However, many companies that I talk to today are challenged with obtaining a single view of key information that

they need to run their business. Let me give you an example I recently encountered within a large coffee producer that distributes one product, with different codes and descriptions across the various markets in which it is sold. The company lost business because it was turning down orders of one kind of coffee bean because it had different product numbers that didn't reconcile with the inventory it had in its warehouse. It turns out that the company had more than 172 number codes for a single coffee bean.

This situation mainly results from the lack of governance and the fact that information is captured many times in many different systems. This causes recurrent data-alignment issues, which hinder smooth and effective operations.

PROVIDING A SINGLE SOURCE OF INFORMATION THROUGH SOA

According to a recent IBM survey of 1,800 IT business executives, the most anticipated benefit of the business investing in its top three IT initiatives was information availability. This tells us that the business expects that its investment in IT will result in better access to the information it needs. However, according to the December 2005 IBM CFO Survey, only 18% of CFOs feel that their companies can adequately integrate and deliver key business information. Your company cannot become flex-pon-sive* without a solid and trusted view of your key information.

Information that is trusted and delivered in-line and in context can be a catalyst to innovation, enabling companies to optimize their operations, reduce their risk, and discover new business opportunities. Simply by improving visibility into business operations, companies are better slated to compete effectively. But when duplicate or contradictory information is scattered throughout multiple locations, complete and accurate facts cannot be easily assembled or trusted. Information integration solves this by giving people, processes, and applications a single view of the truth. SOA enables this single view to be made accessible to the entire enterprise, ensuring that consistent governance is always

enforced. It also provides more flexibility to change, by insulating application changes from information changes.

Beyond just a single view, however, is the additional business value of information. Organizations not only want access to the right information at the right time, but they also want that information to work for them. According to the 2006 IBM CEO Survey, more than 60% of CEOs believe their companies need to do a better job leveraging information. The business value of information is increased only when information is analyzed as a whole. The shorter the cycle is between information retrieval, cleansing, analysis, and action, the more effective a company can be. SOA allows this to be done in-line, providing closed-loop decisions that enable companies to respond more quickly to change, recognizing and acting on opportunity, and mitigating risk.

Ultimately, business executives are searching for ways to improve their use of information, and to empower information to make them wiser. As Dr. Martin Hofmann from Volkswagen AG once said, "Today 70% of the time of our people is spent in searching for information, and only 30% in making intelligent decisions. We want to flip the ratio, providing 70% of time for intelligent, analytical decision making and only 30% administrative work."

Information should be a catalyst for innovation. It should proactively uncover opportunities for optimization, risk reduction, and growth. SOA provides the foundation for taking information that is currently at rest and turning it into information in motion, making it a more fluid participant in your business rather than just a historical record.

THE ELUSIVE SINGLE VIEW OF INFORMATION

Most companies today acquire data in multiple forms from multiple sources. The ability to provide access to consistent and relevant information across applications and processes can be a competitive advantage. This goes for information on products, customers, suppliers, financials, employees, and many other information sources.

While the business benefits of a single view of information can be found across all categories of information, it is often easiest to describe the benefits when you look at customer data because almost everybody has personally experienced the side effects of poor customer data quality. Companies without a single view of your information send you multiple mailings, fail to recognize purchases you make or accounts you hold across different channels, and often provide you with poor service. Conversely, when a company has a complete view of your information, it can offer you personalized products, services, and offerings, and provide extremely high levels of service.

The businesses that do this really well integrate customer data that resides in multiple applications and databases spread throughout the company, and provide the ability to use diverse types of customer data (structured and unstructured) that's being collected to better understand and serve each customer's unique needs. When you look at your business, do you have isolated islands of information and applications that are spread across your environment? Are you able to identify your most profitable and loyal customers, and provide them with superior service and personalized products? Have you reviewed your customer's application and information portfolio to identify redundancies, areas of inefficiencies, or noncompliance with business practices and processes? Do you need to reduce the risk associated with and improve the time to value for new applications or projects that use customer information?

Of course, customer data is just one example. Any data that is reused in many places throughout an organization is susceptible to disaggregation. And because this typically is the information that runs the business, it also can provide great benefit when it is considered and managed holistically. In some cases, it is more about regulatory compliance, or reducing risk, where financials or other information needs to be seen as a whole. Regulations such as Basel II and Sarbanes-Oxley force companies to take this approach, but in other cases, regulations can address another type of risk, such as fraud detection and crime resolution.

As an example, consider the New York City Police Department. Officers needed on-scene insight from billions of records across multiple police databases so that they could have a single view of the truth. They needed to correlate arrests, complaints, summonses, homicides, shootings, locations, 911 calls, and more. Having one view of the information in a timely fashion means the difference between life and death. With a single view of the truth, information reaches detectives within minutes instead of days or weeks. They can perform rapid trend analysis and have a way to quickly identify repeat offenders.

When going down the path toward a single view of information, business leaders need to consider how to clean up the mess they already have, and then how to set up an infrastructure that allows this important information to be managed more effectively and holistically moving forward.

To achieve a single view of information, businesses need to discover and understand information sources, relationships, and business contexts. As with the coffee bean example given previously, company executives need to do an inventory of all the types of data, content, and information to determine where and how the information is used in the company. This technical understanding can then be used to rationalize and harmonize a complete and accurate view of information across systems, using information management technology and best practices. Industry models can help to align this view with a proven industry-specific perspective, to help optimize business processes and align information with business partners. Ultimately, the rules used to rationalize and harmonize the view, along with the information in the view itself, can be published as shared services in a SOA—to achieve the highest levels of accessibility, consistency, and flexibility.

However, simply cleaning things up once is not good enough. Businesses also need a way of maintaining the integrity of this view over time and managing this vital information as a complete whole. This is where an approach called master data management comes in, which provides a set of shared services to manage some of the more common types of business data, including customers,

products, suppliers, and employees. Master data management enables applications, processes, and portals to reuse a common set of services to manage all aspects of these types of information centrally. It then takes the responsibility of synchronizing all the systems that store and use different pieces of this information so that the whole organization is using the same complete and accurate information. The best part is that it reuses a lot of the same information integration services that were used to create the unified view in the first place—this means that if these rules need to be changed over time to adjust to business changes, they have to be changed in only one place.

Not only does this provide the entire organization with accurate and reliable information, but it also makes the business more flexible. As things change, it becomes a lot easier to adjust. In fact, the service-oriented approach underlying this enables your information sources to easily change over time, without forcing applications, processes, and portals to change.

You should ask these questions in this area:

- Have you provided a single, integrated point of access to the information, applications, people, and processes that your customers, suppliers, and partners need to complete the task at hand?

- Can you deliver consistent customer service across all delivery channels, from agent to Web, to speech, to self-service, and enable customers, partners, and suppliers remote access to business information, applications, and processes across a variety of networks, device types, and modes of interaction?

- Have you provided your partners and suppliers with the ability to capture, access, and utilize both structured and unstructured data to help increase levels of collaboration with your company?

- Is external access to critical information assets properly secured to ensure that only the right people have access?

- Can your partners and suppliers intelligently search for relevant information that's contained in all of your company's information and data stores?

- Does your IT infrastructure have the ability to scale to meet unpredictable workloads, and do you have a storage-management strategy in place to handle increasing volumes of the data that's being captured?

- Have you evaluated capital acquisition and financing alternatives to improve capital investment efficiency?

By working on a single view of the company's information, business leaders can see a number of benefits, including the ability to integrate and use both structured and unstructured data to deliver a unified view of information and to provide secure, personalized access to relevant information and applications. But just having the information or a single version of the truth is only a part of the solution. Taking this information value to the next level for business agility is the next part of the puzzle.

ADDING VALUE TO INFORMATION

The ability to capture, organize, integrate, transform, analyze, and use information to create value is a goal of most companies. This enables businesses to proactively identify customer needs and exceed their expectations, improve customer-oriented processes (such as product development and service after sales), and achieve better differentiation of products, along with improving information sharing and collaboration. Thus, companies can increase the productivity of employees, business partners, and suppliers.

Data analysis has tended to be passive in most companies, done after decisions have already been made, in hopes of finding guidance for future decisions. However, increasingly, companies are moving toward real-time analysis based on streaming in-line analytics. This ensures that decisions can be made on the fly within processes, allowing processes to adjust accordingly. This type of sense-and-response environment provides a much higher degree of business agility, enabling organizations to adjust fluidly to change on a continuous basis.

This approach assumes that the single view is in place and leverages that centralized knowledge and its shared services. Upon this foundation, information is extracted, cleansed, analyzed, and transformed as it flows, providing the insight that people and processes need to make accurate decisions and to calibrate their processing and decision making to the precise operational situation at any instance in time.

Here the lines between business processes and information begin to blur, and organizations become more dynamic—capable to innovate within every process, within every transaction, and within every decision.

How do you know how you are doing here? Can you know whether you are using your information effectively? Ask yourself the following questions:

- Does your organization have the necessary analytical tools to better understand operational and historical trends and key performance indicators?

- Do you have the ability to integrate analytics across functions within your business to deliver a consolidated view of your company's performance?

- Do you need to connect disparate applications so that information can be shared across your company?

- Do you have islands of operational and historical information spread across your company that are contained in multiple data stores?

- Do you need to drive more value from your existing applications by aggregating disparate IT resources to reduce the time required to execute complex statistical models?

- Do you need the ability to analyze IT data, to predict and avoid potential future violations of service-level agreements?

- Do you analyze information after the fact, or do you embed analysis in closed-loop processes?

CASE STUDY
STOREBRAND

A well-recognized name in Norway, Storebrand rose to prominence due to its readiness and ability to meet the challenges of new situations. To maintain its reputation, ensure continued brisk growth, and improve its focus on customers in a highly competitive market, Storebrand sought to become a more agile business, one able to flexibly and quickly respond to customer needs. Achieving its goal, however, required overcoming significant hurdles: integrating its disparate products and IT infrastructures, and then finding an optimal way to query its product and customer data.

Many of Storebrand's products and subproducts have their own IT solutions and associated business processes. Storebrand wanted to link all its products and processes to simplify and expedite orders, increase product customization, create product packages, speed time to market for new products, and improve quality control, all while driving down costs. More recently, the company has sought a way to efficiently store and query transaction data to improve its ability to respond to customer requests and to make timely and informed business decisions.

To create a unified and responsive information architecture for handling orders of financial products, Storebrand developed an SOA—applications and information that can be broken apart as components and reused via a web services interface to create new business processes. A business services gateway based on web services handles incoming transactions and provides Storebrand's legacy applications with reusable business services. Storebrand's integration architecture offers distributed transactions while also providing consistency and synchronization among legacy system applications.

continues

Enhancing Access to Data Improves Customer Service

With its SOA, Storebrand can more flexibly handle orders. It can provide customers with around-the-clock access to account information, accept orders 24×7 online, and control transaction flow to legacy systems to avoid performance bottlenecks. Storebrand has been able to shrink order-processing time for many products. For example, an application for a license to implement a pension plan previously took up to three weeks to process but can now be completed in 10 minutes. Faster processing gives Storebrand the ability to handle five times the number of customer orders. Much of the manual data re-entry done by individual departments has also been eliminated, leading to fewer mistakes, higher quality, and more efficient customer service.

CASE STUDY
REGION VÄSTRA GÖTALAND (VGR)

Region Västra Götaland (VGR) is the second-largest region in Sweden, with 1.5 million citizens and 49 municipalities. As a government organization, VGR is responsible for the delivery of healthcare, business development, infrastructure, culture, tourism, and environmental services to its residents and visitors.

Like many public institutions, VGR uses the Internet to effectively and efficiently share information with its various constituents. However, as the volume of data published by VGR staff grew, it became increasingly difficult for employees and citizens to find information when they needed it or even to know exactly what information was available.

More than 50,000 VGR employees across 100 organizations publish documents on various departmental, agency, and hospital Web sites. One hospital site alone maintains more than 70,000 PDF files. Yet, because each Web site relied on a proprietary search

engine capable only of searching documents within its pages, users had to visit multiple sites to find answers to their questions. For example, a citizen seeking information about regional diabetes care had to individually search the Web sites of 17 different hospitals and 130 healthcare centers. As a result, citizens often couldn't find the information they needed and simply called agency staff directly for help.

At the same time, without a comprehensive picture of what information was available, employees spent substantial time searching for files and would often re-create documents that already existed elsewhere within VGR.

VGR executives sought a single search architecture that would enable employees and citizens to search millions of documents across hundreds of sites by simply entering a keyword or phrase. Integrating information in this way would help reduce the time spent hunting for information, enable VGR to get more value out of existing information, and, ultimately, drive greater collaboration between employees and citizens.

But VGR also wanted a solution for the future built on SOA supporting its strategy to deliver information as a service.

Delivering information as a service enables VGR to create a new type of organization, one in which employees and inhabitants can more easily share expertise and discuss ideas to promote regional health and development.

COLLABORATION AS AN ENTRY POINT

A major growing entry point in the innovation evolution is collaboration. Featuring both internal and external linkages, collaborative innovation separates winners and losers. Successful companies no longer believe they have a lock on innovation inside the firm. As one CEO said, there exists "a lot more capability and innovation in the marketplace…than we could try to create on our

own." In fact, outperforming companies source 30% of their ideas from the outside, and CEOs are attributing their newer innovative ideas to outside influences—specifically, to business partners and clients. Reports indicate that, beyond any other factor, collaboration has demonstrated the clearest correlation with financial performance. Regardless of the financial metric—revenue growth, operating margin growth, or average profitability over time—strong collaborators have consistently come out on top.

Centered among many different facets of collaboration are people—the fuel of collaborative innovation. Company employees are critical to what makes a company unique and differentiates it from its competition. When a company integrates business partners and customers with its employee team, it ignites a powerful new source of fuel for collaborative innovation.

We are witnessing profound and exciting changes in the global business environment:

- The Internet changes everything.
- The virtual office is becoming pervasive.
- People are compelled to collaborate.
- People are pervasively connected to each other.
- People are pervasively connected to information.
- People have more access to expertise and knowledge.
- People need to make more time-efficient, well-informed decisions.

Collaboration is about enabling human and process interaction with consistent levels of service. Companies that focus on collaboration among people will improve their productivity by giving their employees and outside partners the ability to create a personalized and consolidated way to interact with other people and information in the context of business processes. In other words, through a common interface, a collaborative business environment gives users access to the tools and information they need to do their work with each other. A collaborative environment leverages productivity by providing access to and delivering information where, how, and when it is needed. To produce a collaborative

business environment, companies need to provide a user experience that is intuitive, adaptive, and role based.

ROLE-BASED VIEW TO COLLABORATION

Today collaboration is inhibited because most enterprise information systems are siloed among disparate divisions and departments, providing restricted access to information and transactions. Consequently, data-sharing efficiencies cannot be efficiently leveraged. Considering how applications have evolved within most organizations, one can see a common trend in which the predomination of multiple silos produces confusing data outputs and barriers to collaboration. These applications are usually designed in a departmental fashion, exposing the departmental model and procedures to end users. The context of the user is lost when exposed to multiple sites for access.

Unfortunately, the departmental model undermines the success of collaboration because it places a significant usability challenge on the entire company. Line-of-business users are at the mercy of their IT organizations to gather, assimilate, and consolidate the information required from disparate databases and organizations. These time-sensitive requests for information can take days to weeks to deliver. At the same time, IT organizations are taxed with requests for queries and reports whose time and attention deflect from IT innovation. Consequently, end users are increasingly at odds with their IT organizations, further protracting the collaborative effort.

The right approach in solving this problem involves designing a single interface with collaboration in mind. The first step to collaboration is *understanding the audience*—provide the proper context and deliver the right content, applications, and processes based on that audience's role. A role is simply the function a person performs for a specific organization, such as finance or marketing. The role modeling can be extended by defining the person's specialization (options trader, for example) and what contextual information he needs to do his job most effectively.

By delivering to the user a composite view that allows interaction with multiple back-end systems as if they were one, collaboration becomes easy. Users not only have access and control to get what they want when they want it, but they are furthermore encouraged to share and collaborate *across and outside* their enterprise. Consolidated access to the content, applications, and processes—relevant information provided all in one view—adds the value that produces greater productivity, reduced costs, and a fertile ground for incremental innovation across the organization.

Portals are the foundation for collaborative business environments, playing a vital role as the single point of access for users through which integrated data and application services actually reach or touch the user. Portals are the platform through which access and delivery can be extended to not only multiple users, but also multimodal devices, including cellphones, hand-held devices, browsers, and thin or thick clients. Portals, performing an essential aggregation service, bring together key information and processes in the form of services from across the enterprise, providing a secure role-based view to individuals across the value chain. The portal's role-based view improves operational efficiency through a more effective use of resources.

EXPANDING THE PORTAL WITH COLLABORATION TOOLS

Beyond the value of the portal as a collaboration platform, additional collaboration tools can further leverage productivity and efficiencies across the enterprise. Unified instant messaging, Web conferencing, and voice communications are tools that can be leveraged to improve communication, particularly in today's growing virtual and pervasive business environments. With an increasing number of employees working from various locations—home, office, hotel, car, and the air—the need for integrated collaboration tools becomes critical to user productivity. Web-conferencing tools are replacing face-to-face meetings, VoIP systems are displacing PBXs, and instant messaging has become the virtual knock on the door for a two-minute chat. When these tools are based on open standards, their extensible nature can provide even greater collaborative value. An instant-messaging tool's capability to support

plug-ins enables users to tap into voice and video services or access data from other applications within the instant-messaging client. A sales manager, for example, can have instant access to a rep's percentage of quota when the rep pings him by having the data extracted and displayed alongside the rep's picture and telephone number and other vital information. By integrating these types of communications tools with business processes and services, companies become more collaborative, more agile, and more responsive in the marketplace.

CASE STUDY
BROWARD COUNTY PUBLIC SCHOOLS

Broward Public Schools needed closer monitoring of student/teacher performance to help them comply with No Child Left Behind (NCLB) legislation. They had relevant data in 300+ siloed applications that weren't integrated. Being one of the sixth-largest and one of the fastest-growing school districts in the U.S., Florida's Broward County Public Schools (BCPS) has more than 274,000 K–12 students who come from 168 countries and speak 55 languages. An annual budget of $4.2 billion operates 138 elementary, 42 middle, and 28 high schools, as well as 6 adult vocational institutions, 10 centers, and 38 charter schools. The school district employs nearly 40,000 personnel, including 19,000 teachers.

Interacting with so many disparate systems was difficult, and it became impossible to use these valuable systems to Broward's greatest advantage. They needed a way to flexibly and easily pull together the relevant pieces of functionality into a customized, role-based view so that employees could interact with the systems in a unified, collaborative way.

Their challenges are like others in the public school system. Like other schools receiving public funding, BCPS was challenged to comply with No Child Left Behind (NCLB) legislation that puts funding in jeopardy if students do not perform well on standardized

continues

tests. But the district's more than 300 siloed IT applications made it difficult to consolidate student performance data and create relevant reports. With limited visibility into student progress, it was nearly impossible for administrators to implement curriculum changes and make informed decisions. It needed a way to monitor student performance and quickly respond to deficiencies to comply with NCLB legislation and increase the overall quality of its education.

To accomplish these goals, they created a flexible, adaptable, collaborative solution built on the principles of SOA. In this case, they started with a role-based portal that will provide teachers, students, administrators, and parents with 24×7 access to services and applications. This people entry point project treats the various sources of function and information within the various systems as services that can be strung together by users to create a way to interact with all the resources a user needs in one location. With its initial pilot complete, Broward is now in the first of a four-phase implementation over next four years. Now the district's 2,000 administrators leverage the portal to monitor school resources, generate reports, and track student attendance, grades, and assessments. In future phases of the project, they will also be able to correlate business factors—such as how much money is spent per student—with student achievement, allowing the district to optimize its resources. Teachers can access student data and share resources to boost standardized testing scores by aligning curriculum with test content. Students will be able to access class assignments, student resources, and calendars, and to collaborate with peers. Because the portal is designed so it can be deployed in multiple languages, non-English-speaking parents will be able to participate in their children's educational processes.

Benefits to this collaborative SOA solution include:

- Administrators can generate reports in just minutes instead of a week using services instead of traditional approaches, enabling faster awareness of and response to performance problems.

- Three hundred formerly separate systems can be accessed through one interface, improving insight into performance district-wide and expanding resources for all parties.

- The ability to track student performance will help to increase test scores, to ensure compliance with NCLB legislation.

- Increased collaboration will be possible among administrators, teachers, students, and parents.

THE BOTTOM LINE: THE NEW LANGUAGE OF BUSINESS

As you can see from the business-centric entry points, business services are critical. In each of these entry points, you see the link that service in SOA has to the business—either information as a service, a business service used as a step in the process, or a service being showcased to a user in a collaborative fashion. These pre-built services are based on industry best practices and policies. Technology truly serves as a link to the business and yields no surprise that the Cutter Benchmark survey shows that more than 63% of SOA projects today are driven by the line of business.

In addition to serving as a linkage point, the value of the business-centric entry points is both cost savings (such as that of reuse and connectivity from Chapter 4, "SOA as the DNA of a Flex-pon-sive* and Innovative Company," and Chapter 5, "SOA Key Concepts"), but also how businesses can see real revenue growth through this business—IT focus. Remember, this is a journey (see Figure 7.5). The foundational entry points of reuse and connectivity are a basic requirement before moving on to higher value. According to IBM's Institute for Business Value in the "The Business Value of Service-Oriented Architecture" (2006), 97% of customers justified their SOA deployment in cost—and in addition to this cost benefit, 100% realized improved flexibility, 71% reduced risk, and 51% experienced increased revenue. These benefits were realized by going beyond the IT foundational entry points of reuse and connectivity, and diving deep on the business-centric entry points that truly allow that new language of business to come alive. Figure

7.5 is a great view of all the SOA entry points of reuse, connectivity, people, process, and information come together. In addition, it shows that concepts we covered in Chapter 6 serve as underpinnings. The SOA design, and Service Security, management and virtualization are all linked to the principles of SOA governance. I love this picture as it allows me to see how all the pieces we have been discussing really come together in a logical fashion.

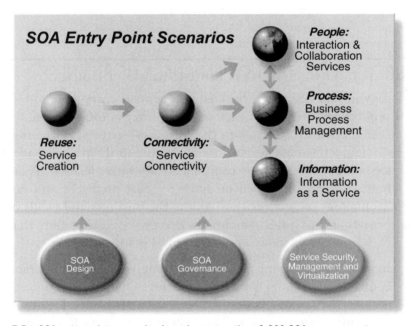

Figure 7.5   SOA entry point scenarios based on more than 3,000 SOA engagements

In Figure 7.6, you start to see from that study that you can use levers to discuss the business value of SOA with your line-of-business owners. This framework focuses on three critical focus areas of reducing risk, assisting with compliance, and improving flexibility. The flexibility value drivers and the profitability value drivers serve to demonstrate areas of thinking in your design. For instance, as you look at your company's desire for improved flexibility, things that will drive that area are things like the ability to

change, the ability to enable new products and services to be introduced quickly, and the ease of integration. Those attributes then drive more thoughts around the link to profitability factors. This table serves as an example of questions that you should be thinking through in your case for the value of deploying BPM and SOA. It enables you to start to think through the benefits to the business that these entry points bring to the table.

Figure 7.7 starts to bring in an approach to enable you to view the business benefits in a timeline and a way to begin thinking through your business justification, allowing your company to reach that flex-pon-sive* stage. As I travel around the world, one of my most demanded presentations is around SOA. However, an equally demanded presentation especially to IT audiences is my presentation on building ROI or business justification through a min-MBA like seminar. Given that most CIOs today are business leaders—true Chief Innovation Officers—they want their teams thinking not just about the technology, but also about the business impacts and outcomes. Figure 7.7 starts to get at some of those concepts.

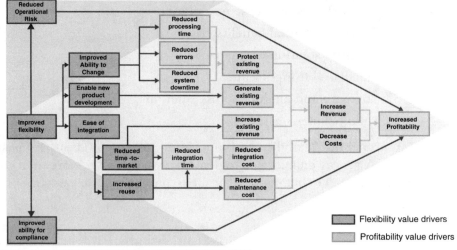

Source: IBM Institute for Business Value "The Business Value of Service-Oriented Architecture" 2006

Figure 7.6 A framework guides the examination of the business benefits of SOA for the nontechnical user.

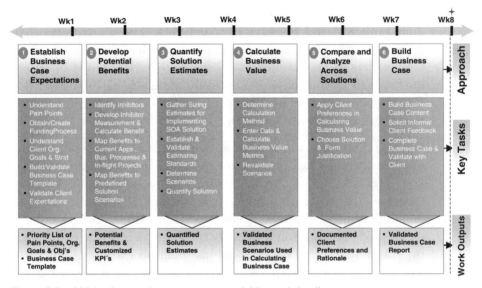

Figure 7.7 SOA business value assessment activities and timeline

The steps to think through include these:

1. Establish business case expectations.

2. Develop potential benefits.

3. Quantify solution estimates.

4. Calculate business value.

5. Compare and analyze across solutions.

6. Build business case.

Approaching flexibility and innovation in a methodical and business case way enables you to demonstrate that IT is more than just a focus on IT, but more of a focus on innovation and business results.

SUMMARY

Achieving business flexibility requires approaches like SOA and BPM that give leaders the ability to act decisively and organizations the agility to rapidly change. The three entry points into flexibility offer a way for all companies to explore how they begin their journey. The use of process, information, and collaboration is core to every business leader.

On the business side, people, process, or information provides a way to start with a discrete project while building out the larger vision. As you can see from the examples given in this chapter, these entry points provide business leaders with a way to align their business goals with their IT goals.

For guidance on which of these entry points to start with, an SOA assessment tool is available at www.ibm.com/soa/assessment. After you answer a set of questions about your business goals and your maturity on both IT and business attributes, the tool provides a recommendation based on the database of results to date, with the most valued place for your organization to start. In addition, it starts to lay in the plan for a business case.

Regardless of where you begin your journey, learning from others is the fastest and easiest way to gain success along the way. You are on your way to being a flex-pon-sive* company enabled by SOA. The next few chapters link in other relevant technologies, such as Web 2.0, and then go into case studies and lessons learned.

8

What about Web 2.0 and SOA? Are They Related?

We have spent a lot of time discussing service oriented architecture (SOA), but what about Web 2.0, PHP, AJAX, and the plethora of other IT alphabet soup that exists today? SOA is the key to IT and business flexibility—flex-pon-sive*—and, therefore, is the key to unlocking your business potential. Web 2.0 is about connecting people and ideas through communications that are real-time and efficient.

The communication mechanisms vary, ranging from podcasts, wikis, and feeds to social networking. Flexibility is the key driver of Web 2.0 success—the flexible delivery of data through the combination of services and disparate data sources through mash-ups, real-time data feeds, and rich interactions. Web 2.0 drives the consumption of services. The key is to tie the flexibility of Web 2.0 to service-oriented principles of loose coupling, encapsulation, and reuse that are the heart and soul of SOA. SOA and Web 2.0 are not just for the techy; they are made real by everyone who utilizes the rich collaboration and communication of the Internet today.

The linkage between Web 2.0 and SOA is important for businesses to understand. Web 2.0 is composed of many enabling technologies, such as PHP, AJAX, RSS, REST, and others. The Web platform is changing from transactional interconnection of computers to Web 2.0; this will allow businesses to interact with customers in more collaborative and efficient ways, and it is already opening up new opportunities for business services, application services, software services, and infrastructure services. Enabling Web 2.0 functionality requires increased infrastructure flexibility, which can be supported by a robust service oriented architecture (SOA). Both AJAX and REST are enablers for SOA. For example, REST can be used to expose services, and AJAX is used to build front ends. This is why I believe that the combination of SOA and Web 2.0 will become the new language for business.

Because this linkage is important to understand, let's start with the basics of defining Web 2.0 and its value proposition. Then we move into the critical linkage points between SOA and Web 2.0:

- What is Web 2.0?
- Web 2.0 and SOA: the advantage for flexibility
- The Web as the next platform
- Business models enabled

WHAT IS WEB 2.0?

Let's start with a definition of Web 2.0, as we did for SOA. Because we are delving into the world of the new, I went to the Wikipedia and other sources (see Figure 8.1). The term *Web 2.0* refers to a second generation of services available on the *World Wide Web* that lets people collaborate and share information online. In contrast to the first generation, Web 2.0 gives users an experience closer to desktop applications than traditional static Web pages. Web 2.0 applications often use a combination of techniques, including public *web service* APIs (dating from 1998), *AJAX* (1998), and *web syndication* (1997). They often allow for mass publishing (web-based *social software*). The concept includes *blogs* (check out my blog live at www-03.ibm.com/developer-works/blogs/page/SOA_Off_the_Record) and *wikis*.

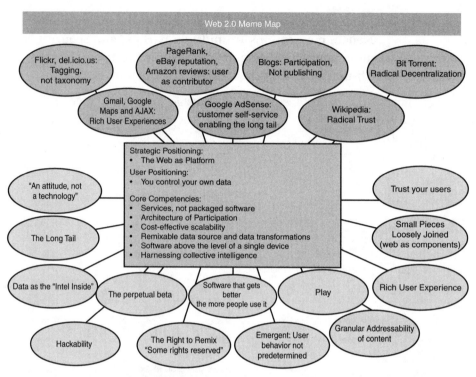

Source: http://www.oreillynet.com/pub/a/oreilly/tim/news/2005/09/30/what-is-web-20.html

Figure 8.1   The Web 2.0 approach contains many powerful ideas.

These examples of Web 2.0 usage can help make this real:

■ The Wikipedia itself is a use of Web 2.0 techniques and social philosophies. The dictionary is driven by content from sources all over the world.

■ IBM's usage of Web 2.0 in response to the effects of Hurricane Katrina was to provide a "mash-up" human resources application to aid displaced job seekers throughout the region. Because of the ease of Web 2.0 development, it took only a matter of a few days (or, as Rod Smith of IBM describes it, "the five-minute app") to build the application leveraging PHP, Google Maps, and Google Earth. Leveraging through SOA services, integrated search interfaces blend two external job boards into one application. This IBM-driven response also gave service providers the opportunity to contribute

significant raw material to user mash-ups such as allocation, presence, connections to multiple parties, and security constraints, and to become an integral part of the build, buy, or mash-up decision at their enterprise customers.

Many more examples of Web 2.0 usage exist, as shown in Figure 8.2 from "Social Computing" (Forrester Research, Inc.; February 2006).

Social networks Technology that allows users to leverage personal connections.	Linkedin Facebook orkut	MySpace friendster	P2P file sharing Sharing media files over a network powered by users who act as both client and server.	BitTorrent HoZoA gnutella.com	
RSS An XML standard that lets users collect and read content feeds.	Bloglines Yahoo! Feed Burner Pluck	NewsGator	C2C eCommerce Buying and selling among consumers via the Net.	Amazon.com eBay craigslist uBid.com	
Open source software Publicly available software that can be copied or modified without payment.	The Apache Software Foundation OpenOffice.org Linux MySQL		Comparison shopping sites Sites that allow consumers to compare products or services.	PriceGrabber.com Froogle Shopzilla	
Blogs Online diaries of text, photos, or other media.	Blogger Xanga Gawker	TypePad MSN Spaces Weblogs.com	Podcasts Online audio or video that users can download to a device.	Odeo Podcast Alley Juice	PodShow
Search engines Services that find Web content based on user-specified criteria.	MSN Google Yahoo!	Ask.com Technorati America Online	Wikis/Collaboration software Shared publishing software or site that allows users to edit content.	JotSpot Wikipedia Groove Networks	Basecamp Socialtext
User review portals Web portals that allow users to search for peer reviews on a product or service.	TripAdvisor Insider Pages CNET.com Game Rankings.com	ReviewCenter	Tagging Metadata assigned to items like photos or Web pages to facilitate searching and sharing.	del.icio.us Flicker BEA	Shadows Digg

Figure 8.2 Many entities have been labeled as Web 2.0, all with different functionality, utility, and business impact.

In simplest terms, Web 2.0 is a maturing of the Web that has been with us for some time. Over the past decade, the wild and wooly frontier of the Web has been tamed into a practical set of design principles that guide the creation of new technologies, standards, and business models, and that are reshaping the basic philosophies of IT. The emphasis is on simplicity, speed to value, solutions that include the end user (in fact, an end to the distinction between "developer" and "user"), community building, and, above all an emphasis on software function delivered in the form of network services.

Underlying Web 2.0 popularity is the trend of creating rich media through the flexible integration of disparate data sources and services borne on the Internet. The value proposition of Web 2.0 is similar to that of SOA—allowing change to occur without a lot of pain. Also similar to SOA, it requires a cultural change. Web 2.0's adoption has grown due to an expanded audience of developers—including line of business, departmental, and consumers—who embrace the ability to compose the end processes and create applications.

Web 2.0 is about the creation of relationships. This point is critical because this relationship view causes some of the shake-up. Because sites are social, users interact with each other and businesses can directly interact with their customers. This form of interaction is different than in the past because companies are both receiving and providing real-time information in new and innovative ways. It is really about social networking (many-to-many) instead of a one-to-one relationship with user.

Web 2.0 enables change in a culturally different way, featuring software that gets better the more people use it, services, unpackaged software, participation, informal publishing (such as blogs), and small pieces loosely coupled (remember our discussion that a key to SOA was loosely coupled services). The Web 2.0 philosophy is that social interaction is king. Blogging on hot topics drives the socialization and the wisdom of crowds. The Web as a platform is built on emergent behaviors such as openness, trust, and perpetual beta.

Collectively, these ideas form a rich conversation about the way we design and use technology to help us create value. They represent a shift from applications to services, from local to network, from concentrated to distributed, and, most important, from task-oriented to process-oriented design of software. From a technology perspective (see Figure 8.3 from "Social Computing" [Forrester Research, Inc.; February 2006]), the Web 2.0 umbrella is very broad as well—virtually anything that allows discrete, modular function to be surfaced to the user in a rich Web context is termed "Web 2.0." These components typically share one feature: They can be easily assembled together to provide a rich user experience

in a Web browsing context. Web 2.0 sites such as Flickr, Google mail, or Jotspot bring user experience to a much higher level than we typically expect from a Web page. These Web 2.0 composite applications are often referred to as mash-ups.

Source: http://en.wikipedia.org/wiki/Web_2.0

Figure 8.3   Innovative technologies proliferate around Web 2.0.

The term *mash-up* originated when DJs "mashed together" pieces of several existing songs to create a new song. They might pull a beat from one song, guitar from another, and singing from a third to produce something nobody had ever heard. In the Web 2.0 world, a mash-up is a quickly built composite Web 2.0 application that combines capabilities from existing Web-based applications in a new way to create new value for the user. Mash-ups represent the practical bridge between SOA and Web 2.0. If a Web 2.0 mash-up represents the coming together of information from disparate sources, SOA infrastructure provides those information sources. Scalable, dynamic, and accessible over the Web, SOA services are the raw material for Web 2.0 mash-ups. For example, the technology Flickr offers is delivered as a mash-up. The geography-based navigation of pictures is done with a mash-up. The rest is done

with AJAX and straight Web application technology. However, Flickr is often composed within mash-ups offered by other business service offerings.

Together, SOA and Web 2.0 fulfill the promise of flexibility and agility for a business process. Web 2.0 mash-ups provide the framework to leverage those business-process building blocks to deliver information to people rapidly and flexibly.

In an enterprise context, Web 2.0 enables workers who don't have technical knowledge to build ad-hoc collaborative "enterprise mash-up" applications on their own to address immediate business needs. By using readily available and intuitive tools such as "mash boards," they can assemble existing content, wire it together, and share it with their key coworkers, customers, and business partners to facilitate business in an exciting new way.

If you remember back to our value propositions of SOA, it was all about flexibility through the entry points of people, process, and information, and cost cutting from the entry points of reuse and connectivity. These same critical factors relate to Web 2.0 as well. In the next two sections, we explore that linkage.

WEB 2.0 AND SOA: ADVANTAGE FOR FLEXIBILITY

Forrester references Web 2.0 design as a "bottom-up innovation approach led from the customer/user's point of view" (see Figure 8.4). Innovation requires change, and change drives a need for flexibility, so we can start to see the value of leveraging Web 2.0 while deploying the flexibility in SOA. It strengthens the value proposition through its use of technology. For example, Web 2.0 uses a lightweight version of service orientation called Representational State Transfer (REST). REST has become perhaps the single most widely deployed form of service orientation because of its simplicity. It is also easier to mash up or create added value by combining other services based on REST in a new or interesting way, again enabling IT for change and flexibility. Without a robust SOA environment, the demand of knowledge workers, as they create dynamic applications, can cause critical failures.

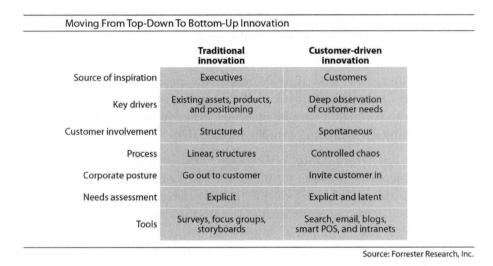

Moving From Top-Down To Bottom-Up Innovation		
	Traditional innovation	**Customer-driven innovation**
Source of inspiration	Executives	Customers
Key drivers	Existing assets, products, and positioning	Deep observation of customer needs
Customer involvement	Structured	Spontaneous
Process	Linear, structures	Controlled chaos
Corporate posture	Go out to customer	Invite customer in
Needs assessment	Explicit	Explicit and latent
Tools	Surveys, focus groups, storyboards	Search, email, blogs, smart POS, and intranets

Source: Forrester Research, Inc.

Figure 8.4   Forrester references Web 2.0 design as a bottom-up innovation approach led from the customer/user's point of view.

With the increase in flexibility, the usability requirements have also increased. With the use of Asynchronous JavaScript and XML, known as AJAX, the usability of a site can be a level of magnitude better than a synchronous site. AJAX is not really new, but is a combination of existing technologies: XMLHttpRequest, JavaScript, CSS, and XML. AJAX is asynchronous; it allows in-page server requests so you no longer need to refresh the whole page when you want the user to interact with the server.

Both AJAX and REST are enablers for SOA (see Figure 8.5). REST can be used to expose services, and AJAX is used to build front ends. REST is a lightweight approach to interconnecting front-end and public Internet services, and the use of more structured services in back-end systematic services is advised. REST has its pros and cons. It is easier because it is less structured. But that lack of structure is an issue for enterprises that are betting their business on SOA for mission-critical business functions. Most companies want to know that their interfaces and invocation semantics are well documented and are being enforced. This is why we believe

that the combination of SOA and Web 2.0 will become the new language for business: This approach yields greater delivery speed, customer affinity, and ROI for Web initiatives.

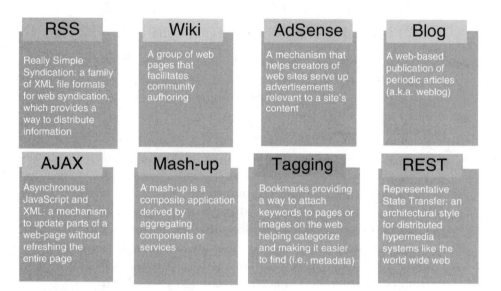

RSS

Really Simple Syndication: a family of XML file formats for web syndication, which provides a way to distribute information

Wiki

A group of web pages that facilitates community authoring

AdSense

A mechanism that helps creators of web sites serve up advertisements relevant to a site's content

Blog

A web-based publication of periodic articles (a.k.a. weblog)

AJAX

Asynchronous JavaScript and XML: a mechanism to update parts of a web-page without refreshing the entire page

Mash-up

A mash-up is a composite application derived by aggregating components or services

Tagging

Bookmarks providing a way to attach keywords to pages or images on the web helping categorize and making it easier to find (i.e., metadata)

REST

Representative State Transfer: an architectural style for distributed hypermedia systems like the world wide web

Figure 8.5　Web 2.0 has given rise to a wave of new tools and techniques.

THE ENTRY POINT LINKAGE

As the new language of business, Web 2.0 and SOA are both about weaving preexisting services and processes together into useful new business applications. The business impacts include reducing the overall effort of development, improving functionality, promoting data consistency, and enhancing responsiveness to customers—all of which adds business value. Because these are joint value propositions, the next question is how to begin. When we discussed the SOA entry points, we referenced the five most common ways to begin: people, process, information, reuse, and connectivity. Thinking through how each of these is positively impacted by combining the technology underpinnings gives companies an increased competitive advantage by leveraging these five entry points together:

- **Process**—Changes the ways businesses interact with their customers, whether part of the Fortune 1000 or small companies.
- **People**—Changes and enhances collaboration, builds contextual relationships.
- **Information**—Facilitates knowledge sharing.
- **Reuse**—Accelerates sharing of prebuilt libraries and code.
- **Connectivity**—Enables you to exchange information within and outside of your business.

If we think about the impact of Web 2.0 on the SOA entry points of people, information, and process, the value of both technologies becomes clearer: The SOA foundation provides information in the form of network-accessible services. Web 2.0 mash-ups collect and present the relevant information to the people on whom the business depends—customers and employees alike. And the management of the process provides the business logic, according to which the information and people are brought together. This collaboration creates a collective innovation, with new ideas being brought in from both inside and outside the company (see Figure 8.6).

The other two SOA entry points, connectivity and reuse, are implicit dependencies for this all to work. Connectivity is important in two ways—as the basic delivery mechanism for the functionality and in the form of the open standards that allow for discovery and use of new sources of information without a lot of prerequisite integration work. Because of this ubiquitous access to rich and plentiful information sources, the ability to reuse is greatly enhanced, accelerating all new development.

As we see in Figure 8.7, Web 2.0 brings to the table the ability to collaborate, create, combine, and distribute information and assets in a new way. To do that, Web 2.0 and SOA enabling Web 2.0 functionality require additional resiliency to existing enterprise infrastructure, and can be mitigated by a robust SOA. In the conceptual architecture of SOA, Web 2.0 exists at the "people" layer, where mash-ups rapidly provide the interface to the business process when and where it is needed. As an SOA breaks down the silos of application functionality and reorients enterprise IT to be better aligned with business process, Web 2.0 begins to break down the distinction between "inside" and "outside" the firm.

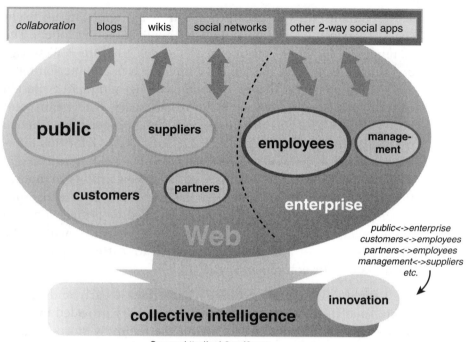

Source: http://web2.wsj2.com

Figure 8.6   Using Web 2.0 to enable dynamic collective innovation

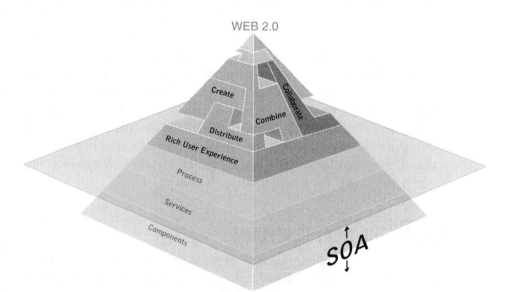

Figure 8.7   Web 2.0 and SOA: the flexibility advantage

The common examples of Internet Web 2.0 applications might seem too extreme for many enterprise application developers. The examples of being able to mash up Google Ads into a Web page don't make any sense for someone building a fixed-function teller application interface. In fact, dynamic, ad hoc, and rapid evolution of user interfaces might seem downright scary. The main point here is that Web 2.0 is not an all-or-nothing proposition. You can get utility from small doses of Web 2.0, such as AJAX for rich interaction, without needing the rest. Conversely, rapid, iterative, and social software might be a technique for driving prototype innovation. Such a prototype can then be harvested during rigorous development processes for use in more fixed or critical function environments where the enterprise wants to lock down on the interaction model and disallow customization that could create business unit or compliance risks.

With rapid development techniques of "release early and release often," and the lower technical barriers to entry provided by composite applications and reuse, a dialogue naturally starts to grow between developer and user. This conversation begins as feedback about the user experience or the delivered function, but, if nurtured, it can deepen to address the "why" and the "how" of what the enterprise is trying to do with its business process. Further encouraged, this conversation can spread to include the entire firm and its customers and can lead to radically different business models. When the customers are given the reins, the enterprise becomes a platform for their creativity. This is a daunting challenge for firms because it requires ceding control, which can be very scary. But properly harnessed through the principles of Web 2.0, the collective intelligence and massive resources of a vibrant community can far surpass those of the firm on its own, especially when leveraging SOA for business flexibility.

THE WEB AS THE NEXT PLATFORM

Looking back in time, companies have gone through a number of platforms that have allowed them to compete in the business world with a technology advantage. Starting with the mainframe era, going through client/server, and moving into the Internet era,

the value of platforms has changed as the technology has advanced. SOA enables these platforms to compete for success—with SOA vendors playing a role as pure players and as enablers for others, such as Yahoo! and Amazon, which offers "services" in the market. These changes have allowed companies to magnify the value of a keystone position through ecosystem innovation and investment.

Think about MySpace.com, which leverages many of the philosophies and technologies of Web 2.0. According to Wikipedia, MySpace is a *social-networking web site* offering an interactive, user-submitted network of *blogs*, profiles, groups, photos, MP3s, and videos, along with an internal *e-mail* system. According to *Alexa Internet, as of August 2006*, it is the world's fourth most popular English-language web site and the sixth most popular in any language. It is the most popular web site in the *United States,* accounting for 4.5% of all web site visits (note that it is possible that other sites have a greater number of unique visitors). MySpace has gradually gained more popularity than similar web sites, to achieve 80% of visits to online social-networking web sites. The other intriguing example is YouTube.com. (YouTube.com was purchased by Google in 2006.) YouTube is a company that was founded in February 2005 as a way people around the world could see videos, produced by anyone, through a web experience. Everyone can watch YouTube, and, as they say on the site, they are "broadcasters of tomorrow." The impact of these Web 2.0 types of computing as a platform for the future leads businesses to ensure that they are leveraging the Web platform.

BUSINESS MODELS ENABLED

The impact of Web 2.0 and SOA on businesses' economic structures will vary. However, we do know that many areas of the business will be impacted.

For marketing and sales, all processes will be impacted. Related to my own business, the blog impact now outmatches many of the traditional mechanisms for communicating with customers. This network of influencers through blogs and wikis is an interesting

relationship—creating flexibility in who your audience is and how you reach them. Even the thought of having a relationship online with someone you've never met is an interesting paradigm. It is worth digging deeper into the psychology of this type of spontaneous, anonymous, and yet instantly personal interaction, and what it can mean to businesses—both in terms of marketing and sales, but also in terms of customer care and maintaining account control and loyalty. For businesses to continue their drive for flexibility, Web 2.0 and SOA now allow for a new kind of marketing. This new business model allows for community-driven relationship models and more organic selling. Given the ways that users can now gain access to try before they buy, a community that will want to try it before buying will be a challenge for the next-generation sales team.

For IT, development cycle times will be reduced and the time to market will become a key metric of success. With the mash-up capability, even small and medium businesses will be able to produce strong business functionality for a reasonable cost. Couple this with the value of SOA, and the future will see maximum flexibility. For example, a system integrator called Sysdat helped Gautzsch, a seller of lawn and garden products (a small business) in Germany, integrate its existing systems with Amazon.de, allowing it to expand through online sales. Gautzsch used collaborations to choreograph the interaction with Amazon.de and used an ESB to manage the external connectivity. The company picked a high-impact project as the place to start and was able to get online in three weeks, with full ROI being achieved in three months. I predict many such projects in the future. Also, don't forget that the increased ease of creation will present new challenges to management and security.

End users will experience a shift in expectations. We have already started to see the effects of this digital economy as many of Don Tapscott's insights permeate businesses today. With the ease of mash-ups, end users might not even need to wait for IT; they will begin to develop their own creations of the applications that meet business needs.

For CEOs and business leaders, this means they need to be thinking through how the new world will view flexibility. According to Ray Lane's Software 2006 Keynote (*http://news.com.com/ Web+2.0+meets+the+enterprise/2100-1012_3-6066138.html*), new rules will be in effect in the next generation:

- Serve an individual need
- Seek viral, organic adoption
- Provide contextualized, personal information
- Deliver instantaneous value
- Utilize the community and social relationships to understand the user

SKILLS REQUIRED FOR THE NEW BUSINESS MODELS

Web 2.0 as a computing model is emerging for building and deploying content-centric applications. As a result, economics in business change. A lot of new applications are now affordable and being used to access and compose SOA business and data services. With those changes comes a need to review your skill plan to ensure that your company understands the new programmable Web with technology skills required in such areas as PHP, AJAX, RSS, Atom, REST, microformats, wikis, and mash-ups. The roles of programmers, Web developers, and UI experts will become critical. The new world will reward those who know content integration and application logic as well as content manipulation and interfaces. According to the U.S. Bureau of Labor Statistics, it is estimated that there will be more than 100 million U.S. users of Web 2.0 mash-ups by 2012 (see Figure 8.8).

The business skills required for this new opportunity include breakthrough thinking, ideas more in sync with the concepts of relationships and social networking, and the ability to leverage the knowledge collected from a variety of sources—some from typical routes of information and others spread out over the Web.

For example, makers of the movie *Snakes on a Plane* leveraged comments from blogs and wikis to modify and add scenes to their movie. The makers expected huge turnouts from their "social networking" Web 2.0 style of their script. But as we have just begun to see the numbers roll out, the figures have yet to bear that out. Hindsight being 20/20, the network leveraged the technology to its advantage for the target audience who were on these Web 2.0 wikis and chats, but next time it needs to also focus on the population with the buying share of wallet. The combination of this added business insight with the technology would have dramatically impacted the bottom-line results.

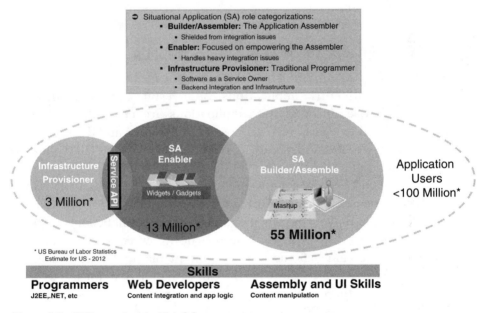

Figure 8.8 Skills required for Web 2.0

In the case study that follows, you read about an entertainment company that successfully started to leverage the power of SOA and Web 2.0.

CASE STUDY
PILOT PROJECTS UNDERWAY AT IBM

One of the challenges in IT today is the length of time to develop applications. With businesses getting more and more time-to-market focused, this time factor really comes into play and can create a barrier between IT and business. The combination of SOA and Web 2.0 technologies is giving rise to a new class of applications that IBM is referring to as Situational Applications. A Situational Application is data- and content-centric, and addresses the needs of an individual or workgroup. These applications can be centered around an event (for example, a budgeting cycle) or a relationship. The targeted "developer" is a business professional. While the typical IT-developed application is measured in years (years to develop and years of use), a Situational Application is measured in minutes, days, and months—minutes to develop and days or months of use. Historically, due to the short lifespan, these application requests were unsatisfied due to the cost of development versus the anticipated benefit. However, data and content exposed through SOA combined with Web 2.0 technologies change the application-development economics.

IBM is actively piloting a number of concepts related to Web 2.0 technologies, including the concept of a Quick and Easy Development Wiki (QEDWiki) for development of Situational Applications. Leveraging the convenience of a wiki, a business-domain expert develops a Situational Application by dragging widgets onto a wiki page and hooking them together (or mashing them up). While this approach allows the knowledge workers to address their specific requirements, enterprise security policies and governance can be enforced by controlling access to the underlying services and widgets. So how are these concepts being applied?

continues

Media and Entertainment

Historically, companies within the Media and Entertainment industry have been on the forefront of technology advances to enhance their end product—content. A recent example is the shift to digital technologies. However, there have not been similar advances in the processes that drive the production of content. While there are robust applications that support individual parts of the process (e.g., transcoding), oversight and management of the end-to-end process is largely manual due to the proliferation of tools with proprietary interfaces. To address this challenge, IBM has developed MediaHub—an SOA infrastructure designed from the ground up to handle the needs of content producers. When combined with QEDWiki, users have a role-based dashboard that gives them visibility and control over the process events within their domain. One pilot involves a fundamental process within the industry—"long form processing." This process includes the ingestion of content for editing and eventual archiving into a content-management system. The workflow includes multiple handoffs between both applications and people. Using MediaHub, the supporting applications are able to communicate and pass content through the MediaHub Enterprise Service Bus (ESB). This gives the applications a common interface for receiving and posting events. The workflow is orchestrated by the process engine within MediaHub. QEDwiki is the producer's dashboard. Through the dashboard, the producer can drive the process (e.g., submit the ingested content for transcoding or editing, view the content), and track the progress of the content through the entire process. Also, by mashing up process events with application log data, the producer can identify where productivity and process improvements are warranted.

For companies that expose services as a business, Web 2.0 will provide them with new revenue opportunities because it allows easy consumption of their services. Dun & Bradstreet (D&B), the

leading provider of business information, has exposed four services through the StrikeIron Web Services Marketplace:

1. **D&B Geo Point**—Provides access to rooftop geographic information (latitude and longitude coordinates) for use in your pre-screening marketing and sales processes. It is available on businesses across the U.S., Canada, Germany, and the U.K.

2. **D&B WorldBase Marketing Plus**—The most efficient way to gain basic marketing information about a potential prospect, such as business name, address, D&B D-U-N-S Number, fax, phone, and trade style, plus business intelligence such as executive names and titles, financials, number of employees, import or export code, branch indicator, and more.

3. **D&B Business Credit Quick Check**—Perform low-risk credit assessments and prescreen prospects with D&B's core credit-evaluation data. Information includes company identification, payment activity summary, public filings indicators, and the D&B Rating.

4. **D&B Business Verification**—Provides programmatic access to D&B's many business reports, including rich business and credit information reports that can greatly enrich any business intelligence initiative.

A QEDWiki pilot was recently completed that retrieved and rendered business information from Salesforce.com using its D-U-N-S number. Upon selection, the business was mapped using the Geo Point Web service and Google maps. Detailed information was retrieved using the WorldBase web service and was rendered when the mouse was passed over the business location on the map.

By D&B's recognition of this need and being able to supply a way to get to this situational information, they are able to leverage Web 2.0 and SOA in a "business growth" opportunity by making services easily consumable.

SUMMARY

Since innovation requires change, and change drives a need for flexibility, the value of leveraging Web 2.0 while deploying your architecture based on SOA makes your technology environment built for change and flexibility. Web 2.0 and SOA are both about weaving preexisting services together into useful new business applications. The connection in the technologies is clear: both AJAX and REST are enablers for SOA. REST can be used to expose services, and AJAX is used to build front ends. The business impacts include reducing the overall effort of development, improving functionality, promoting data consistency, and enhancing responsiveness to the customer—adding business value. It is imperative for business leaders today to ensure that they understand what Web 2.0 is and the advantages that SOA and Web 2.0 can bring to the table. The Web will be the next major platform in play, and understanding its impact on the business model, end user, and other groups within a company will serve to be a critical part of a company's future competitiveness. It cannot be forgotten in the flex-pon-sive* world in which we live that this new language of business involves the marriage of both SOA and Web 2.0.

III

How to Implement Flex-pon-sive* in Your Business

9

The Top 10 Don'ts!

We've covered a lot in this book on how to drive your business toward flexibility and growth through innovation. By now you realize the importance and meaning of flex-pon-sive*. A flex-pon-sive* company is one that responds with lightning speed and agility to rapidly changing business needs. To get to that goal, I focus in this chapter on what not to do. We had the top list of lessons learned in Chapter 5, "SOA Key Concepts." But I always learn from my mistakes—what to do different and what to do better. As such, I wanted to make sure that I included not only what your company should focus on, but what you should avoid with the top ten don'ts. I got this idea watching David Letterman last night while poring over scores of customers who have already started their focus on flexibility. I want to cover the lessons that others have learned, in hopes of sharing that knowledge.

The top ten don'ts for your flex-pon-sive* journey are listed next; this chapter walks through each one.

1. Don't expect maximum business without SOA.

2. Don't just do technology; it is a transformation of the way you do business.

3. Don't throw everything out.

4. Don't bite off big projects all at once.

5. Don't forget to set expectations.

6. Don't expect to do this without a culture modification through governance.

7. Don't forget the right skills.

8. Don't expect the flexibility without open standards.

9. Don't do this alone—leverage partners who have experience.

10. Don't do it without a strong plan because the first step is the most important.

Each of these "don'ts" is based on a wealth of SOA engagement experience and a true focus on business models and innovation for flexibility. I share that learning so that you can leverage the experience and leap ahead in your quest for competitiveness.

1. DON'T EXPECT MAXIMUM BUSINESS WITHOUT SOA

They say that French is the language of love, and I say that SOA is the language of business flexibility. SOA is an approach that draws IT and Business together and drives a discipline toward flexibility. Of course, we've heard this before, but it is truly different. One of IBM's top architects, Rob High, and one of IBM's top SOA consultants, Jason Weisser, summed it up this way:

> SOA is the link to business. It is the an approach to architecture that enables the flexibility required for innovation across the board. Why? We discussed in detail the role both XML and web services play in SOA. They are the glue like HTTP is the glue for the internet. Web services allow companies to have the necessary IT support so the business can be viewed as a set of services.

From a brief technology perspective, the key technologies to SOA, XML, and web services had better accommodate change. Said ever more strongly, SOA-based technologies enable you to build for change! For example, it is possible to add or reorder elements in an XML business object without breaking code. The same applies to WSDL, another standard prominent in SOA. From a technology viewpoint, older approaches, such as RPC or CORBA, do not allow this flexibility.

Additionally, web services offer the flexibility of having learned from the mistakes of previous methods (such as CORBA and RPC). The designers of web services learned that it needed the flexibility to support both asynchronous messaging and remote procedure calls. Before, support for one was there, and the other was added later. Just as with a house, building additions is never as efficient or as flexible as designing it in the beginning.

In addition to this flexibility enablement, other enablers include language independence. XML renders more naturally into multiple languages, such as C, Java, COBOL, and so on.

Because SOA is based on these two critical elements, web services and XML, it is built for flexibility. It enables businesses to be on demand and to be able to respond to whatever the market throws at them.

As we discussed in Chapter 1, "The Innovation Imperative," flexibility and cost savings will continue to be crucial goals. Key to attaining these goals is an SOA strategy because it helps companies save money as they implement on demand flexibility.

2. DON'T JUST DO TECHNOLOGY—IT IS A TRANSFORMATION OF THE WAY YOU DO BUSINESS

Okay, so I just told you to look at SOA, where it is not technology. IT is an approach. SOA does require business processes that are represented as services. However, the most successful companies don't consider this to be an IT-led journey. In fact, they view it as a partnership between business and IT.

For example, consider St. George Bank, Australia's fifth-largest bank. It's one of the top 15 publicly listed companies in Australia, employing more than 7,500 people. Its national operations span all aspects of the financial industry, including retail banking, institutional and business banking, and wealth management.

Customer satisfaction is of utmost importance to the bank, and it cannot afford to have IT challenges distracting it from its customers and business, which is why reusable services make so much sense. The cost of new product development and the time to market are greatly reduced, enabling the bank to be flexible to business drivers while minimizing the cost to make necessary changes.

At St. George Bank, the enterprise architecture team is co-located with the business. Greg Booker, Head of Group Architecture, explains:

> I have two architects working on the same floor as the business leaders in commercial, and I have two architects working with the retail folks, so they're not locked away in an IT center, completely disconnected from the business. They are people that understand the business pressures or business issues from a day-to-day perspective, and the business is also able to reach out and touch those guys and talk to them.
>
> We're able to communicate to the business, in terminology they appreciate, like "fee to market," "reduced complexity," and "reduced costs," all of which they want to hear about. They don't want to hear about the fact that it's a bunch of reusable components that are linked together with web services and all the rest of it.

"This level of engagement is critical," concludes Booker.

St. George Bank is well along the path to achieving a flexible business model, and what makes the difference for the bank is the true partnership between the business and IT. This is not about the technology, but about the way you do business.

One of my most-demanded presentations to CIOs and their teams is actually not about SOA, but is a mini MBA course. The best-run companies have IT teams that understand the business. Get your business requirements in clear view, and then make sure you have a mechanism to ensure that those are taken from the business down to the technology. The advice around governance is one of the secrets of success that all customers called out.

3. DON'T THROW EVERYTHING OUT!

You can go after success in many different ways. But one thing that I have observed is the success of those who don't rip out the years of knowledge, best practices, applications, and technology. If we take a look at the examples throughout this book, the common thread is that all of them inventoried what they had and ensured that they selected an approach that allowed them to leverage current resources. For most of the companies that I've worked with, the whole premise going in is that the cost savings from the initial efforts will provide the fuel for future strategic investments.

Reuse has been talked about for a long time, but previously, technologies have never really been successful in bringing about large-scale reuse. And reuse has only focused on technology not elements of business process and knowledge. SOA addresses head on, with a focus on breaking down the roadblocks that have hindered reuse efforts in the past.

Reuse involves two areas:

- Technology reuse
- Business process or model reuse

Both are powerful concepts. Let's first look at the concept of technology reuse, which is the most prevalent way that companies today are seeing the realization of SOA's value proposition around cost cutting. Remember when we discussed the service repository and a service registry in Chapter 7, "Three Business-Centric SOA Entry Points"? The repository is used during development as a catalog of services. It's where integration developers can go to see the services they have available to reuse. The service registry is used

during runtime to hold all the "metadata" about a service—such information as the service description, usage, and versioning information, for example.

A way that we look at technology reuse at IBM is that the break-even point for reusing a service is 1.6. That means that the first time you have reused a service (meaning, used it a second time), you are saving money. Reuse of services reduces costs by helping to eliminate duplicate development and maintenance.

The other area of reuse is that on the business side. This involves reuse of business logic. For example, suppose a company has a variety of customer services running on a federated model where each business unit operates autonomously and is supported by its own IT organization and infrastructure. The result would be that the same business process and supporting applications are implemented in many ways. The challenge of building a unified view of the customer across all the business units brings home the impact of reuse of business logic. Many companies will select the best practice for customer information and will standardize that best practice into a single federated view—thus reusing the best practice process. This is one reason why the SOA approach is used when companies have done a lot of mergers or acquisitions. A lot of times mergers and acquisitions bring into play a lot of duplicate processes. Thus reuse of the best practice or business model.

Reuse of services helps companies standardize business processes. So reuse both saves money and helps companies run in a more consistent and efficient manner by helping to eliminate overlapping and potentially conflicting services within the organization.

4. DON'T BITE OFF TOO-BIG PROJECTS

Thinking incrementally about how to get there is critical. It is not just about the dollars that tended to be reinvested, but more about proving and showing the value of success to the organization.

Have you ever heard about Zeno's paradox? Zeno of Elea (circa 450 B.C.) is credited with one of the best-known paradoxes about

the Tortoise and Achilles. (Achilles was the great Greek hero of Homer's *The Illiad.*) It is an interesting paradox and has been around for a long time. The story begins with a turtle and Achilles discussing a race. The turtle challenges Achilles and asks for a head start. In the end, they don't race because the turtle convinces Achilles that because he gets a head start, and because Achilles must continually make up that distance, the turtle would always win. His argument was that Achilles would have to cover half the distance, then half the remaining distance, then half the remaining distance, then half the remaining distance...and so on forever. The consequence is that Achilles would never win.

Rather than tackle Zeno head-on, let us pause to notice something remarkable. Suppose we take Zeno's Paradox at face value for the moment and agree with him that before I can walk a mile, I must first walk a half-mile. With the number of small distances, adding all those distances should just give me back the finite distance I started with. And poor old Achilles would have won his race.

The trick here is to understand where you need to go and then to begin with small projects that help you get there. We discussed several key starting projects—around people, process, and information—in Chapter 5. These entry points help businesses pursue flexibility through SOA the right way: by taking a project-based approach and demanding that each project deliver real business value. A recent study of more than 500 companies, conducted by Mercer Management Consultants, showed that the surveyed successful companies are approaching SOA from entry points of integrating people, processes, information, or a combination of all three. So learn from your initial SOA projects by making sure they are small, well defined, and quick to implement.

5. DON'T FORGET TO SET EXPECTATIONS

Many people I talk to about these projects start by asking me if I know of a return on investment (ROI) calculator to help them with the business value of their projects. Although ROI is important in the business world, more important is showing your CEO that business flexibility through SOA is the way to go—not just in ROI,

but by setting and managing expectations within the business. That being said, ROI is a critical element. Why is ROI important? According to Gartner, a project with an associated ROI is 60% more likely to be approved, and in a recent issue of *InformationWeek*, more than 82% of IT decisions require an ROI. From McKinus 2007 study, maybe a first one to explore is integrating in your partner process.

My team created a self-assessment test that you can take to identify your company's business problems and deliver an ROI estimate. These tools provide a set of interview questions to be used with both the business leaders and the IT leaders. The resulting output delivers ROI business cases, key process models, and a solution proposal.

The tool delivers a high-level business case with an ROI and validates the business process that the company has chosen. It then also ensures that the SOA architecture is proposed in sync with the company's level of SOA maturity and skills, including specific skill recommendations.

In Figure 9.1, you can see that this tool takes our advice of always lining business and IT together. Then it assists with the types of common problems seen in business today. Figure 9.2 then shows the fields that are prefilled with data, with default values that match the company profile using the Alinean/IDC database of more than 20,000 customers. This supports multiple industries, countries, and customers' sizes, and pulls in industry average cost metrics.

In Figure 9.3, you see the estimated top-level benefits and some indirect benefits that might be difficult to measure. The results for costs, shown in Figure 9.4, help a company articulate its costs, such as IT or skills training. The tool then calculates an ROI as shown in Figure 9.5. Finally, as shown in Figure 9.6, a sample report is produced.

This review is just one example of some tools shown in the industry, but it is one of my personal favorites. To gain access to use this tool, go to www.ibm.com/soa.

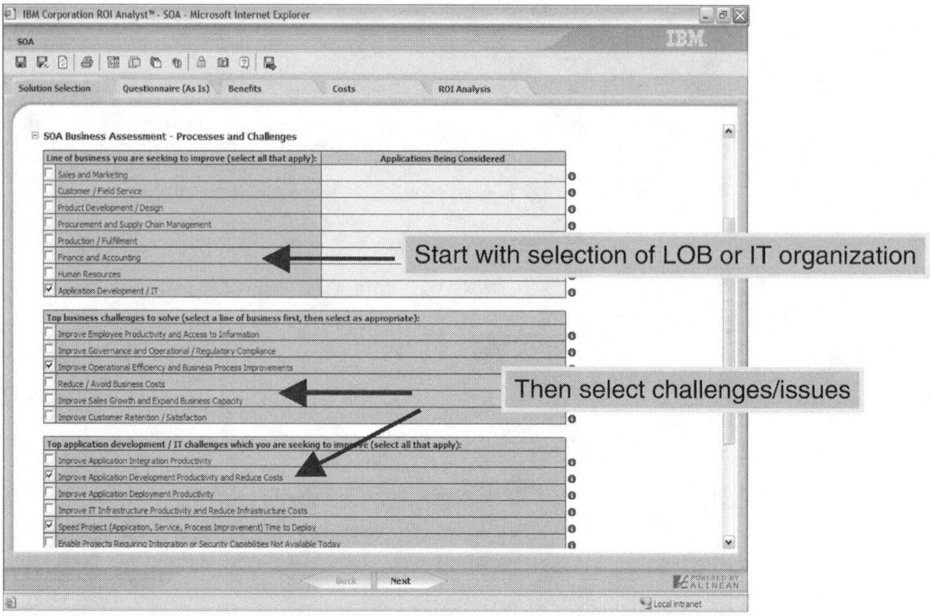

Figure 9.1 Solution selection—business/IT challenges

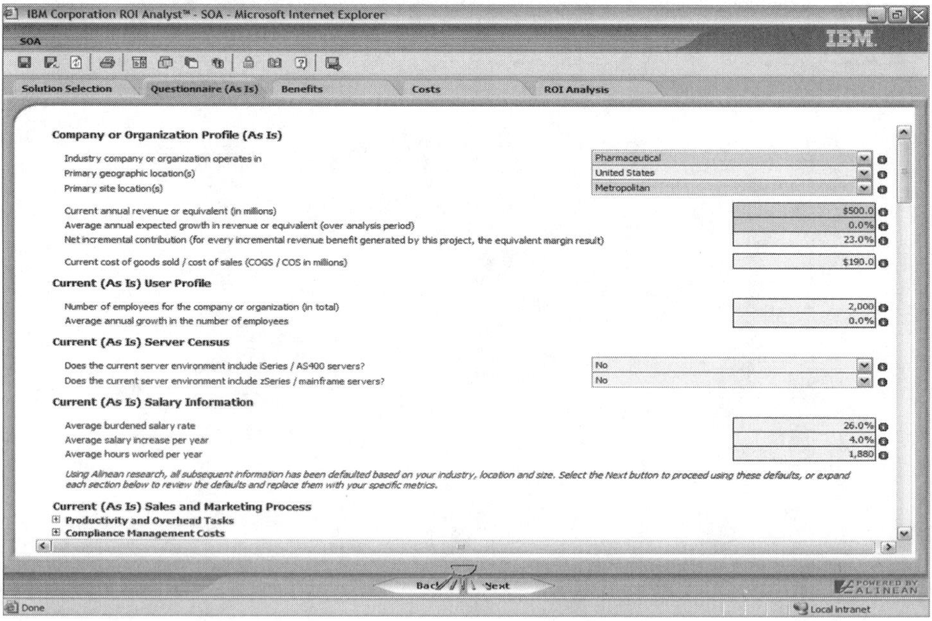

Figure 9.2 SOA questionnaire

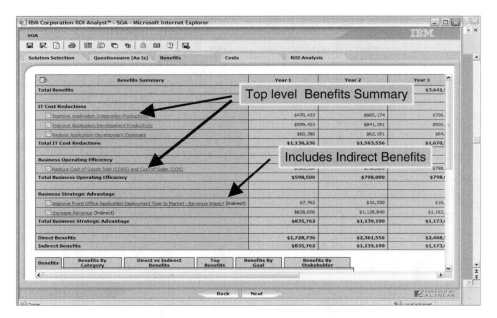

Figure 9.3 Benefits of SOA

Figure 9.4 Costs of implementing SOA

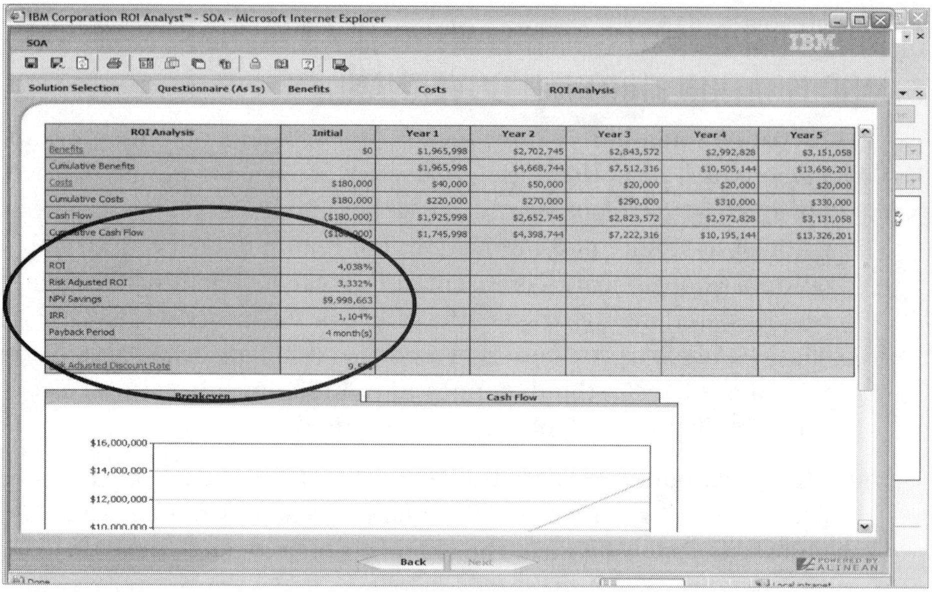

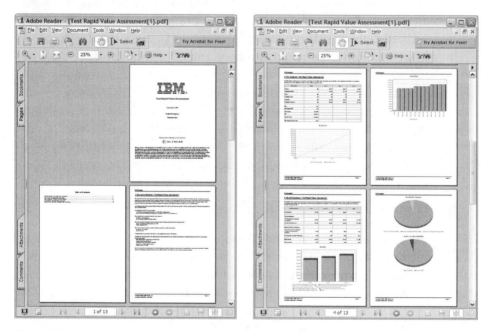

Figure 9.5 ROI analysis

Figure 9.6 Sample report

6. DON'T EXPECT TO DO THIS WITHOUT A CULTURE MODIFICATION THROUGH GOVERNANCE

If you remember *Who Moved My Cheese?* (Johnson and Blanchard, 1998), the notion of change being a good thing to drive business is the focus of the book. For pursuing competitiveness through flexibility and innovation, the notion of ensuring that the cultural change occurs is essential for success. Gaining flexibility requires a company to view the world in horizontal, not vertical, slices. It involves the notion of a partnership between IT and business that changes the dynamics of the relationship. And because they create and drive change, governance is critical.

The Governance model should be directly linked from a company's business strategy to IT strategy. It helps customers establish tailored decision rights in the organization and implement the policy, measurement and control mechanisms necessary to carry out those decisions. Effective governance helps free teams from the uncertainties and challenges of trying to figure out who needs to agree on what so they can focus on creating and delivering innovative business solutions. A recent study from IT analyst research firm, Gartner, confirmed the need for governing an SOA environment. "In 2006, lack of working governance mechanisms in mid-size-to-large (fewer than 50 services) post-pilot SOA projects will be the most common reason for project failure (0.8 probability)." Part of the need for Governance is that it helps drive cultural change. How is cultural change driven in an organization? A governance model drives cultural change through the award system, the management system, and the process of funding.

Cultural Items to consider include:

1. How to bring IT and Business together. More importantly, how to not just bring them together but to foster teamwork and a common way of viewing the business challenge. Given the focus now on horizontal processes, not just siloed ones, a way of approaching this alignment is required. Reenforcing new working styles will be an important part.

To do this effectively, strong processes are an important cultural element for the change to be successful.

2. Need for new skills and how to make those new skills sought after. For the technology side, for example, SOA may be a sole motivator as technologists can learn new skills and influence strategic IT decsions. So to effect the culture positively, to communicate this aspect would be an important element in the value of the change. And for the business team other motivators to learn new skills must be explored for your specific company. One customer I worked with focused on the business process skills and had a special program to communicate when the team members were certified on certain horizontal processes.

3. How to deal with funding models of shared services. Making sure the goverance model addresses the way to fund work for the common good, and communicating across the organization will be a critical element of the change. A company in Europe I worked with had everything in place and was stalled until a funding model for several shared services was defined.

4. How to award for the right focused work. For example, recognition for those who author reusable assets versus patents needs to be taken into account. Monetary awards for individuals or teams may be considered, especially for early adopters. Think back to the IBM example in Chapter 10, "Case Study: IBM."

5. How to measure results (business terminlogy) now on a horizontal scale.

Without a governance mechanism across the corporation, a cultural change can not occur that helps to focus on horizontal processes, versus siloed ones. Most customers use the governance model to map their requirements, policies, and procedures to execute new business plans based on SOA and help with the necessary cultural changes. Identifying required cultural and behavioral changes and getting the executive stakeholders to support the required changes are the keys.

7. DON'T FORGET THE RIGHT SKILLS

As we have surveyed the companies who have attended our SOA executive summits, we have found that the number-one gap for companies beginning this journey is the lack of skills. This process does involve a cultural change, it does involve evolving your IT, and it does involve a focus on the business view in three years. Therefore, having the right skills is important. Before you begin any project, focus on a skills inventory—both what your company needs for the future and what you have today is required. Figure 9.7 shows a sample of the type.

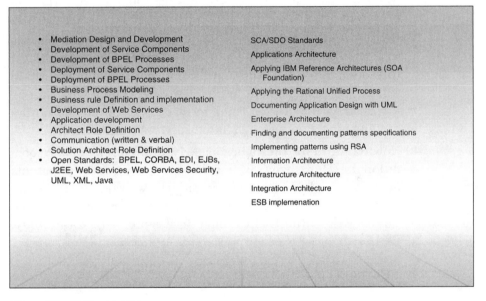

- Mediation Design and Development
- Development of Service Components
- Development of BPEL Processes
- Deployment of Service Components
- Deployment of BPEL Processes
- Business Process Modeling
- Business rule Definition and implementation
- Development of Web Services
- Application development
- Architect Role Definition
- Communication (written & verbal)
- Solution Architect Role Definition
- Open Standards: BPEL, CORBA, EDI, EJBs, J2EE, Web Services, Web Services Security, UML, XML, Java

SCA/SDO Standards

Applications Architecture

Applying IBM Reference Architectures (SOA Foundation)

Applying the Rational Unified Process

Documenting Application Design with UML

Enterprise Architecture

Finding and documenting patterns specifications

Implementing patterns using RSA

Information Architecture

Infrastructure Architecture

Integration Architecture

ESB implemenation

Figure 9.7 Skills checklist

This journey is a team effort that focuses on IT and business as the enablers of flexible business processes.

CASE STUDY
YAMMAR COMPANY LIMITED

A great case of a company focused on SOA skills and capabilities is Yanmar Company Limited. Founded in 1912, Yanmar Company Limited today has more than 15,000 people and 16 sites in Japan as well as 22 subsidiaries in other countries. It is part of the Yanmar Group that has lines of business that span energy, industrial, marine, agriculture, and environmental with diesel engines representing its core business. Yanmar Group also manufactures gas engines, but most are diesel that are used in marine, agricultural, and lifestyle or consumer-based business.

Supporting the Yanmar Group's IT efforts—information processes for the design, development and management of systems and networks—is the privately held Yanmar Information System Service Company (YISS). With 156 employees and seven operation sites in Japan, YISS's challenge was to ensure that they will have the talent and skills for the company's future growth. While developing talent, they also need to meet the needs of the business.

Juggling both the business requirements and IT requirements, YISS needed to support new business models and TCO. IT needed to reduce development time and cost and increase quality. Like many other flex-pon-sive* companies, this was a critical point where business and IT aligned their goals. As business and IT converged, management decided that SOA could better respond to the requirements. In an incremental fashion, they piloted a project after they developed their SOA skills and capabilities.

YISS's first selected SOA project was a distribution application that included management, inventory control, and search. They broke apart this business process into services. The approach was to turn a component of the process into a service. Now this process can be offered as several services. Given that this application had been

continues

tightly coupled, SOA allowed the YISS team to loosely couple the application service and reuse it, which provides flexibility. Along each step, the YISS team developed talent and skills that were crucial to the project and, most important, to the business. One of the big benefits to YISS is the talent and skills future that SOA is driving as part of its corporate mission.

For YISS, SOA is very efficient. Business flexibility is affected by the IT flexibility. Now for them, IT is not a hindrance. With this project, IT encourages and guides the business development. The existing tightly coupled environment of YISS was not flexible, but SOA allows companies to combine different services. Now YISS publishes those services on the network so they can accommodate changes flex-pon-sively*! This whole project was created to support the business goals.

As YISS President Sadayuki Nishimura said, "In this project, SOA enabled innovation and flexibility!" And it would not have happened without.

8. DON'T EXPECT THE FLEXIBILITY WITHOUT OPEN STANDARDS

On the IT side, a set of mandates enables flexibility. Open standards such as BPEL, WSDL, XML, and others are not optional. Before you look at vendors, make sure you review the support and commitment they have to open standards. In this area of business and IT alignment, there are more on the horizon, ranging from refinement of SCA/SDO to new breakthroughs in the industry standards required to solidify the alignment between IT and business. Open standards enable a company to create solutions that are reusable. This means they are portable and/or interoperable. Open standards matter more today than ever in the history of computing.

Let's face it, all companies live in a heterogeneous environment. This concept used to bog us down, but now, with open standards,

that reuse is a reality. See Figure 9.8 to review just a few of the critical standards that exist today and, more important, some great work that is going on to drive the new standards needed in this area around industry-specific standards.

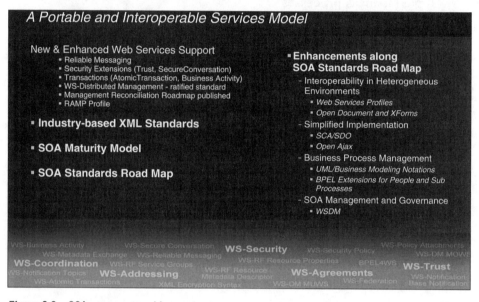

Figure 9.8 SOA openness enables customer reuse.

9. DON'T DO THIS ALONE—LEVERAGE PARTNERS WHO HAVE EXPERIENCE

A robust ecosystem of partners helps you by bringing in qualified people and skills that you can trust to move your company's project forward. Independent software vendors and systems integrators are gravitating to driving this linkage of IT and business, and are becoming more skilled with SOA. A partner community can expand access to key assets and skills.

Because business flexibility through SOA involves sharing best practices and assets, a few vendors, such as IBM, have set up business catalogs. The business catalog has reusable assets from a number of partners. The value here is that a company does not have to re-create the best practice; instead, it can use one that

exists in the industry. For example, in a quick search of the IBM SOA business catalog, you can see some examples of the type of content that is available. Here are six sample business industry process models, showing best practices in a reusable form for simple business processes:

- **Banking**—The Mortgage Application process documents completion and review of a customer mortgage application through the mortgage lending decision.

- **Insurance**—The New Business Life process documents completion, routing, underwriting, and creation of a policy.

- **Retail**—The Product Invoice Payment process documents receiving an invoice and comparing it to the original purchase order, and reviewing a damage report through the payment path.

- **Telecom**—The DSL Provisioning process documents prequalification of customers and the entering/releasing of the DSL order.

- **Industrial**—The Supplier Forecasting process documents a supplier request, a review of the responses, and the generation of the purchase order.

There's even one leveraging reusable services from Amazon, called Amazon E-Commerce Service. The potential here is phenomenal if your company is willing to partner.

Amazon E-Commerce Service (ECS) exposes Amazon's product data and e-commerce functionality. This enables developers, Web site owners, and merchants to leverage the data and functionality that Amazon uses to power its own e-commerce business. ECS 4.0 makes it extremely easy for developers to build rich, highly effective Web sites and applications. Service highlights include these:

- Access product data from Amazon.com, Amazon.fr, Amazon.ca, Amazon.de, Amazon.co.jp, and Amazon.co.uk

- Retrieve detailed item information, including prices, images, customer reviews, and more

- Earn money using your Amazon Associates account

Amazon is just one of the companies leveraging the SOA Business Catalog to share its services. You can also find reusable, standards-based business components from SEEC for building composite applications in the insurance industry.

SEEC components provide policy lifecycle management, new business, distribution/channel management, and claims-management capabilities as a shared-service layer, integrating information and transactions across multiple, existing back-end systems of record (legacy applications or packages). Because each component is licensed and sold as an individual service, you can purchase only those services that you need when you need them.

Component highlights include these:

- Each SEEC business component is a loosely coupled, "atomic" service that performs a discrete business function.

- Components are built to industry standards (ACORD, web services, and J2EE), and are licensed with the source code, to maximize reuse and flexibility, and avoid proprietary lock-in.

- The business components are exposed as a WSDL, which can be invoked by a web service process server or custom J2EE clients.

- Components accept a request from a client; process the request applying business rules and error handling, where appropriate; retrieve the required information from appropriate systems; and return a response to the consumer requesting the information.

This is just an example of more than 3,100 assets currently in the SOA business catalog. IBM plans to expand the catalog to a marketplace of more than 10,000 assets by the end of 2007.

10. DON'T FORGET THE IMPORTANCE OF THE FIRST PROJECT—PLAN AHEAD

The first project will demonstrate to the organization the value that the overall project will bring to the business, so the first project needs to be carefully planned.

Think through the basics even though you are starting small. First, select a well-defined application or business process area. Use a blueprint to establish an initial target architecture. Establish an enterprise architecture and infrastructure based upon SOA principles to enable your journey, and make sure you inventory what you have. Remember that the organization probably will be looking for reuse, so leverage the existing data and back-end processes. Next, establish the right governance structure. This is as important as selecting the right business process and the right technology.

Use the first project to establish credibility and validate financial assumptions, and as a place to "seed" your SOA Center of Excellence (CoE). This CoE will also help your company establish architectural guidelines and organizational infrastructure, to ensure reuse. The first step is the hardest one, so plan ahead by leveraging best practices and patterns of experience. Use experienced practitioners to define the first set of infrastructure and business services.

Remember that even in the first small project, partnership with IT and business is an imperative. There is a talent in bridging the "language" gap: translating business requirements into implementation.

SUMMARY

In summary, understanding what not to do is just as important as understanding what to do. Understand the value of SOA. SOA is about flexible business processes. It's not just doing the same thing as you've done before in a different way. Although you should absolutely approach SOA incrementally, the benefits you can achieve are dramatic. And unlike other IT approaches, SOA is not

just about technology. SOA is really a mind-set and a way of approaching business problems. It supports the flex-pon-sive* company by merging technology, business insight, and thought leadership to create an environment in which innovation can thrive.

How does your company get started? There is no single answer; it depends on your business priorities. In this book, you see that a focus on a real business problem, not SOA, is a critical part of success. If possible, start with revenue-generating applications in small, bite-size hunks. Make sure that you focus on skills by building capabilities. And make sure you have that long-term plan in place that gets your business to the flex-pon-sive* state.

Taking an approach to SOA that is business-centric ensures that you are keeping your investments focused on areas that will mean the most for your bottom line. Whatever your approach, be sure to think through reuse and best practices. Take a portfolio-management perspective and decide what kind of assets you need to run your business. Then figure out where these assets come from. Newly created and reused services are the building blocks of SOA. Reuse gives users flexibility through reduced cycle time and elimination of duplicate processes.

For your first project, have a solid plan with governance at the heart. Governance is critical for success. Use the first project to establish credibility and to validate financial assumptions, to seed your CoE, and to establish architectural guidelines and organizational infrastructure to ensure reuse.

10

Case Study: IBM

IBM's quest to become a more flexible business has produced many lessons for the company. IBM's goal to become a flex-pon-sive* company started in 2002 with a journey from a monolithic, decentralized company to a more flexible business enabled by SOA. The need for transformation was driven by the competitive environment in which the ability to define and execute business process–driven change was a prerequisite for profitability and growth. The underlying technology that would act as a catalyst to support this change was SOA. Over a four-year period, IBM evolved from exploratory activities and pilots to aggressive adoption and acceleration of SOA assets within the IBM solutions-development process. Managing SOA content, created by the development teams, required a strong technological backbone and a governance model that would help direct funding and uphold SOA standards. Successful adoption of these practices enabled IBM to realize the benefits in cost avoidance and increased business flexibility.

This chapter includes several IBM case studies. These are real projects with quantifiable business results and are representative of only a few such SOA initiatives within IBM. Project deployment cannot be successful without a strong governance backbone; that is described in further detail later in this chapter.

The move to SOA is more of a journey than an event. Just as the adoption of enterprise architecture posed a dilemma for CIOs to justify business unit investments in the mid-1990s and early 2000s, SOA poses a similar challenge in today's world of technology. IBM has shown that investments in SOA can generate real, tangible benefits at the project level, but projects are just the beginning of a real journey that nears its end when companies have aligned their business processes to strategic business initiatives, both internally and externally in the marketplace, in a flexible manner. When it embarked on this journey back in 2002, IBM not only set out with business goals and principals, but it also used SOA as the underpinning technology that would enable the company to grow and change in a flexible fashion.

In this chapter, we walk through IBM Corporation's journey—the process it used and some of the results it has begun to see. The secret of its success to date is based on the principle that we have discussed in the book. This section shows several of the topics applied in a real-world example, in an end-to-end fashion.

THE BACKGROUND

IBM was a monolithic, silo-based, global company that had disparate data centers, hosting centers, and decentralized governance. IBM had 128 CIOs, based on both geography and business unit, 155 different data centers, and more than 80 hosting centers that managed an application portfolio of more than 16,000 applications. Business processes were not clearly defined and were redundant across different business units. Functions such as finance, fulfilment, manufacturing, and human resources were executed many times and inconsistently across the company. Even budgets and governance of standards were not consistently

managed. This was not an uncommon practice across companies, especially those similar to IBM that grew over time through globalization and acquisitions.

First, let's start with where IBM began its journey (see Figure 10.1). IBM began the transformation journey in 1992–1993, when Lou Gerstner decided that IBM needed to be an integrated solutions company solving customer problems, not a point-product sales business. IBM was hurting financially as well, so costs had to be cut. The Gerstner vision, combined with the need to cut costs, led to some of the structures IBM has today and the focus on several key initiatives. IBM was a company with a very silo-based view of the world. In addition, ownership of processes was done by division. For example, the supply-chain process varied by division, depending on the way the line of business defined its optimal view. Because each division business was "unique," it drove more than 16,000 applications within IBM overall. With this background, IBM began to see that this model would not take the company into the future.

	1992	2005
CIOs	128	1
Host Data Centers	155	6
Web Hosting Centers	80	7
Network	31	1
Applications	16,000	4,190

Figure 10.1 IBM's transformation simplified infrastructure and governance.

These business goals drove the need to become flex-pon-sive*:

- Focus on competitive processes (such as supply chain and improved human resources) within existing IT spending
- "Shifting the mix" to higher-margin business
- Improved decision making

During the early 2000s, IBM set out its plan for the next several years. IBM really began the SOA journey in 2002. It was originally considered another opportunity for cost-cutting, but it evolved into more of a responsiveness play. IBM prioritized its projects, starting with the total buyer experience, the supply chain process, a workplace for employees, and the IT enablement for the most flexible IT system to support the business. But before real process work was begun, a new governance model was needed.

IBM realized early on that to truly transform the company, all the redundancy across business processes needed to be driven out of the infrastructure. This required several stages. In the first stage, separate and distinct business units were defined and consolidated under one management system. This required a tighter organization around product lines and a move away from "lines of business" that sold many products, across many product lines, across many geographies. At the same time, a strategy evolved around standardization and utilization of a common IT infrastructure using common networks, hosting centers, client platforms, and technologies to drive redundancies out of the infrastructure. Sunsets of applications were a common occurrence, but most of these were driven more by cost reduction than by a change to common processes.

Cost-reduction targets were achieved, but the changes to the business were just not enough. IBM realized that the real value of transformation would not happen until IBM aligned its business processes across business units and product lines. True transformation began when IBM started to align investments to deploy standardized processes such as supply chain management, total buyer experience, human resources, and workplace (to enhance employee productivity).

IBM successfully implemented standards to manage its transition from 2002 to today by creating and adopting governance boards that would ensure direct investment in transformation projects, provide a strategic architectural roadmap, and provide a well-defined migration path to complete IBM's transition to being a flex-pon-sive* company.

THE GOVERNANCE MODEL

The key for most successful companies begins with aligning business goals with IT's, to support those goals. A key way that IBM decided to drive the alignment was through a solid governance model. For IBM, that governance model was linked directly to its business strategy and crossed both IT and the business. Success could not be achieved without that tight coupling and linkage going forward. IBM's governance model included four essential elements.

CIO-LED ENTERPRISE INVESTMENT REVIEW BOARD (EIRB)

The EIRB is a body of decision makers, as shown in Figure 10.2. The process transformation executives selected operational executives and business transformation executives who own horizontal processes across IBM and IT. The EIRB helped to do two things: to discuss the decisions and their impact horizontally across the corporation, and to drive the decisions at a higher level. If a company is looking at investments at the department level, it will probably make different decisions than if it is making decisions for the larger good. The goal of the board was to ensure that the bigger decisions would support the new IBM direction. To design the decision, all the business units had to work together.

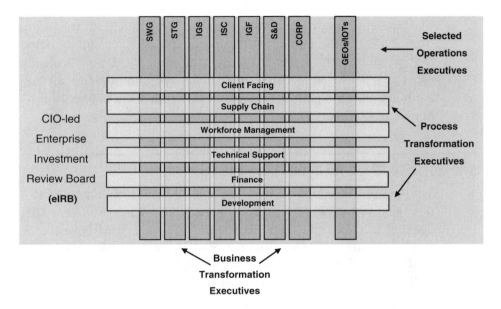

Figure 10.2 CIO management system: improving organizational capability

THE ENTERPRISE ARCHITECTURE COUNCIL (EAC)

The EAC sets cross-unit architecture directions and priorities. As shown in Figure 10.3, they drive cross-unit processes and applications as well as the information architecture. The group sets the target architecture (blueprint) and migration roadmaps to provide portfolio insight. In Figure 10.4, you can see how the group also drives and tracks architecture implementation, and resolves cross-unit problems and issues. It fosters innovation around the driving technologies, such as web services, end-to-end integration, and reuse.

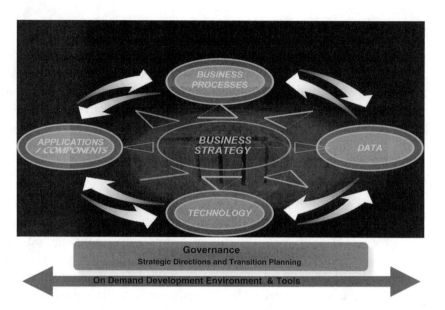

Figure 10.3 Enterprise architecture tightly integrates the business and IT to create an ongoing way to use IT to sustain and grow the business.

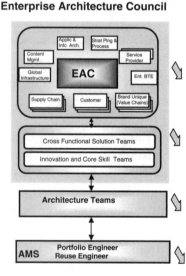

Enterprise Architecture Council

Enterprise Architecture Council

- Set cross unit Architecture Directions and Priorities
- Drive cross unit Process/Applic / Info Architecture
  - ➤ Target Architecture (Blueprint), Migration Roadmaps
  - ➤ Provide portfolio insight
- Drive and track architecture implementation
- Resolve cross unit problems and issues
- Provide focus for 'on demand' innovation – web services, componentization, e2e integration, reuse engineers

Cross Functional Teams

- 'Solution' cross unit problems and issues
- Define key elements of the Target Architecture
- Drive pilots for 'on demand' innovation, e.g., SOA
- Integrate approved solutions into the Enterprise Architecture
- Define required Standards, Guidelines

Unit Level Teams

- Implement agreed processes, architectures & standards
- Define and reuse enterprise components
- Review projects at required DCPs for compliance with agreed standards and Blueprint implementation criteria
- Track implementation progress and issues

AMS Portfolio Engineer

- Ensure compliance with strategic architecture across a logical set of solutions
- Identify project level opportunities for reuse and harvesting of SOA assets

Figure 10.4 The EAC consists of a main decision-making body that drives cross-unit objectives and leverages the extended enterprise.

CROSS-FUNCTIONAL TEAMS

To supplement the EIRB and the EAC, IBM set up cross-functional teams to create solutions for cross-unit problems and issues. This cross-team drives pilots for innovation such as SOA, integrates approved solutions into the EAC set architecture, and defines required standards and guidelines.

UNIT FUNCTIONAL TEAMS

Finally, IBM also set up unit functional teams. From the EIRB, processes and other key decisions are made and set as mandates across IBM. The unit functional teams implement agreed-upon processes, architectures, and standards. In addition, they are tasked with defining and reusing enterprise components, reviewing projects at required checkpoints for compliance with agreed-upon standards and blueprint implementation criteria, and tracking implementation progress and issues.

All these groups work together within an IBM governance model to drive the success of IBM's strategy through the business and IT.

THE JOURNEY

We have already discussed that this journey is best done in small projects that lead to a bigger vision. As shown in Figure 10.5, the journey we will walk through occurred over a four-year period. Not until after a few steps were taken in the right direction did IBM set up its official enterprise governance structure. The governance model drove transformation on the way IBM did business with the Enterprise Investment Prioritization (e-IRB), encouraging enterprise thinking and having a collaborative enterprise architecture board accelerated SOA.

So how did the journey really begin? IBM initially chose SOA as a technology play. The team pulled together views of future technology capabilities and explored web services, which, at the time, was an up-and-coming thought. By piloting web services in a project, the team saw the benefits, not only in the cost savings, but in

making the developers more productive; and more important, changes could be made much more easily. Given IBM's journey to become a flex-pon-sive* business, the technology team did a "look back" and built metrics to demonstrate a case for leveraging web services and, later, SOA as the base for the transformation. For IBM, SOA started as a technology play and grew into the strategic business-flexibility driver.

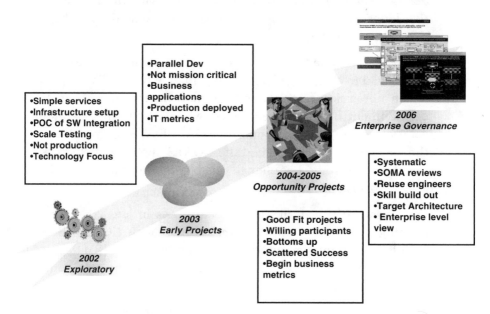

Figure 10.5   Evolution of SOA in IBM

THE FIRST PROJECT

IBM first chose a contained project called COATS, which stands for Customer Order Analysis and Tracking System. It accepts IBM's complex hardware orders from business partners, customers, and salespeople, and it routes those orders to more than 20 different manufacturing plants. These orders are broken down into a bill of materials, special directions for the plant, and configuration. As IBM produced more products, the business process had to change to be flexible enough to handle the customization needs and new technology.

The challenge with COATS is that it is a 25-year-old legacy system that was having difficulties keeping up with today's realities, which included increased complexity of orders, increased volumes of orders, and more plants. The rigid underlying technology inhibited performance of the application as well. For example, COATS processed order transactions in batches, which sometimes caused delivery scheduling discrepancies among systems and occasionally delayed shipments and revenue streams. With the new competitive landscape, the volumes were growing tenfold, and the same throughput was required.

To make these changes for the new requirements, the legacy application had to be changed. As Howie Miller, CIO for IBM, explained, "Each new release took about six months and more than 8,000 development hours to prepare. So when IBM went looking for a good place to test the promise of SOA, COATS rose to the top of the list. When we approached the COATS application changes, we knew that we could not change this big, monolithic application all at once overnight."

IBM began to transform the order process in late 2004, thereby pushing the IT team into leveraging SOA with COATS. Because SOA is usually implemented in incremental pieces, IBM decided to drive the changes to COATS over time due to the impact to the business and the cost.

For IBM to achieve success in its order-management transformation, the IT team needed to work closely with the manufacturing experts at the plants to define their business processes in process-modeling language to accelerate the deployment.

SOA AND REUSE ARE ALIVE

With SOA techniques, instead of having everything done in code, IBM created business rules and, from the business rules, drove the code that is the engine behind the process. To improve adaptability to changing business requirements, legacy COATS business logic has been converted into workflows of reusable services,

including externalized business rules that are adaptable in real time by a business analyst.

The COATS application has evolved from a big, monolithic application to a set of web services components and SOA building blocks that has produced fabulous results. What we've learned is that SOA is much more than just a technology—it's about modeling your business processes and implementing measurements within those business process models. The changes with SOA allow for faster execution. IBM transaction processing time has gone from 10 minutes to 4 seconds and has seen a 25% improvement in development.

IBM saw those results from the key linkage in the capability level. Business executives—similar to the manufacturing plant owners in the COATS example—set their strategies. It could be selling more in emerging countries, selling more through the Web due to reduced cost, or, similar to the COATS example, responding to a more complex business environment. Here in COATS, IT decomposes those business challenges into business capability, such as improved Web-based configuration tools, pricing delegation process, and so on. IT then mapped those requirements into the enterprise blueprint. In that mapping process, the IT team began to find shared services.

To date, IBM has more than 100 shared services stored in a registry and repository, with a goal of having more than 200 shared services by 2007. Specifically, IBM had 12 different order acceptance, validation, and scheduling applications that could be replaced by the new COATS services, and more than 47 different billing applications that are targeted to be replaced by just a handful of shared services. As a company designs for reuse, it must take into account other business unit needs. The value of the enterprise architecture (EA) is that the roadmap helps an IT group spot the areas that can be proposed for reuse. IBM used a methodology to analyze the business processes, to be able to identify where there could be shared services. The architecture enabled IT to target shared services.

In addition to finding shared services in the current legacy view, the process that IBM has now put in place enables the team to steer investments being made toward this shared-service view. Now, when multiple applications or new functions are planned, the architecture team looks at business fit and strategy fit, and helps the overall group select one to support the reuse culture.

The benefits from SOA are enormous, to date, and IBM expects more in the future—that's why it is heavily investing in SOA. See Figure 10.6 for a qualitative view of the overall benefits from IBM's strategy.

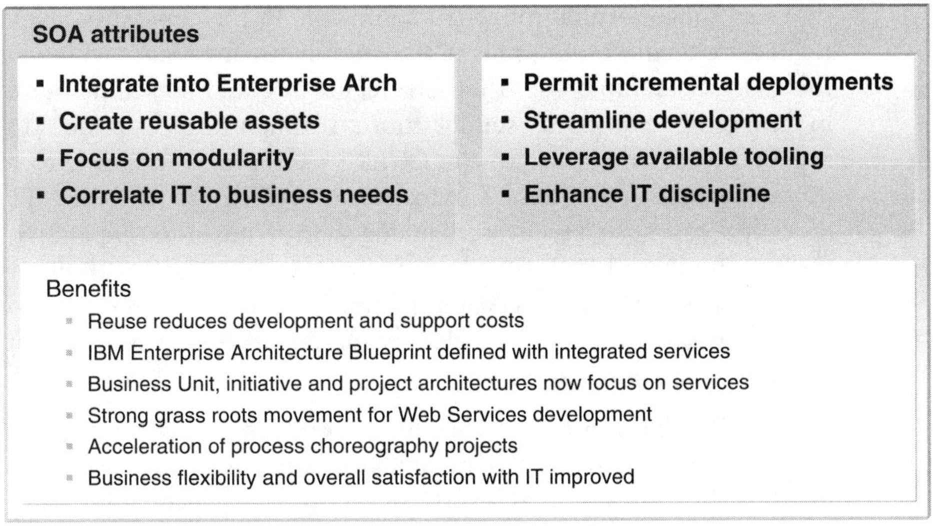

SOA attributes

- **Integrate into Enterprise Arch**
- **Create reusable assets**
- **Focus on modularity**
- **Correlate IT to business needs**

- **Permit incremental deployments**
- **Streamline development**
- **Leverage available tooling**
- **Enhance IT discipline**

Benefits
- Reuse reduces development and support costs
- IBM Enterprise Architecture Blueprint defined with integrated services
- Business Unit, initiative and project architectures now focus on services
- Strong grass roots movement for Web Services development
- Acceleration of process choreography projects
- Business flexibility and overall satisfaction with IT improved

Figure 10.6 SOA benefits for IBM's internal IT strategy

SET EXPECTATIONS

One of the great things that IBM did was to set expectations and to track return on investment (ROI). Investments to spark the initial project activities were made directly by the CIO. By providing the skills, techniques, tools, and infrastructure, the CIO's office was

able to insert itself into critical projects while the business units gained the benefits at no additional costs to themselves. In fact, the business units found that not only were their projects delivered before the planned dates, but enhancements to projects were easier because of the flexibility left behind by the adoption of SOA. This led to a snowball effect from an investment's perspective. IBM process transformation executives (a cross-process management team) and business transformation executives (business-unit solutions executives) agreed to adopt funding guidance from the CIO to set aside a large, multi-million dollar fund in 2007 that would be directed specifically to the creation and reuse of SOA assets.

Today at least 15 different case studies have been completed, and several more are underway as IBM heads into 2007.

The other interesting thing that IBM did was not just focus on the IT metrics. The company established business metrics beyond cost reduction. SOA is more than a cost-reduction play, and most transformational efforts cannot be fully realized with just a focus on cost. In IBM's case, business leaders sit on the EIRB with IT, so these metrics are crucial because the board decides how the funds in IBM are spent and invested. The business leaders are looking for metrics that show progress in flexibility and responsiveness.

So note the evolution that IBM went through over the years. What first started as a technology play grew into a business initiative. Shared services started as technical assets and became viewed as sharing best practices. But you have to start somewhere. IBM started with programmer productivity, the number of shared assets, how many are reused, and so on, to measure the effectiveness in a distribution curve. But as Howie Miller noted from one major EIRB, he would report the metrics and the "business leaders would just sigh. They were really not interested in the fact that developers are more productive." The IT team learned very quickly that the business pays the most attention to the flexibility view—how quickly IBM can impact flexibility, change process, and respond to customers. Those are the most exciting metrics.

BUSINESS IMPACT METRICS

Over time, the IBM IT team started working on business impact metrics. For another example, in addition to the COATS project, let us deep dive on the technology group's project, called "factory in a box." The technology group is setting its manufacturing strategy with a focus on outsourcing. In concert with IBM's innovative philosophy, IBM has chosen to focus on what it deems to be its competitive advantage and to allow others to perform those tasks that are competitive to them. Because this outsourcing is a key part of the strategy, the way that the technology group manages outsourcing was of concern to the IT group. When the technology group decided to outsource a component such as the back end, it usually took three weeks. In addition to the time, it typically took down systems, and the plant suffered from outages.

So working together, the business and the IT teams created an innovative concept called "factory in a box." Although the factory in a box has a lot of parts, for this illustration, it is a set of services that allows for an open interface into the back-end systems. Leveraging these SOA techniques, it is now a two-hour process. Now this metric is something that excites the business side—going from three weeks to empowering an outsourced supplier is now a two-hour process. Now the technology group can just turn it on and off. The outsourced company gets the interfaces, and the business gets an immediate boost, with the business metrics show a strong up-tick

Going back to our COATS example with the hardware ordering system, previous batch-mode process took one to two days. But with the new business metric leveraging the reuse and process flexibility of SOA, COATS order processing went from 10 minutes to 4 seconds. Now these are the types of metrics that get people excited (see Figures 10.7 and 10.8).

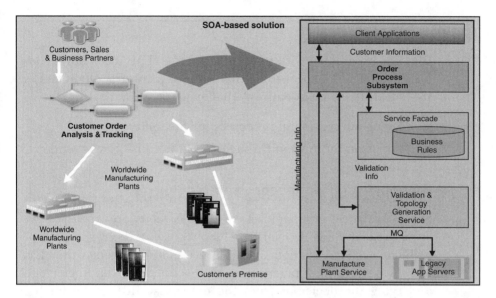

Figure 10.7 A customer order analysis and tracking system implements core business processes of the integrated supply chain.

SOA-based Solution
- Flexible architecture that supports the ongoing transformation of COATS into highly adoptable application
- Real time transaction processing
- Legacy business logic converted to externalized business rules and workflows of reusable services to improve adaptability to changing requirements
- Business process modeling and workflow generation - reduced analysis, design and coding time
- Generation of sense-and-respond metrics

Powered by
- Software
  - WebSphere MQ, Portal, WebSphere Application Server, WBI-SF, DB2
  - Migrating to WebSphere Process Server and WebSphere Business Monitor
- Tools
  - Rational XDE, WBI Modeler, WSADIE, Rational Software Architect, WebSphere Integration Developer
- IBM patterns for e-business, SOA and ESB

Results
- Order transaction processing time reduced from 10 minutes to 4 seconds
- Ability to make on demand changes to the run time workflow, through easily selectable rules
- 25+% reduction in development time/cost
- Reduces the development costs per cycle
- SOA Reference architecture and best practices that are being replicated across IBM and clients
- Hardened IBM Service-Oriented Modeling and Architecture (SOMA) method

Best practices/lessons learned
- Incremental implementation of services provides early buy-in and a non-disruptive migration path while managing expectations
- Align business/IT architectures through service modeling
- To develop agile business processes, address full services life-cycle – from modeling to monitoring – supported by methods and tools
- Follow an iterative design and incremental development

Figure 10.8 Customer order analysis and tracking system redesign—transforming legacy system

THE CULTURAL CHANGE

IBM has progressed with its transformational projects, but a company should not expect to do this without a cultural modification. IBM faced these main cultural challenges:

- Focus on horizontal processes for flexibility
- Focus on innovation through reuse, not just new invention

FOCUS ON HORIZONTAL PROCESSES FOR FLEXIBILITY

Similar to most companies today, IBM's focus on processes was done in silos. Each division has its own way of doing things, typically in a siloed fashion. The biggest cultural change that IBM drove from a process perspective was around its governance model and tying the decisions from the enterprise IRB to the funding model. Because each business felt that it had to drive its business, without a governance mechanism across the corporation, the cultural change to focus on horizontal instead of siloed processes would not have occurred. For example, IBM offers a variety of customer services running on a federated model in which each business unit operates autonomously and is supported by its own IT organization and infrastructure. The result was that the same business process and supporting applications were implemented in many ways. The challenge of building a unified view of the customer across all the business units really brought home the amount of cultural change IBM needed to go through. There is still more to be done, and a gentle balance between everything being done in a centralized versus autonomous way is being shaped on a daily basis. IBM has based this part of the cultural change on its governance model.

FOCUS ON INNOVATION THROUGH REUSE, NOT JUST NEW INVENTION

IBM has a strong culture and history of an award system that honored those who created new ideas and products. For example, not only does the company market its number of new patents every

year, but it is truly a badge of honor for the technical community to receive a patent. (I even focused on getting a patent for an analysis engine with very specific help from the IBM patent community.) A tiered model exists for patents—the more patents that a person has, the more rewards the individual can achieve. For SOA, a culture of reuse—not just invention—is key. In fact, one of the key value propositions and one of the early keys to ROI is the reuse that a person can achieve.

Given IBM's history, the team again led a revolutionary advancement to reward reuse. In fact, the award system directly mirrored the award system used for patents, clearly signaling to the team that new values were going into place. Now the IBM system rewards a person when he or she adds an asset to the common registry and repository. Next, very similar to the patent tiering scheme, when the asset is reused the first time, there is a set recognition that exponentially increases until the asset is reused for the fifth time. The resulting change in the IBM technical community was to drive for services that were more inclusive than simply requirements from the local division.

In addition, IBM runs an annual technical achievement event that includes the number of patents as one of the key success criteria. Now the event is geared to patents and reuse. And the list goes on. Certifications and promotions are also tied to the reuse culture. The point here, as Howie Miller explained to me, is that all major forms of recognition are linked—dollars, public recognition, and advancement. This cultural change of taking the enterprise view instead of just your unit view has started taking hold. Although there is much to be done, IBM has started the drive to demonstrate that innovation does not mean that you have to create something new. It means applying business knowledge to reuse something that you already have. The right levels of incentives are needed to impact the cultural change, and they consist of not just one element, but the entire collection, to truly send the signal throughout the organization.

THE RIGHT SKILLS

As companies, like IBM, progress with transformational projects, they should not expect to do this without skill transformations. The main skilled workforce challenges IBM faced were as follows:

- Technical skills
- IT and business alignment skills

TECHNICAL SKILLS

The right technical skills were required to achieve IBM's success. Because IBM adheres to the open source strategy, a strong depth of open source knowledge and leadership was a key factor. In particular, the technical skills that IBM grew from within its own boundaries included web services and a good foundation in XML, AJAX, SCA, SDO, and the other key elements for SOA. Although this might seem like a "101" lesson to be learned from IBM, from the last survey done at the SOA executive summits that touched more than 15,000 customers around the world, the number-one concern with pursuing SOA was having the required skills.

IT AND BUSINESS-ALIGNMENT SKILLS

Although the technical skills are crucial, several people in IBM who were involved in the projects discovered that the hardest skill to find was that of people who can transform the business strategy and capabilities needed into the capabilities needed for the IT architecture. The search for those with deep skills in both worlds became gates for the projects. In the COATS example, the skill required to figure out that order validation should be a shared service because IBM does this in multiple places, and then identify other shared views such as tax calculation, takes both great business skill to see the component view and technical skill to determine the right-sized service.

Having spent time trying to find these special skilled people, IBM realized they were hard to find and has since set up university programs to help prepare the next generation of skills. In particular,

IBM focused on the needed skills in Business Process Management (BPM), project management, and supply chain process skills, in addition to the technology side of the equation.

Other very specific SOA efforts include, IBM and Georgetown University that announced that in the Spring of 2007, two new curricula will be added to address the growing demand for information technology (IT) skills that can empower an organization to more rapidly respond to changing marketplace conditions. Both of the new programs—one for IT professionals and one for undergraduates and graduates—are designed to teach all students about service oriented architectures (SOA). And the focus is on both dimensions of SOA being technology and business. Experience and knowledge of the SOA approach is a valuable asset for professionals and students who want to enhance their marketable IT industry skills while also honing business acumen. While the U.S. Bureau of Labor Statistics reports that IT is among the fastest growing sectors in the economy, it also finds that America suffers from a shortage of qualified IT workers with flexible skills who can readily adapt and respond to ever-changing IT demands. Meanwhile, the business value of SOA continues to gain momentum as industry analysts from Aberdeen Group recently found that nine of every 10 companies are adopting or have adopted SOA and will exit 2006 with SOA planning, design, and programming experience. As the nation's first collaborative SOA Curricula for IT professionals and academics, the programs will provide IT professionals with an intensive, three-day workshop that focuses on real-world SOA skills that can be immediately used in the workplace. For students, the SOA Curricula will provide an opportunity to take courses as part of a Computer Science major to learn the basics of SOA while earning credits and gaining additional, immediately employable IT skills upon graduation. "Working as an SOA educator as well as an SOA consultant provides me with a unique opportunity to fully understand the business and IT needs of organizations today as well as in the future," said M. Brian Blake, Ph.D., associate professor of Computer Science, Georgetown University. "The SOA curricula will provide professors, students, and IT professionals with an innovative, collaborative forum to

extend the classroom learning experience and develop crucial IT skills that are in high demand.

Today most universities' computer science programs are focused on technologies; however, IBM is starting to educate universities on BPM. Building from their current courses in process optimization and business strategy, a few business schools (MIT, Duke, and California schools) are now focusing on the entire view.

SUMMARY

The IBM story has many lessons that can be applied to companies with similar goals of business flexibility and cost reduction. As in the rest of the book, IBM's success can be boiled down to these essentials:

- **Alignment of business and IT**—For IBM, this occurred through the governance model.

- **Acknowledgment of the journey**—For IBM, this was small, focused projects that leveraged SOA.

- **A set of expectations set and met**—For IBM, this was a mandate and a secret to success.

- **A view of where the gaps were**—For IBM, this exposed shortfalls in the cultural and skills areas that were addressed.

IBM focused on the areas in which the company could gain competitive advantage, similar to many on demand flex-pon-sive* companies in the market. IBM's journey is not complete, but it has begun.

11

Putting It All Together

I am on the North Carolina coast today, and I am surprised to learn that more than 2,000 shipwrecks have occurred off these coasts. Why so many? Hurricanes, treacherous shoals, unpredictable weather, and war caused the majority of the wrecks. My family and I rented jet skis and went exploring around the area to check out and learn about the history. It was neat to see how many other captains had "learned" about the ways to predict and avoid such hazards in the area and were able to successfully reach the North Carolina shore.

In the same way, this final chapter helps companies create a plan for their journey toward innovation. A set of guiding principles and goals is the focus of this chapter as you continue your flex-pon-sive* journey.

GROWTH, BUSINESS FLEXIBILITY, AND INNOVATION ARE THE RESULTS OF A FLEX-PON-SIVE* COMPANY

In some ways, today's business environment is similar to the Internet era, when in the rush to embrace the Internet and to get a competitive edge, companies became preoccupied with e-commerce. In fact, instead of imagining a hybrid world, everyone said that "clicks would replace bricks" and that retail would be changed forever. Others thought that it was about more than transactions; they saw the larger vision of e-business. E-business was a new way of doing business. You can see the similarities to where we are today—the rush to adopt emerging technology and the misconceptions that business changes suddenly instead of gradually.

And today there is a bigger world emerging on the horizon. From the work that IBM has been doing with business leaders and from its client engagements, they have produced a study by the Institute for Business Value (IBV) on the business value of flexibility and SOA in this new world. The results showed that those companies moving to the flex-pon-sive* world were seeing the results in flexibility from SOA; 97% justified their first SOA project based on cost, 100% saw increased business flexibility, and 51% showed increased revenue growth. The 30 customers who produced these results are plunging into today's innovative and flex-pon-sive* world with an understanding that was lost in the e-business world. This new model requires that businesses change, but at an incremental pace. This study complements the CEO study that we analyzed at the start of this book, which showed that companies were primarily pursuing growth again and only secondly cost-cutting. Since that study was completed, competitive pressures have only increased—due to advances in technology, the rapid advent of globalization, and the consequent flat world. If there's any change, it's the insertion of an important qualifier—profitability. Profitable growth is now at the top of the list.

And in a follow-up study, our recently released Global CEO Study 2006, 765 CEOs in every major industry told us that the pressures

to achieve profitable growth had introduced a new mandate—the need to innovate:

- Two-thirds of the CEOs believe their organizations will need to introduce fundamental, radical changes in the next two years to respond to competitive pressures and external forces.
- Fewer than half say they've managed this magnitude of change successfully in the past.

With the growing sophistication about how and where innovation occurs, companies know that business flexibility is the driver. New ideas don't just come from inside their company, but from wikis, blogs, partners, customers, and even competitors. This world requires collaboration to solicit the ideas and flexibility to respond to those ideas. The insight is that CEOs now say that more of their ideas for innovation come from partners and clients than from their own employees.

The interesting commonality here is that all these new ideas come from some sort of collaboration, but to act on those ideas, business flexibility must be a number-one priority.

Among all the CEO areas of focus we examined, business flexibility and collaboration showed the clearest correlation with financial performance, whatever the financial metric—revenue growth, operating margin growth, or average profitability over time. Beyond product or service innovation, more CEOs are looking to business process innovation as a key competitive advantage. As one CEO put it, "Products and services can be copied. The business process and the model is the differentiator." Another CEO commented that new product introductions in his industry offered only one month of market exclusivity before they are duplicated in the marketplace.

This whole discussion is key because it shows that a few of the top areas we need to tackle are the alignment of business and IT, especially around joint goals, and a focus on those processes that will allow companies to differentiate themselves.

This book helps address these key questions:

- What are your company's business goals, and how do you align your whole company, including business and IT, around those goals?

- What governance mechanisms and mandates do you have in place to drive those goals throughout your corporation? Chapter 6, "SOA Governance and Service Lifecycle," addressed how to think through governance, one of the most important indicators for success.

- What flexibility and innovation are needed for those goals to be reached?

- What business processes need innovation to be successful? Chapter 3, "Deconstructing Your Business: Component Business Model," detailed one method to determine the core processes that you should focus on for success.

- How does your company create an environment of innovation and the power to act upon it?

A company cannot continue to succeed if it comes up with some superb ideas through powerful focus and collaboration, but fails to act upon them or is not flexible enough to respond quickly to market forces. Governance and a focus on the right processes coupled with flexibility to act are all critical for a flex-pon-sive* company.

So the bottom line is that companies must have change to innovate. Given that every business is so tied to technology, this conclusion places a premium on the underlying technology that runs your company.

NOW, HOW DO YOU CONVINCE THE BUSINESS?

Behind every successful service oriented architecture (SOA) is the Business. With its promise of using existing technology to more closely align information technology (IT) with business goals, we have seen that SOAs have proven to help companies realize greater efficiencies, cost savings, and productivity.

Still, as many IT managers have learned, without executive endorsement, an SOA will be relegated to the confines of IT as opposed to being recognized as an organization-wide business strategy. While no two organizations are exactly alike, there are consistent themes that arise when aiming for approval to build an SOA.

For those many IT leaders who are facing the seemingly daunting challenge of presenting the importance and value of an SOA strategy to the executive suite, following are ten tips for selling SOA to the Business Leader. A few tips.

1. **Don't call it SOA**: Explain the value and benefits in business terms that reflect the organization's goals such as cost reduction, productivity, competitive advantage, etc. before diving into a technical conversation.

2. **Vision, not version**: Outline the immediate and long-term results from this strategy while avoiding discussions about specific version numbers.

3. **Build consensus throughout the company**: Prove the value of SOA through small, test projects conducted with volunteer departments in the organization. Make sure to include those department leaders when you later roll out the SOA.

4. **Start small yet live large**: When selecting those small test projects, choose to integrate and automate those business processes that can have the most widespread, positive impact across the organization.

5. **Ixnay on the TLA**: While it's easy to get caught up in the technical jargon that is fully understood among peers, remember that three letter acronyms (TLA) can sound as eloquent as pig Latin when trying to convince your CEO of a major, new strategic undertaking.

6. **Get to the powerful points**: Without relying on complex slides that can deter from the true purpose of the meeting.

7. **Conviction and prediction**: Articulate goals for each step along the SOA path. By publicly stating and achieving realistic goals

for the organization based on an SOA—increasing productivity or decreasing costs by XX percent—you can bolster confidence in the project and overall strategy.

8. **Reference third party validation (see the next section in detail!)**: Cite analyst data on the growth and adoption of service oriented architectures and point to relevant SOA success stories within your industry (and by your competitors).

9. **The close**: SOA what? Outline specific before-and-after scenarios of the impact of SOA on your particular organization to help disarm any naysayer and gain CEO approval.

10. **Qualify and quantify**: Set goals, track performance, and refine methodologies at every step along the way. Be sure to share the results with interested parties on a regular basis to demonstrate the success of your company's SOA journey.

The opportunity to evangelize SOA to company executives is rare. To make the most of your extended elevator pitch, remember to articulate business benefits, reiterate bottom line results, and illustrate the company-wide value of an SOA.

SOA AND WEB 2.0 BECOME THE ENABLERS

A flexible business—a flex-pon-sive* business—requires flexible IT. Innovation requires change and SOA makes it easier for companies to change. Given this focus on business flexibility, growth, and innovation, the technology that most expedites these business goals is service oriented architecture (SOA). According to most of the analyst firms, SOA will become the de facto standard for business flexibility and collaboration among companies.

As we discussed in this book, SOA is all about an approach that views a business as linked services and considers the outcomes they bring. Because it is built on open standards, it is a way for businesses to tap into their existing technology investments and flexibly link previously fragmented data and business processes, creating a more complete view of operations, potential bottlenecks, and areas for growth.

As we learned, advances in open standards and software-development tools have made SOA applications easier to develop.

However, this does not mean that everyone is deploying SOA applications; the market is at the early stages of adoption. Services that join together to support business processes within SOA are designed in such a way that different parts can operate independently of one another. Because of this, any one feature can be changed without breaking other parts of the application. This makes companies that have adopted principles of SOA much more responsive to changing business requirements than those that rely on traditional software development, with one feature change potentially derailing an entire application.

The companies that master SOA technology operate more efficiently than their competitors and adapt more quickly to changing business conditions in their industries. And as we discussed earlier, Web 2.0 facilitates the collaboration aspects, and SOA enables the infrastructure for flexibility.

A great example is a retailer deciding whether to issue a credit card to a customer. It could use the technology to tap different sources and pull together information on a customer's creditworthiness and buying habits. A bank can use the same computing services to handle account transfer requests, whether they are coming from a teller, an ATM, or a Web application, avoiding the need for multiple applications. A manufacturer could measure more closely what is happening in its production process and then make adjustments that feed back instantly through its chain of suppliers.

SOA enables profitability through revenue growth and cost cutting. SOA enables innovation through collaboration and flexibility.

Your checklist for becoming a flex-pon-sive* business should include the following:

- Understand SOA and Web 2.0. Chapters 3 and 4, "SOA as the DNA of a Flex-pon-sive* and Innovative Company," start to articulate what you need to consider, but the goal of this book is not to make you technology experts. Rather, the goal is to provide you with enough information to ask the right questions to begin your journey.

- Develop the skills needed to embrace these new technologies.
- Understand the business implications of the new technologies.

LEARNING FROM OTHER COMPANIES IS CRITICAL AROUND THE ENTRY POINTS

The companies that master SOA technology can operate more efficiently than their competitors and can more quickly adapt to changing business conditions in their industries. Meeting innovation priorities requires the ability to change flexibly, and companies should take a business-centric view of SOA (as opposed to an IT-centric view) to achieve these innovation goals (see Figure 11.1). As discussed in Chapter 4, "SOA as the DNA of a Flex-ponsive* and Innovative Company," a recent study of more than 500 companies conducted by Mercer Management Consultants showed that these companies are approaching SOA from entry points of people, process, and information, or all three. The lessons learned from the SOA entry points are furthered by the IBV study about SOA business value. This study of approximately 30 customers reveals some other lessons about revenue growth and cost cutting. 51% of the clients interviewed for this study expected their SOA deployment to grow their revenue, primarily by unlocking the potential of an existing process. To explore this in a real-world setting, review a bank's processes, such as a residential mortgages system, credit card system, or loan-servicing system. Following the IBM case study, an evaluation of those processes should reveal reusable parts, such as "submit loan application," "perform credit check," "determine credit line," or "calculate interest rate." SOA enables IT to recombine these reusable parts to create new products, such as a tailored home equity line of credit. With SOA, the business strategist is free to innovate.

Companies that started from one of these entry points have stories to illustrate the lessons that can be learned from other companies' experiences. Enterprise transformation powered by an SOA is really the holy grail the customer seeks. This enterprise transformation can begin with a set of entry point projects as a way for customers to start their transformation journey.

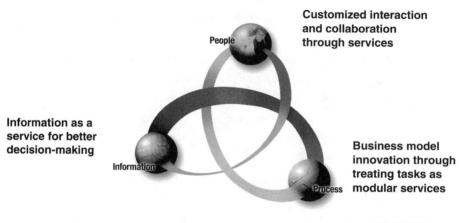

Customized interaction
and collaboration
through services

Information as a
service for better
decision-making

Business model
innovation through
treating tasks as
modular services

Source: IBM Global CEO Survey, 2006

Figure 11.1   Companies are taking an increasingly business-centric approach to SOA.

PEOPLE AND COLLABORATION

CASE STUDY
PACORINI

Pacorini is an international company based in Trieste, Italy. It delivers coffee, metals, foods, and general cargo. The company processes these goods for quality control and schedules them to arrive just when they are needed in the customer's supply chain management (SCM) process. A highly regarded company, Pacorini has 22 locations and 550 full-time employees; it comprises several different companies across three continents and 11 countries. As a market leader in the delivery of green coffee, Pacorini has historically maintained its competitive position by offering timely customer service. Although it used advanced technologies and leading SCM software, the company's internal business processes were not integrated. It was a challenge to manage siloed information and to provide consistent customer service in a 24×7 world. Consequently, Pacorini was concerned about its ability to stay ahead of its competition.

continues

Starting with an analysis of its current business processes to define priority tasks and link them using streamlined workflows, Pacorini built a framework of integrated online processes. The company put into place an SOA to construct information retrieval and work processes using repeatable information services customized to fit every task in a consistent manner. The company has implemented an order-enabled portal solution for both internal and external customers. It has also deployed a system-to-system order-management solution with its largest coffee customer in Italy. Pacorini is now in the process of applying the communications standards it developed with its largest customer to nine of its other top ten customers. In the future, it will extend this solution to customers in metals, freight forwarding, and distribution areas. Online ordering will enable the company to automate approximately 30,000 transactions this year, a projected savings equivalent to four full-time employees.

CASE STUDY
BusinessMart AG

A second example of the people entry point is businessMart. businessMart AG was founded in February 2000 and currently employs a workforce of 28. businessMart conceives and realizes electronic marketplaces and e-business systems for commerce, industry, and handicraft in sectors with catalog-based articles. Measurable improvements and savings are achieved with consistent orientation to the sector processes of its customers and to the in-depth integration of the suppliers and customers' computer systems. The broad spectrum of businessMart's services ranges from conception through technology modules, all the way to the founding of independent, market-leading portal-operating companies. businessMart now carries out the ordering processes of more than 60 suppliers with nearly 3,000 customers and more than 25,000

orders per day. businessMart currently operates two sector portals and additional projects are in preparation.

Better Integration—but How?

The continuous growth of the portals gives businessMart AG increased transaction revenues and clear growth in subscribers. Accordingly, more outside systems need to constantly be connected to the portal. The decisive head start in technology—the far-reaching integration of the suppliers' and customers' computer systems into the portal—was to be expanded even further for a more economical conversion. businessMart went in search of a solution that would significantly simplify the interface management and provide a reliable, flexible, and easily controllable platform for the exchange of business process information.

Conversion of the Architecture

businessMart created an SOA and implemented it throughout the entire portal. Within that context, the technology components were connected in independent, individual modules, or "services." Using the modules, business processes no longer needed to be conducted through the bottleneck of a portal center, but instead could be processed in parallel in the allocated modules. The architecture connects the customer systems with the available applications, using a central interface for all the portal components. Using component architecture enables a significantly faster development. The computer systems of new clients can now be integrated just as quickly as separate modules. Efficient and reusable application modules are created, resulting in software maintenance and care that is significantly more economical. In addition, the consistent use of fallback rules ensures that the system stability is not threatened by the failure of a single (outside) component.

continues

The Advantage of the New Solution

The decisive additional value arises for the customers of businessMart AG through the now unrestricted transferability of individual portal services to outside software systems. The most important portal functions can now also be used directly in the customers' usual software via web service interfaces. To call up product details with pictures, exploded diagrams, operating instructions, or even supplier searches, customers no longer need to exit their own merchandise information computer system. These portal services are seamlessly integrated into the software and passed online from the portal. The customers of businessMart profit from faster and more comprehensive possibilities for intervention: Time-consuming, manual information processes were digitized and have thus been made more economical.

For the integration of the customers' various back-end systems, businessMart uses IBM's SOA-enabled software to connect 16 different SAP systems. Now marketplace participants can simplify the flow of information as well as increase their sales and reduce their procurement costs.

In e-business, the contribution margin killers are unclear order positions that generate manual questions by telephone and annoyances through wasting time. This step can now be processed significantly more efficiently through the portal: If the system recognizes an obsolete article number, an unclear entry of a packing unit, or even a format error, the supplier or the customer is contacted in real time. The supplier or customer can immediately remedy the problem directly in the portal through a correction or by creating a conversion rule.

Well Equipped for the Future

With the transfer of the portal functions to the customers and suppliers' systems, the first step was taken in the expansion of the business model. In the future, companies will no longer exchange

their order information only by means of contacts; they will instead allocate applications and have joint access directly to IT services. A portal will have to take over the role of the interface management to keep the complexity at an acceptable level for the market partner. While in search of a modern technology base, businessMart also found an engine for an evolutionary step.

PROCESS

CASE STUDY
COSCON

COSCON is China's largest shipping container company. As a leader in the shipping and logistics services market, COSCON has 127 container vessels and has shipped more than 320,000 containers to date. Its ships are regularly deployed to ports across the globe, each with its own regulations. To support these diverse requirements, COSCON had an electronic data interchange (EDI) system that consisted of 21 different applications, with a variety of architectures and development languages supported on multiple servers. As COSCON's business continued to grow, its complex IT system hampered the company's ability to respond quickly to its ports of call and its external and internal customers.

To become more competitive, COSCON integrated its existing EDI applications by deploying an SOA. The open standards–based technology approach enabled COSCON to connect its silos of data and software applications to allow its internal business to better interoperate with its customers, partners, and suppliers. This solution leveraged the existing resources within COSCON and augmented it with a solution that improved productivity, allowing for more efficient communication and enabling COSCON to quickly react to changing market conditions.

continues

With countries constantly changing their customs requirements, with a change occurring every two to three days and almost one month per change required in the current system, the need for flexibility—becoming flex-pon-sive*—was critical to deployment. Because of these demands, COSCON chose to implement process integration using SOA. The process entry point was chosen to improve the communication between IT and business as well. Some of the processes COSCON chose to focus on were adding ports and reports that the business side needed. By using the process to create business services of the key tasks, COSCON was able to meet government (customs) regulations and to integrate with many applications in different languages. COSCON deployed an SOA approach to consolidate multiple EDI systems and processes.

COSCON has experienced a dramatic increase in internal efficiency and has achieved higher levels of customer satisfaction. COSCON can now respond more quickly to the changing regulations set by foreign ports. In addition, COSCON has reduced the time it takes to configure and modify its IT system, from two to three months to just two to three days. This time savings and greater development efficiency has resulted in higher customer satisfaction levels and has offered sizable cost savings. In addition, it allows COSCON's business personnel to communicate with IT staff and better understand the IT system, and the IT people can also better understand business operations. As we discussed earlier, this alignment of IT and business is crucial for business flexibility.

"Over the past few years, we have witnessed an increase in demand for our shipping services," said Mr. Ma Tao, Deputy General Manager of Information Technology at COSCON. "This increased interest has placed additional pressure on our business, helping us realize that we needed to revamp and invest in our internal technology infrastructure to position our business for future growth."

CASE STUDY
Automobile Club of Italy

Whether navigating the crowded streets of Rome or maneuvering the narrow roads that hug Italy's coastline along the Adriatic Sea, drivers count on the Automobile Club of Italy (ACI) to deliver emergency roadside assistance.

As the nationwide provider of roadside services, ACI relies on technical support from ACI Global, which maintains a call center that provides 24×7 assistance. ACI Global has agreements with automotive manufacturers, fleet and car rental agencies, tour operators, banks, and insurance companies to provide multiple products and services via its call center. Center operators handle approximately six million contacts annually, using advanced technologies to provide customers with timely and effective service.

The complete ACI operational network includes 3,000 assistance vehicles, 1,000 operating centers, and 5,000 operators.

ACI Global strives to develop, implement, and maintain value-added services that simplify the operations of its customer companies. The firm had been generating such improvements primarily through continually offering customers new and innovative services that encouraged increasingly rapid response times to roadside emergencies. Unfortunately, isolated business processes and outdated software-design efforts limited ACI Global's ability to redefine its business offerings, frequently delaying the delivery of new products and services.

To satisfy customer expectations for new and innovative services and speedy response times, ACI Global wanted to implement a standardized, flexible design infrastructure that would encourage the rapid creation and delivery of new business functions, in turn streamlining several call center processes and shortening service delivery.

continues

ACI Global worked to design and implement an automated call center called "Centrale Operativa" built on an SOA. Now ACI Global staff members can leverage the SOA's open standards capabilities to easily design new support services for customer operators, including automated call-routing systems and improved call tracking and management. The SOA also encourages the reuse of code and processes to further streamline the creation of new services.

ACI Global expects automation and integration to lead to a 20% improvement in customer call response times and a 30% increase in call center operator productivity.

These lessons were learned:

- It was very important up front to involve all the stakeholders.

- Focusing on the business needs made for a smoother production rollout.

INFORMATION

CASE STUDY
PEP BOYS

In 1921, four young neighborhood entrepreneurs in Philadelphia, Pennsylvania, pooled $200 each to start what has become the largest automotive aftermarket retailer in the United States. Today Pep Boys Auto employs more than 22,000 people at its 593 stores in 36 states and Puerto Rico, and reported more than $2.2 billion in sales in 2004. Pep Boys differentiates itself from competitors by being the value alternative to car dealerships, providing exceptional customer service, and being the only retailer that serves all four segments of the automotive aftermarket—do-it-yourself, do-it-for-me, buy-for-resale, and replacement tires.

Pep Boys is leveraging SOA to drive its business goals. In 2003, Pep Boys started to analyze its point of service (POS) and Service Work Order System (for bay service) and realized it did not have the right architecture or applications. The first thing the company did was set up its foundational technical base for SOA with a focus on connectivity and reuse. In this phase of its SOA deployment, Pep Boys leveraged a wide array of existing systems, including IMS/CICS/Old Java. They used a standards-based approach, making approximately 45 calls to back-end systems using web services (WSDL interfaces). They built roughly 200 functional services, with no migration of data required.

For the next phase, Pep Boys extended its deployment to include choreography of several retail processes, including returns and invoicing/billing. They choreographed processes/workflow consisting of 15–20 services. This put the key pieces in place to push new and enhanced functions to its employees in the store. The capabilities enabled by its SOA allowed sales reps to have enhanced, more productive customer interactions. The sales reps were able to turn POS screens around so that they could up-sell and cross-sell using new functionality. At the same time, Pep Boys created and was able to use a single view of the customer for various in-store activities. This is where they focused on the information entry point. The initial pilot was completed in four months at 12 stores, and the total rollout to 590+ stores was completed in April 2005.

Pep Boys started its IT transformation by replacing its outdated POS environment with an IBM Open–POS solution—a next-generation POS configuration built on Java technology–based 360Commerce software running on IBM Store Integration Framework, a specialized instance of an SOA architecture for retail customers, comprising hardware, an operating system, and services from IBM.

continues

The business benefits of this SOA entry point of information in combination with other SOA entry points were that Pep Boys experienced faster checkout and increased responsiveness to customer needs, and enhanced employee productivity and efficiency. "Now we can take debit cards, which have a lower fee rate than credit transactions," explains Pep Boys' Bob Berckman, Assistant Vice President.

CONNECTIVITY AND REUSE

CASE STUDY
U.S. OPEN

The U.S. Open is a tennis event sponsored by the United States Tennis Association (USTA) that is a not-for-profit organization supporting over 665,000 members. It devotes 100% of its proceeds to the advancement of tennis. The USTA leverages SOA to support its business goals and has partnered with IBM since 1990 as its technology supplier. More than 4.5 million online viewers tuned into the United States Tennis Association's (USTA) U.S. Open held in 2006.

The USTA created an integrated scoring system for the U.S. Open. This scoring system helps collect data from all courts and then stores and distributes the information to USOpen.org, the official website of the U.S. Open. The ability to immediately and simultaneously distribute scoring information—with IBM supporting more than 156 million scoring updates for the US Open in 2005—is illustrative of the value and capabilities of a larger technology industry trend known as SOA. The technology supporting the U.S. Open is an example of how SOA can help an organization use its existing computing systems to become more responsive and more closely aligned with the needs of its customers and partners.

For example, umpires officiating at each of the U.S. Open matches hold a device they use to keep score. These devices feed into a

database that holds the collective tournament scores. From there, the constantly changing scoring information is fed to numerous servers that can be accessed through the U.S. Open website. When visitors go to USOpen.org and click the "Live Scores" link, they see the scoreboards for all 18 courts that are updated before the visitors' eyes. This is then used to present visitors with instantly updated scoring information that is presented on the site's On Demand Scoreboards and the "matches in progress" pages.

More specifically, the U.S. Open's scoring system relies on an integration middleware that is a critical part of an SOA. Software acts as an Enterprise Service Bus to transform the messages in-flight from the courts to the devices and to the U.S. Open Web site. A database is also used to support the distribution of the scores and statistics.

Scores and statistics can also be instantly viewed on the Web site and compared with past U.S. Open events and similar competitions. Additionally, IBM technology is helping support the integration of information and statistics related to the tournament, such as individual scores and how they compare with current and past performance of the players and competitors.

When you consider the speed at which these matches are played, you quickly understand how the technology that supports the U.S. Open needs to keep pace as play-by-play results are accurately shared all over the world. The USTA's selection of SOA ensures that fans around the world have a virtual seat to the U.S. Open, with scoring information delivered as it happens on the court.

Linking all of the tournament's information and delivering scores in real time requires a sophisticated information technology (IT) infrastructure that can be easily accessed and understood by USTA subscribers, many of whom are not IT professionals. The USTA is at the beginning stages of an SOA, and the USOpen.org site will be able to accommodate a growing audience of tennis fans worldwide.

continues

In fact, nearly 660,000 fans attended the 2005 U.S. Open, making it the world's largest annually attended sporting event. Also, USOpen.org is among the top five most-trafficked sports event Web sites. The site has seen a 62% year-over-year traffic increase, with 4.5 million unique users, 27 million visits, and 79,000 concurrent real-time scoreboards in 2005. Additionally, since SOAs are scalable and flexible, they can easily meet the demands of the constantly changing USOpen.org Web site and the anticipated heavy site traffic produced by 27 million visits—with each visitor spending nearly an hour and a half per visit.

These case studies show that a central element of SOA is the repeatable business tasks that make up processes with modular, interchangeable software so that reuse is possible. Reuse of these services is one of the main drivers of flexibility. In addition, connectivity through an ESB is a key technology that companies need to select for their needs.

CASE STUDY
SPRINT

In 1899, Cleyson L. Brown sensed the need for a viable alternative to the Bell telephone company and launched the Brown Telephone Company in Abilene, Kansas. In doing so, he began what would become one of the most successful and innovative telecommunications companies in the world: Sprint (www.sprint.com).

After over a century of visionary leadership, Sprint has firmly cemented its reputation in the industry. The company has been first to market with nearly all the telecommunications technologies that inform how Americans communicate today. From the first fiberoptic cable and first digital switch implementations, to the first transatlantic fiberoptic phone call, to the only nationwide Personal Communications Service (PCS) network, Sprint has consistently proven that it is a leader in the telecommunications marketplace.

Sprint now counts over 26 million customers in more than 100 countries, offering them products and services that span traditional phone service, data solutions and Internet services. Sprint's Business Mobility Framework (SBMF) is the most recent extension of the company's innovative heritage and its commitment to providing products and services that help customers find new, more efficient and more profitable ways to do business. The SBMF—a combination of network capabilities, a business approach and a development philosophy—aims to reduce both the cycle times and costs associated with enterprises that want to improve operational efficiency while offering new, mobile-oriented products and services to customers. It enables enterprise developers to extend their applications to mobile workers without having to be experts in mobile technology or the corporate IT environment. As it turns out, the SBMF has opened even more doors than Sprint anticipated.

Focusing on Core Competencies to Tap New Markets

Sprint is adept at serving its customers. For years, the company has rightfully prided itself on exceptional service delivery and support. What the company's management realized, however, according to Rodney Nelson, senior product manager at Sprint, was that the enterprise market was underserved.

"We realized there was a lot of untapped value," says Nelson. "Within our carrier network, we had a lot of services that people wanted." Services, in this case, meant application functions developed internally that could be extended to other companies for inclusion in their applications.

For example, Sprint developed a locator application in response to recent U.S. 9-1-1 emergency regulations that makes cell phone location information available to emergency personnel, who can then use that information to track people in need of assistance.

continues

Sprint realized that this service—the location piece of its application—would be very valuable to customers who manage truck fleets or need to track delivery drivers, or to any company presently using Global Positioning System (GPS) technology.

However, in order to get that value into the hands of the people—the enterprise customers—who could use it, Sprint had to envision and create a gateway whereby enterprise users, regardless of the platforms on which their applications are written, could have access to the service.

Other services include cell phone presence (indicating whether a cell phone is on or off), text messaging and sending voice extensible markup language (Voice XML) messages directly to mobile or wireline phones—integrating voice and data alerts. For example, an airline might broadcast a Voice XML message regarding a delayed flight to everyone on the flight list—to the most appropriate device.

A Standards-Based Path to Success

Since Web services employ standards, anyone, regardless of their technology environment, can make use of the services Sprint has extended. Literally millions of IT developers can include Sprint services within their applications, and can do so easily.

In most enterprises, at least half of the applications are legacy applications, and the other half typically is made up of commercial off-the-shelf (COTS) applications. To integrate new services into these applications would be time-consuming, complicated and expensive. With Web services and Sprint, however, that manual integration is no longer necessary. Developers need only to integrate the Web Services Description Language (WDSL) into the code and connect to Sprint, where the service is run.

The Benefits Are Much More Than the Sum of Their Parts

Sprint has gained numerous new business opportunities, become a leader in the field of mobility workforce enablement and firmly positioned itself to remain a visionary in telecommunications.

Sprint customers that have implemented Sprint's services have seen exceptional cost savings. Developers report that implementation time and effort have been reduced between 40 and 50 percent compared with, most notably, traditional GPS application development. In addition, the time to acquire a location from a cell phone is 30 seconds with Sprint; traditional GPS devices can take up to six minutes. The location information is more accurate, and instead of implementing GPS systems—which can range in cost from US$1,000 to US$3,000—drivers simply need to carry a cell phone, which in some cases is free.

Sprint didn't have to build a whole new IT structure to support this new service. Through its SOA, Sprint just had to unlock and expose capabilities it already had embedded in other processes and applications. This is another great example where SOA is enabling market innovation advantage.

Though in its infancy now, these SOA entry points promise to unleash capability similar to what the Internet—the prior technology evolution of comparable magnitude—already did. Companies employing SOA entry points face more than just technical challenges—there are process challenges and cultural issues, too. In Figure 11.2, you can see an example of how the entry points work in the real world. From the users and consumers at the top, where the services are exposed to people, to the way that processes are broken down into reusable assets made up of application and information components, this picture shows a more powerful, flexible view for companies that can link these pieces together.

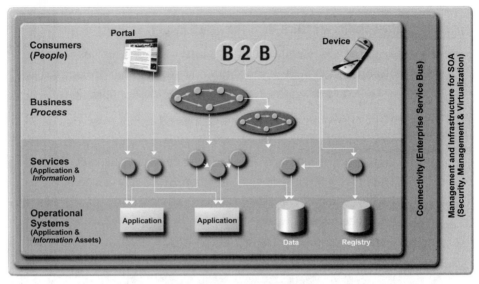

Source: SOA Community of Practice, SOA Solution Stack Project

Figure 11.2   People, business processes, and information sources interact through SOA.

A great way to get started on this flexible IT piece of the equation is to take a self-assessment. In fact, with the assessment at www.ibm.com/soa, you can jointly assess both the business readiness and IT readiness. Answering a set of questions about the business, your technology, and your goals shows your location on a maturity curve. It also suggests projects to begin your enterprise transformation and help you learn the areas before a larger rollout.

You should perform these checklist items:

- Understand what other companies are doing with flexibility and SOA
- Determine how your company can best use an SOA entry point
- Take the SOA assessment to see where your company might begin
- Begin a pilot project to learn the SOA framework

UNLOCK THE BUSINESS VALUE MULTIPLIER

The next step to SOA value comes when you start to link across the entry points of people, process, and information. This is when you start to realize a Multiplier Effect and your company's SOA business value accelerates. Creating entry points for SOA projects can deliver significant value on their own. People-, process-, and information-centric approaches yield results that can deliver strong ROI. However, the power can be exponential when clients apply SOA capabilities to people, process, and information aspects of a business in combination. We call this the Multiplier Effect and it changes the way you approach SOA.

The Multiplier Effect promises to deliver even greater value to clients by linking people, process, and information through SOA. The promise is that businesses will not only be integrated, but also built for change—built to adapt as market conditions demand greater attention by all parts of the business and shifts in resources. It's no great accomplishment to hard-wire a few data-bases to a user interface that, in turn, presents information mapped to a particular process. The real value is in creating flexi-ble linkages of all three entry points in a dynamic environment. Clients are continually upgrading and changing processes, appli-cations, databases, and views in the business. Through SOA, all parts of the business—its people, the key processes, and the criti-cal information—can stay linked and supported through that con-tinual change.

In Figure 11.3, begin your view from the center, where you can see the entry points we have been discussing. The companies that have started their journey have seen a higher ROI by combining the entry points of people, process, and information. This increase in flexibility and responsiveness comes from the focus on BPM and composite business services, which are made up of prebuilt, domain-specific modules that form highly customized applica-tions. Composite business applications will become as predomi-nant as the monolithic applications that exist today.

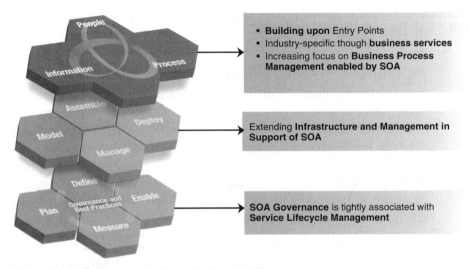

Figure 11.3   The flex-pon-sive* agenda through SOA

Those same companies, which have seen the value of moving up the stack, also see the power of the right infrastructure. Security, management, and virtualization are all different in a highly flexible SOA domain. These infrastructure services enhance resilience and security to accommodate decentralized services.

Add these items to your checklist:

- After your first SOA project, begin to see the linkages of people, process, and information. As you incorporate an SOA approach to address an immediate business problem, progress on the path to a broader SOA enterprise adoption. These projects generally incorporate reuse and connectivity, and involve information, process, and people (see Figure 11.4).

- BPM is more than a technology—it is a discipline.

- Composite applications will blend with monolithic applications. Check out the SOA business catalog (at www.ibm.com/soa) to see where the future is moving.

- Make sure you evaluate your infrastructure and management capabilities to support your SOA projects.

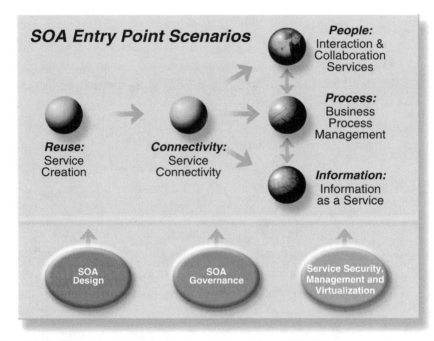

Figure 11.4 SOA entry point scenarios based on more than 3,000 SOA engagements

For a case study on the overall value of SOA and the impact of combining entry points, s.Oliver is a great example. Working with Sandra Rogers, Program Director, SOA, Web Services, and Integration at IDC, we explored this German company's approach to combining the SOA entry points and its best practices.

CASE STUDY
An IDC Case Study: s.Oliver

(From the IDC whitepaper sponsored by IBM, "Service Oriented Architecture as a Business Strategy," doc 204313, November 2006)

Background

s.Oliver Bernd Freier GmbH & Co. (s.Oliver) is a multinational retailer of apparel and accessories for men, women, and children. Founded in 1969 in Rottendorf, the company is one of the fastest-growing

continues

textile companies in Germany. With more than 2,350 employees, the firm currently operates 49 mega stores under its own management and approximately 240 stores that it runs in conjunction with partners. Its continuously revolving collections are represented in 1,000 branded shops and departments, and distributed through 1,330 stores in over 30 countries throughout Europe. s.Oliver's aggressive growth strategy has the company in line to double its revenues from €820 million in 2005 to reach €1.5 billion by 2010, fueled by further geographic expansion and partnering models.

The fashion industry is very fast-paced as companies such as s.Oliver compete to stay ahead of the curve of consumer preferences. The firm must be able to quickly identify trends and turn over new products, continually introducing new styles and products to stay competitive. Such volatility places heavy demands on the firm's IT environment to be in lock-step with the business, with the latest product information, and subsequently support these offerings throughout all operational aspects of the business, from creation through the entire order and fulfillment process.

The company also must frequently enhance its web presence with features to support what has increasingly become a critical go-to-market and partner-integration channel. With its international reach, s.Oliver must support multiple languages and currencies, yet maintain strong brand control.

The Business Challenge

When Stefan Beyler, CIO and board member, joined s.Oliver in 2002, he and his team completely reviewed the company's entire systems and application infrastructure with an eye toward innovation. With many corporate divisions and an expansive product portfolio that typically turns over every four weeks, the firm's overall IT approach needed to be addressed in a whole new way. The company's systems environment had to better reflect the overall business strategy; therefore, according to Beyler, s.Oliver's strategy was

not about installing a new application, system, or server. Its strategy was all about speed and agility. The firm must be able to recognize and exploit market trends in real time, apply modern logistics, leverage e-commerce and mobile technologies, and continue to promote a highly collaborative and creative corporate environment.

The company's IT staff of nearly 100 employees is responsible for worldwide operations, with a shared-services model supported by two major data centers, one in Germany and the other in Hong Kong. s.Oliver's IT environment is a heterogeneous mix of many applications that have been acquired over the past few decades, including two major ERP systems and varied database and information sources. Thus, the team needed to manage a tremendous amount of interface logic (estimated at 1,500 data interfaces), and with such a rapidly changing business environment, keeping pace was becoming a daunting and nearly impossible task. The cost of making changes to application integration logic, which required custom coding, was also a widening concern.

Beyler was faced with the challenge of creating an environment that could readily adapt to new business requirements and processes, and manage increasing volumes of information. With corporate expectations of maintaining efficiency and keeping down cost, holistically changing over the company's existing base of applications was not an option. Utilizing SOA to create an on-demand business environment was determined to be the ideal approach that s.Oliver needed, as it would provide the mechanism to address growth and change, yet allow the IT environment to evolve in an incremental fashion with minimal risk, disruption, and expense.

The SOA Solution

The company created the s.Oliver Federated Integration Architecture (SOFIA). In September 2005, s.Oliver's IT team began

continues

implementing information-centric services to support its highly critical order process and was live in production by the end of February 2006.

One of the critical requirements for s.Oliver's evolving SOA strategy is to utilize technology that can coexist and leverage its heterogeneous application and data resources. It is also important for the company that any new software introduced adhere to open standards for interoperability and investment protection, to minimize future vendor dependencies. The company chose to leverage an IBM suite for BPM enabled by SOA.

Another important part of the s.Oliver IT environment is its use of the people entry point and portal infrastructure to provide access to more than 250 applications and centralized information services, simplifying the user interface and addressing multiple languages the company must support. The portal also enables collaboration and distribution of critical information across the enterprise to facilitate faster processes and decision making.

One of the key business values behind the SOA construct is its inherent flexibility to address change, allowing s.Oliver additional speed to market. This platform allows the IT team to incrementally address new product requirements with minimal impact to upstream applications. The company is recognizing significant cost savings from the reduced efforts of the IT staff to continually maintain hard-wired integration logic.

By applying its SOA strategy, the IT team has thus far been tremendously successful—a sure sign is the volume of requests flowing in from the business. "An interesting point to note," stresses the s.Oliver CIO, "is that the business stakeholders do not see these as SOA projects, nor do they need to have any technical understanding of what a service entails. It is all about providing the business with what it needs."

To facilitate achieving this level of business alignment, normally a business leader is involved with each project to provide that critical link. A team of eight IT professionals is dedicated to the overall SOA strategic agenda. However, for its long-term success, the entire IT community must support the vision and adhere to the reference framework.

Beyler points out the criticality and complexity of outlining and addressing all the processes involved for SOA governance. This includes guidance on how to determine and document requirements, development practices, versioning, monitoring and management, security, and assignment of responsibilities for the many tasks involved in creating and maintaining services. The CIO notes that there is a lot to learn, and it requires a good level of process understanding. The company already had a robust IT governance practice in place; however, it needed to add "SOA thinking" to the equation. To support further automation and SOA governance, the team also anticipates it will leverage a services registry and repository solution in the near future.

Lessons Learned and Looking Ahead

According to Beyler, "SOA is a *business* project, not a technology project," and the most significant contributor to its success is addressing the people aspect of the equation. This involves rallying support throughout the entire IT organization, convincing developers through IT operations to cooperate across the many processes and dimensions of SOA design and governance. One activity that Beyler noted to be extremely useful was arranging for IBM SOA training for the s.Oliver IT staff. He noted it was very helpful to have the workshop's agenda address the many activities and roles throughout the IT and SOA lifecycle.

Success, however, involves cooperation and acceptance across the entire business. Many IT organizations look to corporate management to help drive cooperation in the development and use of new

continues

technology. However, to Beyler, it is the IT department's ultimate responsibility to drive adoption throughout the company by providing good portal and application features and functions that have an impact on the business.

One of the next technical milestones the company has set its sights on will involve combining operational and nonoperational data within its SOA environment, to support both transactional and data warehouse services. Another will be incorporating service orchestration on top of its Enterprise Service Bus to facilitate functional and process service requirements. Another key business requirement for s.Oliver will be to support offline processing; thus, Beyler and his team will be investigating how to incorporate an SOA-managed client capability.

For s.Oliver, SOA is seen as an enabling competitive differentiation for the company, allowing the company to rapidly introduce new products to market across its many businesses and lines. From a business perspective, the company plans to address functional business processes within its SOA environment to take advantage of the flexibility this architecture enables, including tasks involved in bringing products from design through production, supply chain management, and sales.

GOVERNANCE IS CRITICAL

If this book has done nothing else but convinced you of the importance of governance as your company moves forward, then that alone is worth its weight in gold. SOA requires an efficient business and technology governance mechanism to make sure that IT efforts meet business needs, and as a means of controlling what services are deployed and how those services are used.

Governance is designed to enable organizations to realize the full potential of flexibility. It addresses issues that, if left unattended, might be inhibitors to gaining the flexibility and time-to-market benefits associated with SOA—essential issues surrounding the

lifecycle of a service. Effective SOA governance is more than just technology. It calls for a lifecycle approach that integrates an organization's people, processes, information, and assets.

In its internal use of SOA, IBM found governance to be that secret to success. "From our point of view, SOA governance is an integral and significant aspect of our overall IT governance, which includes managing process, applications, data, and technology," said Catherine Winter, Team Leader for IBM Enterprise Architecture Governance. IBM started by identifying the appropriate process and roles/responsibilities set up the IBM Architecture Board to govern and manage the SOA environment. This governance strategy helped optimize IT assets across the entire corporation.

Address these keys to effective governance:

- Establishing decision rights for your SOA environment
- Defining appropriate services
- Managing the lifecycle of service assets
- Measuring effectiveness
- Changing the Culture
- Aligning IT and Business

CASE STUDY
PEOPLE'S BANK OF CHINA

China's federal bank avoids $1 billion in infrastructure and development costs and eases management of the country's treasury by implementing a nationwide real-time tax and customs payment-collection system based on an SOA.

Owned by the Chinese government, the People's Bank of China (PBC) has been the driving force behind the Chinese commercial banking market since 1949. PBC, which serves as a clearinghouse for the Chinese banking industry, employs approximately 100,000 people at 32 first-line branches, 300 second-line branches, and 2,000 third-line branches.

continues

The federally run People's Bank of China (PBC) collects and processes tax and customs payments from all of China's 600 million tax-paying citizens. Historically, the nation's 32 provincial governments would first collect the payments from local banks and then submit the collections to PBC. Delays in this process, as money changed hands from the banks to the provinces and finally to PBC, allowed some provinces to accrue interest on the collections, which complicated management of the national treasury. To simplify and accelerate the process, PBC wanted to collect directly from the local banks. However, such a change would require it to integrate its tax- and customs-processing systems with thousands of different bank systems. The challenge was for PBC to create an efficient exchange system across all of China, without investing massive amounts of time and money in integration-development projects.

PBC can now collect tax and customs payments from the local banks in real time by leveraging a cost-effective SOA. By enabling seamless integration among the disparate banking systems, open standards–based software automatically routes roughly 13 million transactions per day between PBC and the commercial banks, while minimizing the need to hard-code integrations. PBC can efficiently add to or modify the services in the SOA as needed, to accommodate new requirements or implement new functionality with relative ease. PBC has seen business results of an estimated cost-cutting of approximately $1 billion in infrastructure and development costs by taking the SOA approach, and eased management of the national treasury by eliminating processing delays. In addition, it gained business flexibility—flex-pon-siveness*—needed to adapt and improve the exchange system in the future.

To accomplish these goals, PBC built an all-new treasury application infrastructure and SOA that will support more than 800,000 users. Through the SOA environment, they route messages (transactions) to and from the external institutions, handling about 13

million messages per day. To ensure a smooth development process for the system's real-time transaction applications, a team of 20 developers, 10 testers, five analysts, one project manager, and two executives added new processes and development methodologies to the SOA environment. Because of this focus on the Lifecycle of Service Assets through Development and Delivery, PBC will be able to reuse application components to integrate new applications quickly and maintain existing applications easily.

The business value of PBC's SOA environment is that PBC can now easily interface with more than 150 diverse merchant banking, tax, and customs institutions across China, effectively centralizing and standardizing the collection of national treasury information. Using the solution, citizens can submit tax and customs payments online in real time via their bank accounts. Tax preparation that used to require as much as four hours to complete can now be entered and submitted in less than ten minutes.

PBC is able to easily adapt to changing LOB requirements. The integrated environment helps speed the bank's development process and eliminates wasted resources.

In total, the integrated, SOA-enabled system will help PBC save more than $1 billion in national treasury infrastructure, maintenance, and development costs.

INFRASTRUCTURE AND MANAGEMENT COMPLETE THE PICTURE

To realize the value of SOA initiatives, companies are taking a planned approach to extending existing infrastructure and management capabilities in support of those projects. SOA requires thinking about these areas in a slightly different way. By effectively securing the infrastructure across the people, process, and information boundaries spanned by SOA projects, you can save money, reduce risks, and ensure compliance. Managing efficiently to gain

visibility and control of SOA services and the components underneath them is critical for SOA project success.

By nature, SOA services can be virtualized. Making sure the infrastructure to support services is virtualized allows clients to place and prioritize the services for optimal business performance.

Address these keys to effective governance:

- Establishing the right set of security for your services
- Defining management within the context of SOA
- Determining your virtualization needs to drive performance and the right use of resources

CASE STUDY
ING

In 2005, ING became the sixth-largest European financial institution, based upon market value, up six positions from only one year earlier. According to ING executives, this change is a reflection of the company's success in offering innovative and low-cost customer-focused services through a variety of distribution channels, including web services, call centers, intermediaries, and branch offices. However, like many companies out there, ING was facing a growing number of industry regulations and increasing sophistication of its business services. For ING to continue its success, they needed to reduce the time and cost of managing employee access to information while ensuring that staff could quickly respond to business change. Focusing on its entitlement program, ING needed a streamlined approval process that leverages electronic forms and intelligent workflows to enable managers to request and approve authorization requests online. In addition, it was important to their business goals that ING provide a self-service capability so employees could change their passwords without the assistance of help-desk personnel.

The implementation of a common identity management system was a key milestone on the journey to deploying a broader, strategic SOA environment for ING. The removal of security components

from each individual application enabled the implementation of a common, centralized set of security controls. This allows the organization to reduce development and deployment costs, ensures the consistent application of security policy, and provides users with a simple, convenient single-sign-on capability across a wide range of services. The benefit of this decision was a host of business benefits: the total projected savings of €15 million ($20 million) a year, a projected 50% reduction in the number of administrators assigned to support identity management processes within 18 months, an anticipated 25% savings in help-desk administrative costs, the ability to reduce time and cost associated with regulatory reporting, and the ability to reduce turn-on time for new users from 10 days to less than 24 hours.

SUMMARY

To begin the journey of becoming a flex-pon-sive* company takes both business and IT acumen, with a special focus on your business models and processes. As we discussed in Chapter 1, "The Innovation Imperative," your journey begins with a focus on a real business problem, not SOA. How do you grow? How do you become more responsive? How do you ensure that you have the right skills needed on both the business and IT sides? Start small on your journey and build those needed talents and capabilities; in the long run, SOA will enable your success.

Those who succeed have the longer term in mind—they're flex-pon-sive* in a global world—and they leverage the best practices and learning of other companies. Maximize your company's journey with a shorter time to value:

■ Focus on the area that will change the game in your industry.

■ Address the area of focus with flexible IT—and SOA—to begin growing your revenue and ensuring flexibility. The SOA entry points are built on business-centric views and are flexible enough to fit your needs. These entry points are more than just hype; they have solid experience woven into the patterns for success.

- Leverage the best practices of others in your industry and those outside. Remember that the new game is the focus on business models and business processes.

- Implement governance, which is critical for cross-business cultural change and a secure, robust infrastructure that is needed to scale and support your SOA projects and undertakings.

- Include a trusted partner such as IBM that provides both the business acumen and advanced technologies to build your journey upon. Because the world is changing, it is not just about technology—it is about the combination of business and IT.

I started this closing chapter discussing the number of shipwrecks off the North Carolina coast due to the unpredictable nature of the forces of nature and man. Today's time seems to be very similar to that N.C. coast. Your success depends on your business's ability to weather unpredictable times and to drive change into the marketplace. It is an adventure that truly takes you to all parts of the world in a global economy. To succeed, similar to those captains of the sea, you will need tools to enable your success.

This book provided you with several of those tools:

- The Component Business Model, to determine which processes to focus on (Chapter 3)

- The business-centric entry points enabled by SOA, to help your business deploy SOA at the rate and pace you need for real business results (Chapter 4)

- A technology roadmap and SOA reference architecture and lifecycle (Chapters 4 and 5, "SOA Key Concepts")

- The business case approach for innovative ideas around process and models, to serve as a framework (Chapter 7, "Three Business-Centric SOA Entry Points")

- More than 30 case studies and examples that can shed light on others' journeys and lessons learned from more than 3,000 real-world businesses (Chapter 9, "The Top 10 Don'ts!"; Chapter 10, "Case Study: IBM"; and throughout)

- Maturity models, to determine where you are and what the right approach is for your business (Chapter 7)

Regardless of where you start, your journey toward competitiveness in business model innovation is enabled by the new language of business—SOA and Web 2.0. Becoming a flex-pon-sive* company drives your business to new levels of growth and flexibility in the marketplace. It becomes your language for business success.

Glossary

AJAX Asynchronous Java Script, a Web-development technique for creating interactive Web applications. The intent is to make Web pages feel more responsive by exchanging small amounts of data with the server behind the scenes so that the entire Web page does not have to be reloaded each time the user makes a change. This is meant to increase the Web page's interactivity, speed, and usability. (Example: Google Maps)

appliance A specialized hardware and software device. A software capability that is embedded in specialized hardware to enhance SOA deployment runtime.

asynchronous messaging Sending messages that are not in sync with an external clock.

Atom Atom Syndication Format, a standard way for a Web application to check for "feeds" from another Web site. (Example: publish-and-subscribe technique so that you get an alert or feed whenever an event happens that you've asked to be notified about)

blogs Online diaries of text, photos, or other media.

BPEL Business Process Execution Language (pronounced "beeple"). BPEL provides a way to formally specify business processes and interaction protocols.

BPM Business Process Management, a discipline combining software capabilities and business expertise through people, systems, and information to accelerate time between process improvements, facilitating business innovation.

business services   Prebuilt services based on industry best practices and policies. They are unique, in that they provide the higher-level value.

composite business services   Collections of individual business and IT services that work together, along with a client's existing applications, to provide specific business solutions that support the industry and semantic standards common to each industry, such as HIPAA in healthcare, ACORD in insurance, and SWIFT in banking.

connectivity   One of the five SOA entry points, focused on the IT side. SOA connectivity enables you to exchange information among all your assets within and outside your business through a secure, reliable, and scaleable messaging backbone for seamless communication among applications, people, and information sources. Often associated with an ESB.

dashboard   Uses SOA to provide a single view into how your business or IT is operating, unifying fragmented sources of information and applications for monitoring, analysis, decision making, and execution.

digital economy   A term used by Don Tapscott in his book by the same name. Typically, it refers to an economy that is driven by people who have grown up in a world of computers and the Internet, and the changes that it causes on the society.

ESB   Enterprise Service Bus, a flexible connectivity infrastructure for integrating applications and services by performing the following actions between services and requestors: routing messages between services, converting transport protocols between requestor and service, transforming message formats between requestor and service, and handling business events from disparate sources.

event   A significant real-world action or instance that does or does not occur in a specific period of time. Services respond to events in accordance with business rules.

flex-pon-sive* Description of a company that responds with lightning speed and agility to rapidly changing business needs.

governance SOA governance helps organizations meet their SOA goals and vision by establishing decision rights, measurement, policy, and control mechanisms around the services' lifecycle.

information One of the five SOA entry points, focused on the business side. Information as a service is an approach that unlocks information in all its forms from its repository, process, and application silos, providing it as a trusted service to the applications, processes, and decision makers who need it.

long tail (From Wikipedia) The phrase "The Long Tail" (as a proper noun with capitalized letters) was first coined by Chris Anderson in an October 2004 *Wired* magazine article to describe certain business and economic models, such as Amazon.com or Netflix. The term "long tail" is also generally used in statistics, often applied in relation to wealth distributions or vocabulary use.

loosely coupled The ability of services to be joined on demand to create composite services, or disassembled just as easily into their functional components. It is one of the basics of SOA that drives its value of flexibility.

management SOA management helps deploy, monitor, secure, control, and enable business processes, SOA-based services and composite applications, and the supporting IT environment.

mash-up A quickly built composite Web 2.0 application that combines capabilities in a new way to create new value for the user. Mash-ups represent the practical bridge between SOA and Web 2.0.

on demand An enterprise whose business processes—integrated end to end across the company and with key partners, suppliers, and customers—can respond with flexibility and speed to customer demand, market opportunity, or external threat.

open-source software   Publicly available software that can be copied or modified without payment. From Wikipedia, open-source software is an antonym for closed source and refers to any computer software whose source code is available under a copyright license that permits users to study, change, and improve the software, and to redistribute it in modified or unmodified form. It is the most prominent example of open-source development and often compared to user-generated content.

open standards   (From Wikipedia) Publicly available and implementable standards. By allowing anyone to obtain and implement the standard, they can increase compatibility between various hardware and software components.

people   One of the five SOA entry points. According to the industry, more than 50% of companies will begin their SOA journey through a portal, one of the areas of a focus on people as an entry point. People can interact with SOA-based business services and composite applications through an enabling framework of tools and practices.

PHP   Originally derived from Personal Home Page (PHP) tools, PHP is a recursive acronym that refers to Hypertext Preprocessor, a general-purpose scripting language well suited for Web-based development, allowing for the creation of dynamic content that interacts with databases.

podcast   Online audio or video that users can download to a device.

process   One of the five SOA entry points focused on the business side. A process is a set of related business tasks spanning people, systems, and information to produce a specific service or product. The process entry point provides specific tools and services to help streamline and improve processes across the enterprise.

registry and repository   A central reference point within a service oriented architecture that stores and manages services information (metadata). It stores information about what the services

are, how they are used, and how they are interconnected with other components.

Remote Procedure Calls   (From Wikipedia) A protocol that allows a computer program running on one computer to cause a subroutine on another computer to be executed without the programmer explicitly coding the details for this interaction.

representational state transfer (REST)   An approach for getting information content from a Web site by reading a designated Web page that contains an XML (Extensible Markup Language) file that describes and includes the desired content.

reuse   Addresses methods of creating the services needed to execute business tasks by service-enabling existing IT assets, consuming reusable services from an external service provider, and creating net-new reusable services from scratch.

RSS   Really Simple Syndication, an XML standard that lets users collect and read content feeds.

SCA   Service component architecture, which provides an open, technology-neutral model for implementing IT services that are defined in terms of a business function and that make middleware functions more accessible to the application developer. SCA also provides a model for the assembly of business

SDO   Service Data Objects. SDO complements SCA by providing a common way to access many different kinds of data. The specification reduces the skill levels and time required to access and manipulate business data.

service   Self-contained, reusable software module that is independent of applications and the computing platforms on which it runs. Services have well-defined interfaces and allow a 1:1 mapping between business tasks and the exact IT components needed to execute the task.

service orientation   A way of thinking about your business processes as linked, loosely coupled tasks supported by services.

Service oriented architecture (SOA) A business-driven IT architectural approach that supports integrating your business as linked, repeatable business tasks, or services. SOA helps today's businesses innovate by ensuring that IT systems can adapt quickly, easily, and economically to support rapidly changing business needs. It is a flexible architectural style that enables customers to build a set of loosely coupled services for automating and streamlining business processes. SOA helps customers increase the flexibility of their business processes, strengthen their underlying IT infrastructure, and reuse their existing IT investments by creating connections among disparate applications and information sources.

siloed Having a stove-pipe view of your business, with each division or business unit isolated from the rest. Contrast this with a business that takes on a horizontal perspective, looking across multiple divisions when making decisions.

SOA entry points Five distinct but interrelated ways of undertaking SOA projects that encompass both a business and an IT component. The entry points are people, process, information, connectivity, and reuse.

SOA foundation Integrated, open standard–based set of software, best practices, and patterns that is designed to provide what you need to get started with your SOA.

SOA infrastructure As clients adopt SOA, this new simplified, virtualized, and distributed application framework poses challenges for infrastructures that must be addressed to ensure that the new applications can meet their performance, availability, scalability, security, and management.

SOA infrastructure solutions The SOA infrastructure solution from IBM is designed to help you increase business flexibility, responsiveness, and performance by enabling your IT infrastructure for SOA. Start by leveraging your existing IT assets, and then evaluate, design, and implement.

SOA lifecycle   Defines a methodology for conducting successful SOA projects by modeling the business process and the services that will support them; assembling the services into a composite application; deploying the services in a robust, scalable environment; managing and monitoring key IT resources and business metrics; and doing all these lifecycle steps while adhering to solid governance and best practices.

SOA reference architecture   Defines the comprehensive IT services required to support your SOA at each stage in the SOA lifecycle.

SOA scenarios   Define specific SOA projects that customers can implement while focusing on a very small number of targeted software products and/or services per project.

SOA security   Helps create a consistent infrastructure to support SOA projects by enabling user-centric, policy-driven authentication, authorization, and access to applications, information, and data, and consistent enforcement and auditing of corporate compliance and security policy.

social networks   Technology that enables users to leverage personal connections.

UI   User interface.

user review portals   Web portals that enable users to search for peer reviews on a product or service.

virtualization   Supports SOA projects by enabling IT infrastructures to be dynamic and responsive, supporting scaling of services in support of business processes, and improving performance and service-level attainment of SOA deployments by implementing intelligent service workload management techniques.

Web 2.0   Encompasses a range of technologies, tools, techniques, and standards that focus on enabling people to increase the social factor—how people connect with each other to improve how software works. Key principles involve use of lightweight

programming models and standards, and techniques such as mash-ups, wikis, tagging, and blogs for richer user interfaces and improved use of data.

web service A software system designed to support interoperable machine-to-machine interaction over a network. It has an interface described in a machine-processable format (specifically WSDL). Other systems interact with the web service in a manner prescribed by its description using SOAP messages, typically conveyed using HTTP with an XML serialization in conjunction with other Web-related standards.

Web syndication Similar to syndication of a newspaper column. It is the licensing or use of content in multiple places. Typically, it is Web content that someone makes available for others' use.

wikis/collaboration software Shared publishing software or site that enables users to edit content.

WSDL (From Wikipedia) The Web Services Description Language (pronounced "wiz-dull" or spelled out as "W-S-D-L"), an XML format published for describing web services.

XML Web services are based on the Extensible Markup Language (XML). XML is a markup language for documents containing structured information.

INDEX

BOOKS ONLINE
ENABLED

THIS BOOK IS SAFARI ENABLED

INCLUDES FREE 45-DAY ACCESS TO THE ONLINE EDITION

The Safari® Enabled icon on the cover of your favorite technology book means the book is available through Safari Bookshelf. When you buy this book, you get free access to the online edition for 45 days.

Safari Bookshelf is an electronic reference library that lets you easily search thousands of technical books, find code samples, download chapters, and access technical information whenever and wherever you need it.

TO GAIN 45-DAY SAFARI ENABLED ACCESS TO THIS BOOK:

- Go to **http://www.prenhallprofessional.com/safarienabled**
- Complete the brief registration form
- Enter the coupon code found in the front of this book on the "Copyright" page

PRENTICE
HALL

If you have difficulty registering on Safari Bookshelf or accessing the online edition, please e-mail customer-service@safaribooksonline.com.